Negotiating the New Germany

Negotiating the NEW GERMANY

Can Social Partnership Survive?

edited by

Lowell Turner

ILR Press, an imprint of Cornell University Press

Ithaca and London

First published 1997 by Cornell University Press
First printing, Cornell Paperbacks, 1997

Printed in the United States of America

Library of Congress Cataloging-in-Publication Data

Negotiating the new Germany : can social partnership survive? / edited by Lowell Turner.
    p. cm.
  Based on original contributions presented at the conference "The political economy of the new Germany," held at Cornell University, Oct. 14–15, 1994.
  Includes bibliographical references and index.
  ISBN 0-8014-3420-3 (alk. paper).—ISBN 0-8014-8444-8 (pbk). : alk. paper)
  1. Germany (East)—Economic conditions—Congresses. 2. Germany—Economic conditions—1990—Congresses. 3. Industrial relations—Germany—Congresses. 4. Social policy—Germany—Congresses. I. Turner, Lowell.
HC290.782.N44 1997
338.943—dc21   97-29480

Cloth printing   10 9 8 7 6 5 4 3 2 1

Paperback printing   10 9 8 7 6 5 4 3 2 1

® GCIU

For John P. Windmuller

Contents

Contributors

Christopher S. Allen is Associate Professor of Political Science, University of Georgia.

Peter Auer is Senior Research Fellow, Wissenschaftszentrum Berlin.

Michael Fichter is Senior Research Fellow and Lecturer, Freie Universität Berlin.

Gary Herrigel is Associate Professor of Political Science, University of Chicago.

Wade Jacoby is Assistant Professor of Political Science, Grinnell College.

Matthias Knuth is Senior Research Fellow, Institut für Arbeit und Technik, Gelsenkirchen.

Richard M. Locke is Associate Professor of Political Science and Industrial Relations, MIT.

Stephen J. Silvia is Associate Professor, School of International Service, American University.

Lowell Turner is Associate Professor, School of Industrial and Labor Relations, Cornell University.

Douglas Webber is Associate Professor of Business and Political Science, INSEAD.

Kirsten S. Wever is Assistant Professor of Labor Studies and Employment Relations, Rutgers University.

Acknowledgments

This book is based on original contributions presented at the conference "The Political Economy of the New Germany," held at Cornell University, October 14–15, 1994. Chapters were revised for presentation and discussion at the International Industrial Relations Association Tenth World Congress, Washington, D.C., May 31–June 4, 1995. Final drafts were then prepared in 1996 for publication in this volume, with final revisions in 1997. For funding support, the authors thank the School of Industrial and Labor Relations, the International Political Economy Program, and the Institute of European Studies, all at Cornell University, as well as Thomas Kochan and the German-American Section of the International Industrial Relations Association. For important logistical support, we thank Lori Ard, Alison Cable, Jackie Dodge, Tammy Gardner, and Susan Wright. At Cornell University Press, this book was significantly improved by the editorial and organizational work of Roger Haydon, Teresa Jesionowski, and Andrew Lewis.

This book is dedicated to John P. Windmuller, a pioneer in the study of international and comparative labor, a superb teacher, and a truly fine, compassionate human being.

L. T.

Negotiating the New Germany

Introduction
Up Against the Fallen Wall:
The Crisis of Social Partnership
in Unified Germany

Lowell Turner

It is commonplace for both eastern and western Germans to remark, not always in jest and often with bitterness, that they were better off before the Berlin Wall came down. Westerners resent the high economic costs of unification, which have translated into higher taxes and lower paychecks to finance an enormous resource transfer from West to East (about $100 billion per year since unification in 1990). Easterners resent the collapse of their economy, mass unemployment in a formerly full employment society, the stripping away of social benefits ranging from free child care to government-subsidized vacation homes, and the occupation of their territory by Western business, labor, and government officials.

These complaints are symptomatic of the contemporary crisis of social partnership in unified Germany. And indeed it is quite clear that the German social market economy is under extraordinary pressure from a number of directions. Competition on the global market is becoming more and more intense; European economic integration continues to demand social, political, and economic concessions that Germany cannot easily afford. Added to these are the immediate and protracted pressures of German unification. Yet the fate of the German model of economic and social regulation is important far beyond the new national borders: on it depends not only the relative success of German exports in world markets but also the prospects for democratic stability here at the center of the new, post-cold war Europe and the very future of social democracy.[1]

---

1. This is not to say that West Germany was ever as fully social-democratic as other, smaller countries such as Sweden. The interplay between the major postwar political parties blended

This book addresses two central and related sets of questions. First, what type of political economy is emerging in unified Germany? How "West German" is it? Is Germany permanently polarized into East and West or converging on a single, integrated political economy? To what extent is the "coordinated market economy" (Soskice 1991) becoming less, or differently, coordinated? The answers to these questions will affect the outcomes of issues ranging from policy and politics to production organization.

Second, what has happened to the famous German "social partnership" since unification? Do the employer offensives of 1993–1996 in the pattern-setting metal and electronics industries, and in other industries as well, indicate a serious hollowing out or simply a readjustment of the social partnership? What has happened to employer associations and unions since German unification? What will happen to them in the near future? Can German industry hold its own in increasingly competitive world markets with its social partnership relations intact, or is this an outdated and expensive model of the past? Can the social partnership survive decentralization and lean production, or will they undermine and eventually dissolve it?

The articles in this collection focus on the conditions for institutional adaptation in new market circumstances. In the "new world disorder" of an increasingly globalized economy, what happens to the German political economy will have wide repercussions for the pace and shape of economic development throughout Europe. The questions addressed above illuminate broader ones: Will any sort of social market capitalism persist in Germany (and other parts of Europe) as an alternative to the U.S. and Japanese variants of capitalism? Or are we all in time headed down the same road of deregulation, lean production, and union decline? Is Germany now falling apart, as some observers claim, a victim of high costs and/or unification, or are there good prospects for future economic, political, and social success? What does the future hold for social democracy in Germany, Europe, and elsewhere?

On the front lines of contemporary social science research into rapidly changing world events, such questions rarely have "correct answers." Rather, they usually provoke ongoing and sometimes heated debate based on contrasting empirical evidence and analytical approaches. In this book, therefore, we present not one answer to each of these questions but rather

---

important elements of social democracy, Christian democracy, and liberalism in the making of economic and social policy as well as political and economic institutions. But with its strong unions, comprehensive collective bargaining, and other arrangements for labor-inclusive negotiation throughout the political economy and with its expansive welfare state, West Germany —and unified Germany today—has certainly been the large industrial society that most closely approximates a social-democratic model.

a variety of well-argued answers from different perspectives. In the presentation of diverse opinions, our hope is both to offer the truth—none of us in this uncertain world can be absolutely certain that our own well-researched findings and persuasively argued analyses are correct, yet somewhere in this diversity the truth *does* lie—and to stimulate the reader's own critical thinking about changing global markets and the prospects for socially responsible regulation.

THE GERMAN MODEL

This book can only introduce the contemporary debates; it is beyond our scope to spell out in great detail how the German economy works and how its social partnership orientation distinguishes it from other variants of capitalism found in Japan, the United States, and elsewhere. Yet the careful reader will travel behind the scenes and into the workings of social partnership capitalism in a number of areas, from economic policy, to industrial relations, to vocational training. Those seeking a more schematic and detailed presentation of the organization of the German economy should consult other sources.[2] To understand the arguments presented in this book, a thumbnail sketch of the German model should suffice.

Germans refer to theirs as a "social market" economy. By this, they mean an economy organized around market principles such as supply and demand and free trade, yet subject to extensive social regulation. The emphasis on *market principles* means, for example, that the Federal Republic and its major interest groups have throughout the postwar period supported expanding free trade (and indeed the German economy is significantly dependent on exports) and European economic integration. In addition, monetary policy is regulated by a strong and independent central bank, committed at all costs to keeping inflation low in order to ensure the strength and stability of the currency with which market exchanges are transacted. The emphasis on *social regulation* is intended to ensure that the impersonal workings of markets do not interfere with or undermine basic social needs, ranging from adequate income and health care, to organized representation in the workplace, to comprehensive vocational training. Social regulation includes both a safety net and broader social benefits (includ-

2. See, for example, Streeck 1984, Berghahn and Karsten 1987, Katzenstein 1989, Thelen 1991, and Wever 1995. For a concise and useful history of Germany from World War II through unification, see H. Turner 1992. On the problems and processes of German unification, see Huelshoff, Markovits, and Reich 1993; Hancock and Welsh 1994; and Goodhart 1994. For comparative analyses that contrast German economic organization to that found in the United States and other countries, see Hart 1992, Soskice 1990, L. Turner 1991, and Wever 1995.

ing, for example, health care for all and free university education for all who qualify). Part and parcel of social regulation is the concept of *social partnership*: negotiated agreements between strong and well-organized employer associations and labor unions throughout the political economy, from wage bargaining, to vocational training, to regularized input into economic policymaking.

This collection emphasizes the social partnership: the actors and institutional relationships that make the German economy a social market and distinguish it fundamentally from other types of capitalism.[3] Most employers in Germany belong to powerful employer associations organized by industrial sector; around one-third of German employees belong to independent labor unions (most of which are also organized by industrial sector).[4] More telling than membership levels is the fact that for most employees in the private sector, basic pay levels and working conditions are set in comprehensive collective bargaining agreements between employer associations and industrial unions (Jacobi, Keller, and Müller-Jentsch 1992, 236–38).[5]

In addition to collective bargaining, generally negotiated outside the firm for entire sectors and regions, the German "dual system" of industrial relations offers a second basic pillar of representation for employees: codetermination at the firm level. German law provides for elected workforce representation both on the supervisory boards of firms with five hundred or more employees and in the works councils for each workplace with five or more employees. In the latter case in particular, works councillors elected by the entire workforce, blue collar and white, have regularized and ongoing rights to information concerning and consultation and participation in management decision-making processes. Since in most cases works councillors as well as elected supervisory board members are also members of one of the sixteen dominant industrial unions, codetermination provides an additional firm-based level of union influence and ongoing labor-

3. See Hart 1992 for a useful description of alternative ways of organizing market economies, in Britain, France, Germany, the United States, and Japan.

4. Figures vary according to how calculations are made. Typical figures, stable for most of the postwar period, show union membership density ranging around 35 percent. See, for example, Jacobi, Keller, and Müller-Jentsch 1992, 232.

5. Exact numbers are difficult to pin down. Typically cited private sector figures (for 1989 to 1996) range around 80 percent employer association coverage (meaning that 80 percent of all employees work at firms belonging to an employers association) in western Germany and around 50 percent in eastern Germany (where association presence is still quite new). Figures gathered by Stephen Silvia from Gesamtmetall for the metal and electronics industries indicate somewhat lower—and declining—rates of coverage: 74.5 percent of West German employees were covered by comprehensive collective bargaining in 1984, compared to 64.2 percent in 1993.

management negotiation. In practice, personnel decisions in such areas as transfers, promotions, hiring and firing, work reorganization, working hours, and overtime are not made without the consent of the elected works council.[6]

These private-sector processes are mirrored in the public sector, where "personnel councils" play the role of works councils and basic pay and working conditions are set in negotiations between strong unions and corresponding government ministries.

If comprehensive collective bargaining and codetermination are the cornerstones of social partnership in Germany, negotiation and collaboration among organized business and labor also permeate both the human infrastructure of the economy and the processes of economic and social policymaking at the local, state, and federal levels. The much admired and extensive German system of vocational training (in which two-thirds of young Germans receive skills training in multiyear apprenticeships, followed by continuing opportunities for advanced training), for example, is everywhere overseen and actively participated in by both employer associations and labor unions. And the "social partners" are actively consulted in government policymaking, often quietly and behind the scenes but sometimes formally and with great public fanfare, as in 1992–93 "Solidarity Pact" negotiations that set the framework for key economic policy decisions regarding the new states of eastern Germany.

In these and other ways, well-organized and officially recognized social partners—business and labor—establish rules and negotiate important components of the framework in which the German market economy operates.

THE UNIFICATION OF GERMANY AND ITS CONSEQUENCES

The social market model, referred to here as "social partnership capitalism" to indicate the active and central role of organized business and labor, had great success throughout the lifespan of West Germany (1949–1990). Impressive and consistently strong economic performance unfolded over four decades in a society characterized by strong labor and social standards, including high wages and benefits, low income polarization (compared to

6. This is especially true for firms with one hundred or more employees, virtually all of which have elected works councils. Many smaller firms do not have works councils (although they are mandated by law), since employee initiative is required to establish an election committee to get the process started. Since there are no penalties for not having a works council, smaller firms often lack works councils for one or both of the following reasons: the employees lack the interest or initiative to establish one, or the employer has discouraged them from exercising their rights.

other large industrial societies), and strong mechanisms for workforce representation. The authors represented in this book are unanimous in their admiration of key elements of the German model. They diverge in their assessments of the adaptation and resilience of the model in the face of dramatic new challenges in the 1990s.

When in the wake of unification the German economy plunged into a deep recession in 1992–1993, voices were raised on both sides of the Atlantic to argue that German social partnership was an expensive relic of a welfare-state past that could no longer solve the problems of an increasingly competitive global marketplace. In its emphasis on expanded vocational training, labor-management partnership, and a more activist government economic policy, the Clinton administration, and in particular Secretary of Labor Robert Reich, was criticized from the Right as a proponent of the German model just as this model headed into decline.[7] Even admirers of German social partnership wondered if negotiated decision making, strong labor and social standards, entrenched patterns of labor-management collaboration, and strong trade unionism in an era of international union decline could survive in the new post-cold war global economy.

In 1990 the stakes were raised dramatically. To West Germany's stable social market economy—population 60 million—was added overnight a large new chunk of territory, the former East Germany, with a population of 16 million. In the face of currency union on July 1, 1990, and political unification on October 3, 1990, both the eastern economy and accompanying institutions such as public ownership structures and communist-led trade unions collapsed. Western "social partners" were confronted quite suddenly with a vacuum of ownership and representation requiring major organizational efforts. Although both unions and employer associations quickly established a presence in the East and began to negotiate comprehensive collective bargaining agreements, more fundamental questions remained: Could these new actors and institutions transferred from the West sink roots deep enough to make social partnership work in the new federal states—and so in unified Germany as a whole? Would incoming westerners adapt or impose their model in the East? Could economic growth take off in the East, to bring this part of the country and its imported institutions up to western levels, to make unification a reality? Or would the East remain a less developed area, weak in both economic capacity and representation, where individual employers could set lower labor and social standards (as U.S. employers have done in the American South) that in time would undermine the social partnership back in the West? For a host of

7. See, for example, David Gitlitz and Lawrence Kudlow, "The Reich Reich," *National Review*, July 11, 1994, pp. 44ff.

reasons, well-placed scholars of German industrial relations predicted pessimistic and perhaps ultimately disastrous scenarios for both unions and employer associations in the new Eastern states.[8]

As if life-and-death challenges posed by unification were not enough, two other major challenges came into full view in the early 1990s. First, continuing European integration lent credibility to the threat that German employers would relocate their firms and factories to much cheaper locations in southern and eastern Europe. The threat of capital flight or "social dumping" (expressed in the 1990s as a loud and public debate over the viability of *Standort Deutschland,* Germany as a production location) threatened to raise employer bargaining power at the expense of unions', weaken national institutions of regulation, and thereby destabilize the social partnership (see, for example, Mosley 1990 and Streeck 1991). And second, intensified global trade competition and especially the development of low-cost, high-quality Japanese production methods exposed problematic German rigidities in both cost and production organization (see, for example, Kern and Sabel 1990 and Gary Herrigel's chapter in this volume). German industry appeared by the early 1990s to require a major reorganization of work, a daunting task for a rather stable and slow-to-change social partnership.

THE DEBATES

The debates in this collection concern both the actual responses of the social partners to these challenges and the prospects for adaptation and future success. Extreme views are excluded: both the now-discredited "blooming landscape" perspective, which posits a largely seamless transfer of western institutions to the East and continuing rapid adjustment of German industry to new European and global challenges, and the hopelessly pessimistic "iron-cage" perspective, which discounts actor strategies and sees the German social partnership as trapped by impersonal forces of history.

Michael Fichter, Gary Herrigel, and Stephen Silvia all emphasize the crisis faced by social partnership and its current erosion. Fichter emphasizes prolonged East-West tension within the labor unions and the failure of transplanted western institutions to take root in eastern soil. Herrigel highlights western rigidities in work organization, on the part of managers and skilled workers, that interfere with a necessary reorganization of German industry to match the output of Japanese-inspired lean production. Silvia calls attention to the increasing bifurcation of the contemporary German labor mar-

---

8. On employer associations, see Wiesenthal, Ettl, and Bialas 1992. For unions, see Armingeon 1991 and Mahnkopf 1991 and 1993.

ket, which has begun to affect formerly insulated groups such as skilled blue-collar workers, pointing in the direction of an American-style polarization that could well confine the social partnership to a shrinking elite core.

On the more optimistic side, Peter Auer, Lowell Turner, Douglas Webber, and Kirsten Wever emphasize the capacity for continuing negotiated problem solving within the basic social partnership. Auer outlines the basic stability of German social partnership, and especially codetermination, as indicated by bargaining outcomes of 1993–95, while nonetheless calling attention to the millions of unemployed, who are not part of the system and need to be included. Turner points to the dramatic and unexpected strike victory of IG Metall in eastern Germany in 1993 and backs up his assessment of the relative success of social partnership with plant-level case studies. Webber presents broad political evidence, such as the Solidarity Pact negotiations of 1992–93, to argue that pressures of unification have actually promoted a resurgence of key elements of the German model, such as peak-level "corporatist" bargaining between organized business and labor. And Wever, calling attention as Herrigel does to necessary decentralization and reform within German firms, nonetheless argues that entrenched patterns of negotiation and compromise make successful renegotiation within the firm possible.

Other, perhaps wiser voices place less emphasis on either optimistic or pessimistic assessment, examining instead the contingencies present in key areas of economic policy. Chris Allen examines unification-era policy failures and the great danger inherent in what he poetically terms the "siren song of deregulation." Matthias Knuth explains the paradox of social peace in circumstances of massive economic dislocation in eastern Germany as a product of unprecedentedly active labor-market policy efforts, including important (and union-inspired) innovations such as the employment and training company (ETC). And finally, Richard Locke and Wade Jacoby examine the post-unification development of vocational training systems in eastern Germany, comparing Leipzig and Chemnitz to explain the successes and failures of institutional transfer as products of the vitality of local institutions and networks of civil society.

IMPLICATIONS FOR A THEORY OF CHANGE

Three variables emerge as most relevant in the sometimes contrasting analyses presented in this book: global competition and economic restructuring (the environment); existing institutions (structure); and actor strategy (agency). For those who emphasize the crisis, all three are important: global market competition drives change, which is inhibited by institutional rigidity and aggravated by an employer offensive against the rigidities within German social partnership. For those who emphasize adaptation of the German model in difficult circumstances, global markets and the employer offensive drive change while flexible institutions and actor strategies (especially union strategy) shape viable adaptation.

The real differences then are both empirical and theoretical and concern mainly structure and agency—since we all agree about the severity of environmental challenges, from global competition and European integration to German unification. The authors concur that institutions are important, but differ considerably over just how flexible or rigid, how capable of reform, these contemporary German institutions are. To what extent are Germans today trapped in once successful institutions (and corresponding identities, as Herrigel argues) that are no longer up to the new tasks faced, or capable of adequate and rapid reform—a German version, perhaps, of the "British disease"? To what extent can conscious actors shape or adapt the given institutions to solve major new problems? How important are innovative union strategies—or are the actors trapped by environmental and institutional constraints?

Finally, if strategy matters, then what kind is most important? Each author emphasizes a different area, and in so doing stakes a claim for primary theoretical relevance. Fichter, Herrigel, Silvia, and Wever emphasize internal organizational reform, pointing both to the constraints and opportunities in given institutions and to potential actor strategies to reform the institutions in the face of new challenges. Knuth, Turner, and Webber, by contrast, emphasize outward-directed strategy, especially on the part of unions and government, to adapt and reform institutions, policies, and bargaining relationships.

The overarching theme of this volume is conflict and negotiation—a fitting theme for a book on social partnership. Since 1989, the German model has found itself under great pressure; change or at least the necessity of change is driven by dramatic circumstances in the world arena. Existing institutions of the Federal Republic, now transferred to the new states of eastern Germany as well, matter a great deal for German capacities to manage the crisis—and as various authors argue here from different viewpoints, make some outcomes more likely than others. Yet within given institutional constraints, actors in business, labor, and government promote innovative or traditional strategies, which in turn collide with the strategies of other actors. In the end, the outcomes of conflict and negotiation between actors will provide at least the immediate cause for the relative success or failure of both policy innovation and institutional reform.

REFERENCES

Armingeon, Klaus. 1991. "Ende einer Erfolgsstory? Gewerkschaften und Arbeitsbeziehungen im Einingungsprozeß." *Gegenwartskunde* 1: 29–42.

Berghahn, Volker R., and Detlev Karsten. 1987. *Industrial Relations in West Germany*. Oxford: Berg.

Brunetta, Renato, and Carlo Dell'Aringa, eds. 1990. *Labour Relations and Economic Performance*. Proceedings of the International Economic Association conference in Venice, Italy. IEA Conference Volume no. 95. Houndsmill, U.K.: Macmillan.

Ferner, Anthony, and Richard Hyman, eds. 1992. *Industrial Relations in the New Europe*. Oxford: Blackwell.

Goodhart, David. 1994. *The Reshaping of the German Social Market*. London: Institute for Public Policy Research.

Hancock, M. Donald, and Helga A. Welsh, eds. 1994. *German Unification: Process and Outcomes*. Boulder, Colo.: Westview Press.

Hart, Jeffrey A. 1992. *Rival Capitalists: International Competitiveness in the United States, Japan, and Western Europe*. Ithaca: Cornell University Press.

Huelshoff, Michael G., Andrei S. Markovits, and Simon Reich, eds. 1993. *From Bundesrepublik to Deutschland: German Politics after Unification*. Ann Arbor: University of Michigan Press.

Jacobi, Otto, Berndt Keller, and Walther Müller-Jentsch. 1992. "Germany: Codetermining the Future." In Ferner and Hyman, eds., 218–69.

Katzenstein, Peter J., ed. 1989. *Industry and Politics in West Germany: Toward the Third Republic*. Ithaca: Cornell University Press.

Kern, Horst, and Charles F. Sabel. 1990. "Gewerkschaften in offenen Arbeitsmärkten." Soziale Welt 41, no. 2: 144–66.

Mahnkopf, Birgit. 1991. "Vorwärts in die Vergangenheit? Pessimistische Spekulationen über die Zukunft der Gewerkschaften in der neuen Bundesrepublik." In Westphal et al. 1991, 269–94.

——. 1993. "The Impact of Unification on the German System of Industrial Relations." Discussion Paper FS I 93–102, Wissenschaftszentrum Berlin für Sozialforschung.

Mosley, Hugh G. 1990. "The Social Dimension of European Integration." *International Labour Review* 129, no. 2: 147–64.

Soskice, David. 1990. "Reinterpreting Corporatism and Explaining Unemployment: Co-ordinated and Non-co-ordinated Market Economies." In Brunetta and Dell'Aringa 1990, 170–211.

Streeck, Wolfgang. 1984. "Co-determination: The Fourth Decade." In Wilpert and Sorge 1984, 391–422.

———. 1991. "More Uncertainties: German Unions Facing 1992." *Industrial Relations* 30, no. 3: 317–47.

Thelen, Kathleen A. 1991. *A Union of Parts: Labor Politics in Postwar Germany*. Ithaca: Cornell University Press.

Turner, Henry Ashby, Jr. 1992. *Germany from Partition to Reunification*. New Haven: Yale University Press.

Turner, Lowell. 1991. *Democracy at Work: Changing World Markets and the Future of Labor Unions*. Ithaca: Cornell University Press.

Westphal, Andreas, Hansjörg Herr, Michael Heine, and Ulrich Busch, eds. 1991. *Wirtschaftspolitische Konsequenzen der deutschen Vereinigung*. Frankfurt: Campus Verlag.

Wever, Kirsten. 1995. *Negotiating Competitiveness: Employment Relations and Organizational Innovation in Germany and the United States*. Boston: Harvard Business School Press.

Wiesenthal, Helmut, Wilfried Ettl, and Christiane Bialas. 1992. "Interessenverbände im Transformationsprozeß." Arbeitsgruppe Transformationsprozesse in den neuen Bundesländern, Humboldt Universität, Max-Planck-Gesellschaft, Working Paper AG TRAP, no. 92110, Berlin.

Wilpert, Bernhard, and Arndt Sorge, eds. 1984. *International Yearbook of Organizational Democracy*. Vol. 2, *International Perspectives on Organizational Democracy*. New York: John Wiley & Sons.

1 • Unifying Germany: Social Partnership Moves East

1 • Institutional Stability Pays: German Industrial Relations under Pressure

Peter Auer

From the economic miracle *(Wirtschaftswunder)* of the 1950s to its central position in today's European Union, the Federal Republic of Germany has been a remarkable socioeconomic success. In spite of contemporary problems in the wake of German unification, long-term economic strength and social stability remain the underlying realities. This success, both long-term and contemporary, is the product of the institutional setting of the social market economy. This is true because these institutions are both inclusive and stable but allow for flexibility through incremental change.

The inclusive and stable institutional setting, which includes federalism, financial institutions, and a nationwide system of vocational training, is a dense network that permeates, regulates, and facilitates the workings of the market economy in Germany. Two institutions of industrial relations, collective bargaining and codetermination, which bring together the organized interests of business and labor in negotiated relations of "social partnership," are especially important elements of this market environment.

The responses of the institutions of German industrial relations to the contemporary challenges of unification, the Europeanization of markets, and the coming of lean production have consistently demonstrated that an essentially inclusive institutional stability that allows for incremental change has been a powerful factor in Germany's socioeconomic success and its capacity to cope with new challenges. Analyses of West Germany based on

This article is a thoroughly revised version of a chapter in Davis and Lansbury, eds., *Managing Together? Consultation and Participation in the Workplace* (Sydney: Addison Wesley Longman Australia, 1996), and appears here by permission of the publisher.

its relative success in the 1980s (such as Katzenstein 1989) thus turn out to be surprisingly valid for unified Germany in the mid-1990s.

Conventional wisdom differs sharply from the perspective presented here. The OECD, for example, blames contemporary social and economic problems in advanced industrial societies (such as declining economic competitiveness and high unemployment) on structural rigidities, pointing implicitly at inflexible institutions such as those which regulate industrial relations (OECD 1994). The German case, by contrast, demonstrates the positive contribution of stable institutions in a rapidly changing world economy, when those institutions are both inclusive and adaptable.

Important and unpredictable changes have visited the German economic and political system in recent years: German unification, which came as a great surprise to most; European integration, with both progress and major pitfalls; the deep recession of 1992–93; and far-reaching organizational change in the direction of "lean production." These changes pose major challenges for the German system of industrial relations, long seen as a cornerstone of the successful German social market economy. What remains to be seen is how well the German system of industrial relations will be able to cope with these challenges.

INDUSTRIAL RELATIONS AND CODETERMINATION

There are three laws that regulate workplace codetermination in Germany: the law on codetermination in the coal and steel industries *(Montanmitbestimmung)* of 1951, the law on codetermination on company supervisory boards of 1976, and the Works Constitution Act *(Betriebsverfassungsgesetz)* adopted in 1952 and amended in 1972. These laws, together with the bodies and functions they establish (such as works councils at the company level), shape the institutions of codetermination in the narrow sense.

A more extensive view of codetermination, however, must take other institutions into account as well. The most important instrument of labor's influence on the economy—and therefore in a sense the most powerful instrument of codetermination—is collective bargaining. In Germany, collective agreements are negotiated at an industry level between employer associations and industrial unions and have a geographical scope that is either nationwide or regional. Differences between regions are small, and even inter-industry wage differentials are rather minor (Streeck 1987, 3). Although collective bargaining at the industry level is mainly concerned with wages and working hours, other issues, such as training, are also regulated at that level. Kathleen Thelen (1991) emphasizes the importance of this dualism (codetermination at the plant level and industry-wide collective bargaining) to an understanding of German industrial relations. Gerhard Leminsky (1995) underlines how the complementarity of collective bargaining and codetermination is even more apparent today, given that changes in work organization and the spread of "opening" or "hardship" clauses in collective agreements have intensified company-level bargaining.

Other forms of codetermination include trade union participation on the boards of the "self-administered" social security agency and the national employment service *(Bundesanstalt für Arbeit)*, as well as in the organization of vocational training (especially in initial apprenticeships), itself one of the most important sources of the German "industrial consensus" (Streeck 1987, 5).

In fact, codetermination includes all of these elements and their interrelations—with collective bargaining at the center—which together add up to a "flexible coordinated system" (Soskice 1990) providing for bargained settlements on many issues. Although it should be kept in mind that the different elements of this system are all highly interdependent, I emphasize here the basic institutions of codetermination in the narrower sense—codetermination at the board and management levels and on the shop floor.

CODETERMINATION ON COMPANY SUPERVISORY BOARDS

"Montanmitbestimmung," codetermination in the German coal and steel industry, has far-reaching provisions that were not extended to joint-stock companies in other industries. These include parity of seats on the supervisory board and the appointment of a worker director, responsible for social-welfare matters and personnel management, to the management board.[1] The worker director cannot be appointed without the consent of the representatives of labor on the supervisory board. The introduction of this form of far-reaching codetermination happened without resistance even from conservative parties such as the governing CDU (Stein 1976), in part because in 1951, when the law was passed, the memory of how important these key industries had been to Hitler's National Socialism and the war effort was still fresh. For other industries, however, opposition was much stiffer.

Despite trade union demands to extend Montanmitbestimmung to other industries, the Works Constitution Act of 1952 was more limited. Only a third of the members of the supervisory boards of all joint-stock companies and of all limited liability companies with more than five hundred employees had to directly elect representatives of the workforce. It took twenty-five years and a Social-Democrat-led coalition government for another, fuller version of codetermination to be introduced in all joint-stock companies

---

1. Large German companies have both a supervisory board that meets quarterly to make strategic and policy decisions and a management board responsible for day-to-day operations.

with at least two thousand employees. The Codetermination Act of 1976 provided for a parity of seats between shareholders and representatives of the employees on the supervisory boards of such companies; in effect, however, the shareholders retained a majority, since in case of a tie vote, the chairman of the board (always a representative of the shareholders) had the deciding vote. Moreover, one of the "employee" representatives had to come from the managerial staff, and the workers' representatives had no voice in the selection of the worker director.

While codetermination at the supervisory board level is an important means for unions to gain access to information and to influence board decision making, the decisions supervisory boards make are often regarded as relatively unimportant. Members of supervisory boards usually act in an "oversight" role for several companies. But they have been repeatedly criticized for exerting more of a symbolic influence than real control over their management boards, where real decision-making power lies. Moreover, the further away from the shop floor codetermination rights are exercised, the less important the workers themselves consider them. Indeed, workers have sometimes even openly criticized union representatives, especially when they have failed to prevent layoffs, as is often the case in economic downturns (a fact noted by Gülden back in 1977). The "Steinkühler affair" certainly did little to raise worker opinion of union representatives on supervisory boards. Franz Steinkühler, former president of Germany's largest union, IG Metall, and a member of the supervisory boards of Daimler Benz, VW, and Thyssen, was accused of insider trading in two instances, leading to his resignation from these boards as well as from his union presidency. This scandal did lead to questions regarding the activities of union representatives on the boards, but not to any change in policy toward codetermination.

CODETERMINATION ON THE SHOP FLOOR

The Works Constitution Act of 1972 regulates the composition and functions of the works council *(Betriebsrat)*, the organ of representation for all wage and salary earners of a company, regardless of union membership. Thelen (1991) notes that the unions opposed the 1952 law because the CDU government made the works councils legally independent of the unions. The 1972 law, which was adopted under a Social-Democratic government, did not abandon the stipulation that works councils remain technically neutral in industrial disputes, but it did tighten the potential links between works councils and unions by giving works council members rights to perform in-plant functions on behalf of the unions (Thelen 1991, 102). In practice, however, there has always been a strong link between unions and works councils, for most *Betriebsräte* (works councillors) are in fact union members. In the 1990 works council elections (held nationwide, plant by plant, simultaneously), 76 percent of those elected came from DGB (Deutscher Gewerkschaftsbund—the German central labor federation) union lists, and an additional 3 percent from the white-collar DAG (Deutsche Angestellten Gewerkschaft—the German Employees' Union.)(Kronenberg et al. 1991).

Works councils are elected by all employees at companies that regularly employ at least five permanent workers. No employer or management representative sits on the work council (unless a middle or lower-level manager, as an employee of the company, is elected by the workforce, which does sometimes happen).

The size of a works council depends on the size of the firm. Any council having more than nine members may form an executive committee *(Betriebsausschuß)* to run day-to-day business. All companies with more than one hundred employees may have an economic committee of the workforce, which receives information on the company's economic affairs from management. In larger, multi-plant companies, representatives of the plant councils form central works councils, and in large diversified corporations a corporate works council *(Konzernbetriebsrat)* can be formed. Works council members are partially or totally (depending on the size of the firm) freed from work and enjoy special protection from dismissal.

Works councils have participation rights (the right to be informed and to be consulted by management) as well as specified codetermination rights, such as the right to veto certain management decisions in such matters as the classification and reclassification of workers, working-time arrangements, overtime, and to a more limited extent, recruitment and dismissal. Negotiation rights extend to areas such as the scheduling of the working day, vacation plans, job design, training, and the compensation plans that accompany mass layoffs. Works councils have a broadly defined right to information regarding company business. If the works council and management disagree, however, works councils cannot call for industrial action (they have a *Friedenspflicht,* or "peace obligation") but must refer the matter to an arbitration committee. They have no rights in basic wage bargaining but do negotiate pay premiums and certain fringe benefits. With work-time reductions and new flexibility arrangements, including "opening clauses" that allow for negotiated working-time reductions to save jobs, bargaining at the enterprise level is becoming more important, thus enhancing the rights and powers of the works councils (see, for example, the discussion of *Verbetrieblichung,* "company-centered bargaining," in Lecher 1995 and Leminsky 1995).

Participation at the plant level has a second dimension, union representation on the shop floor through the shop stewards *(Vertrauensleute).* During the seventies, the years of shopfloor politicization, the "imperial" behavior of certain works councillors was criticized by the more rank-and-file shop stewards; this nucleus of rank-and-file upsurge, however, did not develop into a serious force in West Germany. Despite some claims that this "genuine trade union representation" should be invigorated as company-centered bargaining *(Verbetrieblichung)* accelerates, and that the "mono-representation" tradition of enterprise unions in the former GDR would facilitate linking old and new structures (Lecher 1995), a comeback of the shop stewards as an important counterbalance to the works council seems improbable. Therefore, this "dualism" does not nowadays constitute an important source of conflict, partially because of the strong influence the unions exert on works councils, an influence strengthened by the 1972 and 1976 amendments to the Works Constitution Act.

Although the institution of works councils is generally seen as a rather powerful instrument of codetermination at the workplace (Thelen 1991; Turner 1991; Streeck and Vitols 1993), some (German) observers remain more skeptical. Wolfgang Däubler, for example, wrote in an interpretation of the 1972 act that "the overall picture is clear: the employer's autonomy to decide on all things concerning the company remains untouched" (Däubler 1975, 22). On the other hand, Wolfgang Streeck contends that especially in large firms the "factual strength of works councils often exceeds their legal power." While this has also led to accusations of "plant egoism," and some authors have identified a trend away from unitary unionism toward plant syndicalism (Hohn 1988), the strength of central industrial unions as such has not been too seriously affected. If anything, union strength has been boosted by such important IG Metall victories as the battle for working-time reductions in 1984 and the defense of the eastern contract in 1993.

The extent of actual codetermination, in any event, is determined not only by legal stipulations but also to some extent by the specific circumstances in (and the size of) different companies.

SMALL FIRMS AND PUBLIC-SECTOR INDUSTRIAL RELATIONS

The Works Constitution Act does not cover all German firms: very small firms (fewer than five employees), which account for about 65 percent of the total, are outside its scope; thus, under the law, works councils are possible in only about 500,000 of the approximately 1.4 million German firms. These 500,000 firms, however, employ 87 percent of the workforce (Wassermann 1989). In addition, the law only allows for the election of works councils; it does not require them. Thus, at the beginning of the 1980s, only 25 percent of companies with fewer than 100 employees had works councils, while in the size class from 100 to 999 employees 90 percent had them (Bosch 1983, 322). There is no legal sanction for companies who fail to install a works council even if there has been a worker initiative to create one (Däubler 1975). The more frequent case, however, is that no initiative is forthcoming to found a council (in face of either employer/owner opposition or workforce inertia). This shows that even in Germany with its highly developed system of industrial relations large numbers of firms remain outside the norms set primarily by and for the large companies (Auer and Fehr-Duda 1989). It appears that this is all the more true of codetermination at the board level: the Codetermination Act of 1976 affected—in the mid 1980s—480 firms, which employed about 27 percent of the workforce and produced half of total output.

Specific conditions apply to the public sector. While a large proportion of the some 5 million employed in the public sector (20 percent of total employment in Germany) is covered by arrangements similar to the Works Constitution Act (the Staff Representation Act, providing for staff councils, or *Personalräte*), and their terms and conditions of work are the result of collective bargaining, the rules for the 1.9 million officially designated civil servants *(Beamte)* are established by law. Wage increases from collective bargaining, however, are generally applied to civil servants as well.

The importance of the differences in codetermination at big private companies, small firms, and in the public sector is difficult to judge. In fact, much less is known about the latter two segments of the economy because industrial relations literature has tended to focus on large industrial firms. Leaving aside civil servants, codetermination at the "office floor" in the public sector, which is highly unionized (with union density of around 80 percent, about twice the national average), seems to be rather analogous to that in the larger enterprises, certainly as far as the legal framework is concerned (Henneberger and Keller 1991). Bargaining is more centralized and has led to a pay and classification scheme that leaves less room for individual adaptation. Only as far as working-time schedules are concerned is there today more scope for workplace bargaining in the public sector.[2]

For small firms, codetermination depends on the presence or absence of union representatives and works councils; as has already been noted, many small firms have neither. In such cases, codetermination depends on the good will of the owner, since there are no other intermediaries between the owner and the workers. Whereas such intermediaries (union representatives or works councillors) are "built-in" at large firms, outside intermediaries (local unions, labor courts) usually only intervene at small firms in case of

---

2. See, for example, *European Industrial Relations Review* no. 233 (June 1993): 27.

conflicts. And while it is true in general that wage levels at small firms are lower and working conditions less generous than at large firms (Wassermann 1989), labor law and collective bargaining provisions apply there as well, so that the sector is not as such "deregulated." And so far, no significant lobby has arisen to fight for an extension of codetermination rights to small firms or their enforcement there.

We can summarize the foregoing by saying that the German institutions of codetermination taken together in their interactions have up to now constituted a powerful instrument for the participation of labor in economic and social developments and have contributed to what Thelen (1991) calls "negotiated adjustment." Until very recently at least, unions have, through these institutional channels, obtained real wage gains, shortened the working week considerably, and successfully dealt with a growing bargaining agenda at company level (e.g., for flexibility of working hours and technological and organizational change). Although union membership is now declining (membership in DGB unions fell from 11.8 million in December 1991 to around 10 million in July 1994) as a consequence of the recession, structural adjustment, and employment losses in the East (see Hoffmann 1995, 101), they are still far more powerful than other European (or American) unions, which have experienced sharply declining density rates and loss of influence.

At the same time, because of changes in the economic and political environment, codetermination (and industrial relations in general) now faces major new challenges. Three areas of structural change—German reunification, European integration, and lean forms of production organization—are among the most important challenges facing German industrial relations today.

LEAN PRODUCTION AND CODETERMINATION

Ever since the publication of *The Machine That Changed the World* (Womack, Jones, and Roos 1990), many German managers have been eagerly striving to introduce lean forms of production into their companies. Philipp Cooke (1993) has shown that many German managers consider *The Machine That Changed the World* a "bible" in their attempts to change outmoded production and labor practices. Faced with the seminal message of the book, "change or die," works councillors and unions have had to respond to this form of rationalization, which—along with recession in 1992–93—has already cost many jobs in the metal industry (between 1991 and 1994 more than 600,000 jobs were lost, 150,000 alone in the automobile industry) and other branches, with more job cuts yet to come despite the economic upturn. The trade union position on lean production is ambiguous, in part because of the vagueness of the concept itself, which includes items to which unions would subscribe: direct worker participation, for example, which for union reformists is high on the agenda (Lecher 1995). The twofold nature of the concept (more participative work organization on the one hand, technical and organizational rationalization leading to employment losses on the other hand) accounts for the ambiguity as far as the unions are concerned. Works councils are entitled, under the Works Constitution Act, to be at least consulted concerning the implementation of lean forms of production, and in certain circumstances they have bargaining rights. But if reorganization does not run against accepted standards of work organization and ergonomics (which lean production often does), they cannot prevent its introduction. And in the face of increasing competition and the growing threat of plant relocation within the EU and elsewhere (such as Eastern Europe), German unions themselves are convinced that production processes in German industry must change. Industry has to get leaner, not as lean perhaps as employers would like (the unions continue to strive for "humanization of work" goals such as long task cycles and autonomy from machine pacing), but lean enough to permit a sound competitive position. Therefore, works councils do not in principle oppose the introduction of lean forms of work organization. Even if in most cases they bargain for the retention of some "fat" as well as for employment adjustment measures to cushion the displaced, works councils risk being held partially responsible for the job losses that accompany reorganization.

Ulrich Jürgens (1993, 3) stresses that while it is still hard to see the concrete contours of policies concerning lean production, "realization of the concept is taking place *within the framework* of the system of co-determination." Jürgen Hoffmann (1995, 102) contends that management, as the "locations of decision making are multiplied," effectively expands codetermination beyond the formal institutions, to work teams, for example, and urges corresponding union policy reforms. Jürgens (1993, 9) also asks whether employment cuts in the recession of 1992–93 reflected, as a "hidden agenda," employer efforts to downsize toward employment levels compatible with lean forms of organization. If so, such a hidden agenda may have spared the unions difficult choices, since employment cuts could not be ascribed directly to lean production. And temporary solutions to avoid layoffs do exist: short-time work (government subsidized) and specific arrangements such as the 1994 Volkswagen agreement on the introduction of a 28.8-hour work week with only partial wage compensation. The social effects of dismissals are also alleviated by the legal obligation to provide compensation plans, with measures to cushion layoffs, an important source of legitimacy for works councils and unions as they negotiate the terms of workforce adjustment. There is, however, a potential conflict in such an approach by the unions, to which Streeck (1987, 40) has pointed in other circumstances: "While it will increasingly become impossible to hide the role of trade unions as co-managers of industrial change—if they are in fact willing to assume such a role—this may give rise to fratricidal ideological conflict with quite uncertain results."

CODETERMINATION BETWEEN REUNIFICATION AND EUROPEANIZATION

Two external changes have had a major impact on industrial relations in general and codetermination in particular. Whereas German reunification came as an unforeseen "shock," the process of European integration has long been on the agenda, clearly gaining in importance with the completion of the Single European Market, the "social dimension" debate, and the Maastricht Treaty with its social chapter.

Unification

The unification of Germany in October 1990 put great pressure on the system of industrial relations in the Federal Republic. This was true even though it was clear well before that date that the West German institutional framework was to be "exported" to the East. As of July 1, 1990, the laws on codetermination, including the Works Constitution Act, became valid for the whole of soon-to-be-unified Germany. The old plant-level representation structures in the East (the BGL, or *Betriebsgewerkschaftsleitungen*) were in many cases simply transformed into works councils (Kirschner et al. 1992; Fritzsche and Rachel 1992; Röbenack and Hartung 1992). The first official works councils elections were held a year later.

The strongest unions, such as IG Metall, which signed up around a million new members as a result of reunification, succeeded through collective bargaining in introducing a temporary ban on dismissals and contributed to the introduction of a favorable system of short-time work (the usual benefits were supplemented by 22 percent of former wages in the metal trades). While the massive use of short-time work prevented layoffs for a year or two, the end of the dismissal ban and later of the short-time work scheme revealed the true extent of job losses, despite an unprecedented use of active labor market policy (expenses for labor market policy peaked at around 18 percent of East German GDP, compared to an EU average of around 2.5 percent). Even so, around 40 percent of all jobs in the eastern labor market were lost between 1989 and the end of 1992.

These figures indicate the dimension of the tasks facing works councils in the new federal states, which were frequently so involved in organizing layoffs that they were simply not in a position to discuss and negotiate new production and new jobs. Another task of the works councils has been the reclassification of jobs according to western job classifications, which also led to some conflicts. In general, works councillors in the East have experienced considerable difficulties in applying and working with the new laws, although (western) German unions have made a concerted effort to train them, as part of a campaign to strengthen the ties between eastern works councils and the unions.

The mere extent of the transformation and crisis seems to be one of the reasons why German scholars have taken a more pessimistic view of general developments and of industrial relations (e.g., Mahnkopf 1991). This position is countered by Lowell Turner (see Chapter 5 in this volume), who sees a successful industrial relations structure emerging. It is true that the dual structure of German industrial relations (collective bargaining outside the firms, internal codetermination and negotiation by works councils within them) has been partially successful. In particular, the successful strike of 1993 in the metal and steel industries (the first in fifty years in the East)—which ended with a compromise favorable for the unions but also acceptable to the employers (although they contend that even the slower pace of wage adjustment to western German levels will cost many jobs)—gave a boost to union representation and works councils. Nonetheless, fears of far-reaching decentralization (through the introduction of "opening clauses" permitting individual plants to depart from central agreements) expressed by Birgit Mahnkopf (1991) remain salient, although such clauses, at least in the metal industries, are only permitted in cases of pending insolvency and with union approval.

In conclusion, the transformation process in the East is at least partially "negotiated," but the terms of negotiation are different from those found in the West: East-West differences in wages, working conditions, and working hours persist, but the benchmarks for all bargaining are now Western German standards. However, given economic collapse and the particular structural problems of the East, together with fact that the current East-West wage differentials are only temporary and thus play no important role in investment decisions, bargaining is under increasingly severe pressure, and the problems are far from being resolved. Only time will tell whether the union strategy practiced in West Germany (centralized, industry-wide bargaining and codetermination placing tight limits on inter-firm differentials) is as conducive to economic development in the East as it has been in *maintaining* an already developed economy in the West.

European Integration

European integration gained a second wind with the passage of the Single European Act in 1985, establishing the single market with its four freedoms (free movement of capital, labor, goods, and services) and the subsequent Maastricht Treaty on the European Union ratified in November of 1993. While the economic program of the single market (basically the deregulation of markets) has received widespread approval, the prospects of the so-called social dimension attached to it are less certain. In some fields, such as workplace safety and health, significant progress toward European-wide regulation has been made, while in other areas achievements are rare and decision processes lengthy. Although the social chapter attached to Maastricht (reserving an "opt-out" possibility for the United Kingdom) now foresees qualified majority voting on most social issues (which greatly facilitates decision making)—and such issues include information and consultation rights for employees throughout the EU—decisions on full codetermination legislation continue to require unanimity (Streeck and Vitols 1993).

German codetermination is the most highly developed, and its example influenced earlier attempts to introduce European legislation (such as the so-called Fifth Directive); but because of opposition from the business community (and the British government), however, only watered-down versions of the German model were included in later proposals. In principle these earlier codetermination initiatives included a range of possible alternative forms, based largely on the existing practices in the different member countries. Still, with the exception of workforce information and consultation in the case of collective redundancies (1977) and the transfer of undertakings (1979), none of these proposals were enacted until the adoption of the Directive on European Works Councils (EWC) in September 1994. The latter is breakthrough legislation for the EU: all multinational firms with at least 1,000 employees in the EU, with at least 150 in each of two member states (excluding the United Kingdom) now have to set up a European Works Council (or its equivalent) for the purpose of informing and consulting employees. Even this directive, however, leaves a lot of scope for different set-ups, since it establishes only minimum rights. Furthermore, since the regulation applies only at the multinational level, existing national forms of codetermination will be left intact. More generally, the principle of "subsidiarity" on which Community policymaking is increasingly based means that detailed regulation is left to individual member states, who were required to implement the directive in national legislation by September 1996. Until then, "preemptive" agreements between employers and unions could be concluded; Article 13 states that obligations do not apply to companies or groups that already have an agreement covering the entire workforce and providing for transnational information and consultation.

Even before the approval of the directive, EWCs (or other forms of trans-European negotiation between management and workers/unions) had been established on a voluntary basis at a growing number of multinationals, partly with a view to avoiding European regulation (*European Industrial Relations Review,* nos. 228 and 229, 1993; Gold and Hall 1992; Streeck and Vitols 1993). The EWC at Volkswagen, established on the initiative of the German central works council in Wolfsburg, may be the most highly formalized of such institutional arrangements; in addition, EWCs were set up at other French and German firms in the early and mid-1990s following formal agreements between management and unions. While not a sufficient condition for success, such formalization is a necessary condition for the stabilization of such structures (Streeck and Vitols 1993).

The new directive will certainly accelerate the establishment of EWCs and other procedures of information and consultation. Cross-national differences, however, will persist. Although none of the national implementation laws will go so far as to establish full codetermination rights, the scope of information to be made available to workers and the institutional features (time-off, number of representatives, composition of committees, and so on) will most likely vary considerably.

As for German codetermination, it is feared that given an unrestricted movement of capital, national differences in regulation will permit "regime shopping"—making it possible for German companies to avoid the costs associated with high social standards by investing elsewhere in Europe, thus putting pressure on Germany to lower its own standards (such as codetermination)(Mosley 1990; Streeck 1991).

Again, it is possible to take a more optimistic view of these trends. Turner (1992) argues that subsidiarity is a two-edged sword: if only soft versions of EU-wide codetermination legislation are agreed upon (as is now the case for EWCs), the German system will remain unchanged. If an attempt is made to harmonize systems EU-wide, German high standards will probably be eroded since such directives would certainly not be based on the highest but more likely on average standards. In the present case, the European Commission's EWC directive leaves national systems unchanged, while adding information and consultation rights at the transnational level. At present it is rather difficult to predict whether there will be a "spillover" effect in which soft transnational regulations erode stronger national regulations over time. Given Article 13 of the directive, it is improbable that the directive's softer EWC requirements will displace established national structures.

The recently adopted "posted workers directive" has much more impact on national labor regulation than the EWC directive. Because of high wages and nonwage costs in Germany, local labor is more expensive to hire than, for example, Portuguese, Irish, or even British workers posted in Germany temporarily. This has caused real problems in certain trades, such as the construction industry in Berlin where local unemployment has risen despite an immense construction boom. In the absence of a community directive, Germany's construction trade organizations were attempting to counter the inflow of cheap labor and agreed, in the 1996 bargaining round, on moderate wage increases and especially on (for German standards) low minimum wages for the 1.5 million construction workers.

Unlike codetermination, which has a rather indirect effect on competitiveness, the posting of workers has a much more immediate effect, so that community regulation to avoid "unfair" competition was necessary.

GERMAN INDUSTRIAL RELATIONS IN THE MID-1990S

So far, Germany's industrial relations institutions, including codetermination, have held up surprisingly well in the face of major new stresses and recent changes in the global, European, and German environments. Not only have unions and employer associations provided a fairly centralized and coherent bargaining and employee-representation structure in the East, but European integration, with the much-feared accompanying pressure of "social dumping," has not really endangered these institutions. The conditions for "negotiated adjustment" (Thelen 1991) continue to exist, and there is reason to agree with Turner's (1992) optimistic evaluation of the resilience of German industrial relations.

This may change, however, in the face of pressures from within Germany itself, pressures reinforced by a trend toward "neo-voluntarism" elsewhere in Europe. At the end of 1993 German employers abrogated—for the very first time since World War II—a collective agreement in the metal industry. Although this was legally permitted (each party being free to cancel an agreement in due time before its expiration), established practice was for the unions to take such initiative. In this case, however, given the severity of economic recession, employers sought a thoroughgoing revision of German wage policies, centered around considerably lower pay levels. The 1994 bargaining round did in fact result in real wage decline. This does not mean, however, that labor's bargaining power has seriously weakened or that the employers have succeeded: rather, German unions have accepted macroeconomic responsibilities and moderate wage settlements (in the metal industry, for example, bargained nominal wages rose only 1.17 percent for 1994, lower than the rate of inflation) in a difficult economic period. Unions also responded to employer concerns for high non-wage costs and accepted, for example a reduction in the Christmas bonus and more flexibility in working hours. With economic upswing under way, the 1995 bargaining round, which included warning strikes followed by a full-fledged strike in the Bavarian metal industry, brought back pay raises (around 4 percent) and confirmed the introduction of the thirty-five-hour work week in October 1995. These recent bargaining settlements, combined with the enhanced firm-level negotiating responsibilities of works councils and new flexibility concerning working hours, confirmed both the resilience of the *core* and the adaptability at the *margin* of the industrial relations system, lending support to an optimistic perspective on German institutional resilience.

High levels of unemployment, however, make it harder for unions and works councils to maintain high social standards in the workplace, opening them to the charge of serving only insiders and exacerbating the problem of labor market exclusion. As lean forms of organization become a reality, negative employment effects might well make it more difficult for works councils to continue to play the role of cooperative "co-managers," the role which in the final analysis, has made them acceptable to management. If there is no substantial improvement in the job market, works councils may soon have to face the dilemma of remaining cooperative and facing opposition from within the unions and the workforce, or becoming more confrontational, thereby disrupting the cooperative climate central to the model of negotiated adjustment. Either way, works councils run the risk of losing some of the legitimacy they have in the past enjoyed.

Again, a more optimistic scenario is possible, one in which unions and employers conclude work-sharing agreements to save jobs. Such a flexible solution was, for example, negotiated at Volkswagen, where 30,000 jobs were saved through the introduction of a four-day work week, entailing wage cuts for 100,000 VW workers in Germany. And "employment oriented agreements" introduced in the 1994 bargaining round in the metal industry permitted firms and works councils to negotiate lower hours with no or only partial wage compensation in exchange for employment guarantees, another sign of the adaptability of the system. The 1996 bargaining round confirms this trend toward a trade-off between moderate wage bargaining and employment security provisions. For example, the recent collective bargaining agreement in the chemical industry, where a 2 percent wage increase comes together with the promise of employers to maintain employment in the sector for the duration of the contract.

The stability and adaptability of the German dual system of industrial relations help the economy weather the ups and downs of short-term business cycle fluctuations and long-term structural changes in a competitive manner. An announcement of "the end of the German model" would be premature at best.

The biggest problem is that millions of unemployed are excluded, sometimes for long periods, from the direct benefits of collective bargaining and codetermination. This is true in spite of indirect effects such as the maintenance of high non-wage costs to finance transfer payments for the unemployed, and the fact that those who keep their jobs through work-sharing agreements do not swell the ranks of the unemployed. However, if no solution is found for mass unemployment, and the introduction of lean forms of organization continues (with the consequence that employment levels will continue to shrink even during economic booms), serious problems will arise even for insiders. Finding solutions for the parallel development of "modernization and marginalization" (Hoffmann 1995, 106) is high on the reform agenda.

Thus, while there are problems in the German model, the basic elements seem to have held. And in light of this analysis, it is precisely the resilience of inclusive institutions, the stability and predictability of basic rules with built-in flexibilities allowing for marginal negotiated change, which is at the heart of Germany's success. Therefore it is important to resist the "siren song of deregulation" (Allen, Chapter 6 in this volume), since deregulation could lead to the destabilization of the German social market economy, an outcome that even dramatic changes in the environment have not yet managed to bring about.

REFERENCES

Auer, Peter, and Helga Fehr-Duda, eds., 1989. *Industrial Relations in Small and Medium-Sized Enterprises.* Brussels: Commission of the European Communities.

Bosch, Gerhard. 1983. "Interessenvertretung in Mittel-und Kleinbetrieben." *Die Mitbestimmung* 7: 322–24.

Cooke, Philipp. 1993. "The Experiences of German Engineering Firms in Applying Lean Production Methods." In ILO, *Lean Production and Beyond.* Geneva: ILO.

Däubler, Wolfgang. 1975. *Das Grundrecht auf Mitbestimmung.* Frankfurt: Europäische Verlagsanstalt.

Fritzsche, Heidrun, and Gabriele Rachel. 1992. *Herausbildung und Probleme der betrieblichen Interessenvertretung und Mitbestimmung im Prozeß der Privatisierung ostdeutscher Unternehmen.* Halle: KSPW, Graue Reihe 304.

Gold, Michael, and M. Hall. 1992. *Information and Consultation in European Multinational Companies: An Evaluation of Practice.* Luxembourg: Commission of the European Communities.

Gülden, Klaus. 1977. *Mitbestimmung in der Wirtschaftskrise: Fallstudie über die Stillegung eines Walzwerbes.* Berlin: Verlag der Arbeitswelt.

Henneberger, Fred, and Berndt Keller. 1993. "Industrial Relations in the Public Sector." *European Industrial Relations Review* 233 (June): 25–28.

Hoffmann, Jürgen. 1995. "Trade Union Reform in Germany: Some Analytical and Critical Remarks Concerning the Current Debate." *Transfer* 1: 98–113.

Hohn, Hans Willy. 1988. *Von der Einheitsgewerkschaft zum Betriebssyndikalismus.* Berlin: edition sigma.

Katzenstein, Peter J. 1989. *Industry and Politics in West Germany: Toward the Third Republic.* Ithaca: Cornell University Press.

Kirschner, Lutz. 1992. *Transformation von Interessenswahrnehmung und Mitbestimmung. Fallstudien aus Unternehmen und Betrieben der neuen Bundesländer.* Halle: KSPW, Graue Reihe 303.

Kronenberg, Brigitte, Gert Volkmann, and Ulrike Wendeling-Schröder. 1991. "WSI Mitbestimmungsbericht 1990." *WSI Mitteilungen* 8: 486–96.

Lecher, Wolfgang. 1995. "Globalisierung und direkte Partizipation. Vorschläge zur Modernisierung der Mitbestimmung." *Gewerkschaftliche Monatshefte* 2: 75–84.

Leminsky, Gerhard. 1995. "Gewerkschaftsreform und Mitbestimmung." *Gewerkschaftliche Monatshefte* 1:21–33.

Mahnkopf, Birgit, 1991. "Vorwärts in die Vergangenheit? Pessimistische Spekulationen über die Zukunft der Gewerkschaften in der neuen Bundesrepublik." In Andreas Westphal, Michael Heine, Hansjörg Herr, and Ulrich Busch, eds., *Wirtschaftspolitische Konsequenzen der deutschen Vereinigung.* Frankfurt: Campus.

Mosley, Hugh. 1990. "The Social Dimension of European Integration." *International Labour Review* 129, no. 2: 147–64.

OECD, 1994. *Jobs Study OECD.* Paris.

Röbenack, Silke, and Gabriele Hartung. 1992. *Strukturwandel industrieller Beziehungen in ostdeutschen Industriebetrieben.* Halle: KSPW, Graue Reihe 302.

Soskice, David. 1990. "Reinterpreting Corporatism and Explaining Unemployment: Co-ordinated and Non-co-ordinated Market Economies." In R. Brunetta and C. Dell'Aringa, eds., *Labour Relations and Economic Performance.* IEA Conference Volume no. 95, pp. 170–211. Houndsmill, U.K.: Macmillan.

Stein, Eddehart. 1976. *Qualifizierte Mitbestimmung unter dem Grundgesetz.* Frankfurt: Eva.

Streeck, Wolfgang. 1987. "Industrial Relations in West Germany: Agenda for Change." Discussion Paper IIM/LMP 87–5, Wissenschaftszentrum Berlin für Sozialforschung.

——. 1991. "More Uncertainties: German unions Facing 1992." *Industrial Relations* 30, no. 3: 317–49.

Streeck, Wolfgang, and Sigurt Vitols. 1993. "European Works Councils: Between Statutory Enactment and Voluntary Adoption." Discussion Paper FS I 93–312, Wissenschaftszentrum Berlin für Sozialforschung.

Thelen, Kathleen A. 1991. A Union of Parts: *Labor Politics in Postwar Germany*. Ithaca: Cornell University Press.

Turner, Lowell. 1991. Democracy at Work: *Changing World Markets and the Future of Labor Unions*. Ithaca: Cornell University Press.

——. 1992. "Institutional Resilience in a Changing World Economy: German Unions between Unification and Europe." Discussion Paper FS I 92–6, Wissenschaftszentrum Berlin für Sozialforschung.

Wassermann, Wolfgang. 1989. "Industrial Relations in Small and Medium-sized Enterprises." In P. Auer and H. Fehr-Duda, *Industrial Relations in Small and Medium-Sized Enterprises*, 143–74. Brussels: Commission of the European Communities.

Womack, James P., Daniel T. Jones, and David Roos. 1990. *The Machine That Changed the World*. New York: Rawson.

2 • The Dilemmas of Diffusion: Institutional Transfer and the Remaking of Vocational Training Practices in Eastern Germany

Richard M. Locke and Wade Jacoby

> The process of unification, it is thus far clear, is more than a simple transfer of economic and political institutions from West Germany to East Germany. In West Germany, these institutions are embedded in the social structure. In East Germany, without this social structure, these institutions exist as a set of parameters that constrain social and political action. There is no reason to assume that the sum of these actions will produce institutions that are identical or even similar to what we have known in West Germany or that they will not transform the institutions that characterize the Federal Republic as a whole.
>
> —Wolfgang Seibel, "Necessary Illusions"

One of the most important debates in contemporary industrial relations theory and policy is whether or not (and if so, how) institutional practices developed in one setting can be transferred to and implemented effectively in another. This debate takes place both at the level of company practice—witness the debate over "lean production" in several manufacturing industries (Berggren 1992; Camuffo and Micelli 1995; Womack, Jones, and Roos 1990)—and in broader policy discussions over the relevance of

A slightly altered version of this chapter appeared in *Politics & Society*, vol. 25, no. 1 (March 1997): 34–65. For helpful comments on earlier drafts, we thank Peter Berg, Martin Behrens, Martin Baethge, Horst Kern, Thomas Kochan, Gary Herrigel, Robert McKersie, Michael Piore, Chuck Sabel, David Soskice, Kathleen Thelen, and Lowell Turner.

works councils in the United Kingdom and the United States (Kochan and Osterman 1994; Rogers and Streeck 1994; Trades Union Congress 1995; Weiler 1990).

Yet there are good theoretical reasons why institutional transfer may be difficult to achieve. No institutional practice stands alone, but rather, as many have argued already, each is situated in a broader institutional and cultural context, which shapes the outcomes it produces (Dore 1973; Mac-Duffie 1995; Milgram and Roberts 1990; Westney 1987). In addition, each of these institutional arrangements also rests on and interacts with distinct sociopolitical relations that shape how they actually work (Locke 1995).

The diffusion of the acclaimed West German "dual system" of vocational training to the former German Democratic Republic, now known as the new federal states *(neue Bundesländer),* starkly demonstrates the importance of local sociopolitical relations for the successful transfer and implementation of institutional arrangements. Despite massive levels of government funding, the presence of the same complementary institutional supports, and the concerted efforts of the country's major social partners, dualistic training arrangements are experiencing significant difficulties taking root in the new federal states. This is due not simply to the particular politics of unification (which entailed the wholesale transfer of West German arrangements regardless of whether or not they were appropriate to Eastern Germany) or even to the paucity of dynamic private firms capable of and willing to train new apprentices but also to the underlying weaknesses of the East German sociopolitical infrastructure (e.g., chambers of industry and commerce, local unions, employers associations, and so on) on which the entire dual system rests. In fact, as this case study of two Saxon cities illustrates, localities with well-developed networks of secondary associations and interest groups capable of coordinating efforts, pooling resources, and sharing information (such as Leipzig) have been able to overcome or at least compensate for these economic and institutional deficiencies and establish dualistic training arrangements. In settings with more limited sociopolitical resources (such as Chemnitz) these new institutions are still struggling to develop.

Following the unification of the two Germanies in 1990—and given the terms under which it occurred, namely, Article 23 of the Basic Law—West German laws, institutions, and economic arrangements were transferred rapidly and on a large scale to the East. West German government agencies, banks, employer associations, chambers of industry and commerce, and unions all moved eastward and implanted themselves quickly. As a result, German unification presents itself as a unique "natural experiment" (Offe 1992) through which to explore the problem of institutional transfer. We focus on Germany's vocational training system because it is often associated with Germany's strong economic performance in the postwar period (Soskice 1994; Streeck et al. 1987). Moreover, because this system is credited with reducing youth unemployment and producing highly skilled and productive workers, it has often been seen as a model to be replicated in other countries (Hamilton 1990; Jeong 1995; Osterman 1988). Thus an understanding of the micropolitical and social foundations on which the "dual system" of training rests could provide useful insights into *both* how this system actually works and under what conditions it may be diffused to other contexts.

The remainder of this essay is divided into four parts. The first section sketches in highly stylized terms the key features of West Germany's "dual system" of vocational training. Part 2 then describes the preexisting training arrangements in the former German Democratic Republic (GDR) and the process through which the West German model was transferred to the new federal states. The third section presents evidence documenting the difficult diffusion of West German practices to the East. We will examine both aggregate data for the new federal states as a whole as well as a case study of two major industrial cities in Eastern Germany: Leipzig and Chemnitz (the former Karl Marx Stadt) in order to illustrate the importance of underlying sociopolitical relations to the development and performance of these institutional arrangements. The final section of this paper will ponder the significance of these findings for not only the German case but also for the way we think about institutions in our analyses of contemporary employment relations.

Our findings are based largely on field research conducted in Germany between May 1992 and April 1995. This field research involved archival work as well as over fifty interviews with academic, government, business, and labor leaders at both the national and local levels. We also visited numerous government agencies, business associations, chambers, unions, and companies in the former German Democratic Republic.

BASIC FEATURES OF THE WEST GERMAN VOCATIONAL TRAINING SYSTEM

Approximately 70 percent of German youth (16–19 years of age) participate in the so-called dual system of initial, vocational training.[1] This system is typically seen as an effective way of combining work and learning. By matching apprentices to prospective occupations and firms, it allocates

---

1. This section draws heavily on Streeck et al. 1987, Soskice 1994, Osterman 1988, Casey 1991, Lynch 1992, Bosch 1992, Harhoff and Kane 1993, and Wever, Berg, and Kochan 1994. Adult continuing education (*Fortbildung* and *Umschulung*) is not considered here.

labor resources efficiently, smooths the school-to-work transition, and reduces youth unemployment. And because the system provides German firms with highly skilled workers, it is often seen as facilitating firm-level adjustment and the introduction of new technologies. In fact, there is an abundance of published material on various aspects of the German system of training, much of it written with an eye to replicating these practices in other national settings.

The German training system has three key features: (1) the role of the social partners in developing the content and regulating the implementation of training programs; (2) the shared investment in training made by private employers, the government, and individual apprentices during the training process; and (3) the role of the local chambers of industry and commerce (or craft chambers) in certifying the quality of the portable skills gained through training.

In this system, apprentices attend public vocational school one or two days a week, where they are taught both general subjects like mathematics, history, and languages and the underlying "theoretical principles" associated with their future occupations. They spend the remainder of the week working at a firm, where they acquire practical skills by taking part in the ongoing production process. The apprenticeship is based on a training contract between the individual apprentice and the employer. While the required general school training is funded by the state governments, the costs of in-firm training are covered by the firms. As part of their contribution, the apprentices accept wages that are between 25 and 44 percent of the skilled wage rate during their three years of training.

As in other advanced industrial nations, firms in the Federal Republic choose whether or not to participate in this system. Even during normal times, most generally choose not to. Only about 20 percent of West German firms conduct training at any one time. A web of laws and regulations set the standards to be met by training firms, develop and periodically revise the curricula offered in the schools, and institutionalize the participation of the unions and employers associations at the federal, state, sectoral and local levels of the system. According to the Federal Vocational Training Law of 1969, all youth under eighteen are eligible to be trained in any one of the 374 (1991 figure) officially recognized occupations. The content of the training programs on the shop floor is determined at the federal level. Unions, employers' associations, state governments, and the federal government (through the Federal Institute for Vocational Training—BiBB) negotiate the curricula and the types of occupations to be covered by an apprenticeship. At the plant level, training is provided by certified trainers employed by the firm and monitored by the works councils. National standards are maintained through a set of examinations administered locally by the chambers which cover both the theoretical and practical aspects of training. Apprentices who pass these exams receive certificates recognized all over Germany. Certification and quality control of training programs ensure the portability of these skills.

The supporting institutions and secondary associations involved in designing and monitoring the apprenticeships are central to the functioning of the German system. Paul Osterman (1988), David Soskice (1994), and Wolfgang Streeck and his colleagues (1987) describe the important role played by the local chambers of industry and commerce (or craft chambers) in this training system. Aside from examining individual apprentices and determining the eligibility of individual firms to train apprentices, these local chambers employ full-time staff to provide an array of services to assist firms in developing and/or improving their training programs. Representatives from the chambers also meet regularly with union leaders, local school administrators, and officials from the local offices of the government employment agency *(Arbeitsamt)* to coordinate activities and ensure both that there are sufficient numbers of apprenticeship slots for each year's youth cohort and that the training provided meets well-established standards. In short, the German system of vocational training requires both a dynamic private sector and an articulated network of other organizations and associations in order to function properly.

Despite this positive and static picture, Germany's vocational training system currently faces a number of problems, including a mismatch between existing apprenticeship slots and youth increasingly interested in pursuing the *Abitur* (gymnasium matriculation certificates); a significant reduction in the number of apprenticeships slots, including in the leading metalworking sector;[2] a predominance of training slots in smaller, more artisanal firms where the quality of training and prospects for long-term employment are mixed;[3] a need to adjust the vocational focus of the current system to the requirements of both high-tech and service firms demanding completely different skills and to manufacturing enterprises restructuring along new, more flexible lines—lines that blur traditional craft boundaries;[4] and finally the tremendously difficult and lengthy process (caused by drawn-out negotiations between the social partners) required to reform outdated training programs (Casey 1991). Certainly the West German training system has

2. The dramatic decline in the number of industrial apprenticeships can perhaps best be appreciated through the following example. In 1987, 51,637 new training contracts were signed for metal working occupations. In 1993, only 27,490 new contracts were signed in the same occupations. Declines in other industrial sectors (such as electronics) appear even more severe. For more on this, see Baethge, Baethge-Kinsky, and Hendrich 1995.

3. For more on this, see Casey 1991 and Osterman 1988.

4. See Baethge 1995 and Sabel and Herrigel 1994.

weathered hard times in the past. But almost all of the managers, union officials, academic experts, and government representatives we interviewed made it clear that they believed the current system was in flux.

These various concerns notwithstanding, Germany's dual system of training, like virtually all other social, political, and economic institutions of the Federal Republic, was transferred wholesale to the East. Thus since unification in 1990 West German employers' associations, chambers of industry and commerce, government institutions, and unions have all invested enormous resources in recreating dual training practices in the new federal states. The various difficulties and dilemmas that have arisen from this process of institutional transfer—especially the insistence on reproducing a set of arrangements that seem poorly matched to the needs and interests of private firms and youth—have exposed some of the latent problems facing West German training arrangements.

VOCATIONAL TRAINING IN THE "OTHER" GERMANY

The central feature of the system of vocational training in the East before 1990 was state authority over training, which led to important differences from the "dual system" in the West. The German Democratic Republic's "hybrid" form of training was essentially a compromise between traditional German dual apprenticeship arrangements and the COMECON practice of unified firm-based training. As in the Federal Republic, however, East German apprentices spent time both in schools and in firms.

East German vocational schools had two principal forms: the *Betriebsberufsschulen,* which were located within the firms and enrolled about 68 percent of the East German apprentices in 1982, and the *Kommunaleberufsschulen,* which were controlled by local communities and taught the rest. The community schools serviced small firms primarily, especially in sectors that could not afford their own training facilities.[5] Over the course of the 1980s, training became increasingly concentrated in the *Betriebsberufsschulen,* by the final years of the GDR, these schools accounted for about 80 percent of all vocational training.[6]

Most East German youth entered vocational schools after successfully completing the mandatory ten-year *Politechnische Oberschule.* Apprenticeships usually lasted two years and, as in West Germany, were regulated by

5. See Zimmermann et al. 1985, 333.
6. See Degen, Walden, and Becker 1995. In addition to the two forms of part-time vocational schools, full-time *Fachschulen* were also an important part of the East German system. Some pupils went to *Fachschulen* after their apprenticeships for more specialized or advanced certificates; others went directly to the *Fachschulen* from the *Politechnische Oberschulen* to learn school-based vocations.

training contracts between individual apprentices and training firms. Like the Federal Republic, the GDR had a constitutional clause about free choice of occupation. But unlike in the FRG, East German citizens also had a constitutional duty to finish at least a partial apprenticeship (Zimmerman et al. 1985, 330). These two principles often conflicted. Central planning heavily restricted the range of vocational choices available to East German youth. Thus by the late 1980s, only about 50 percent of East German apprentices were being trained in their first choice of occupations or in related fields.

Firms that trained in the GDR were generally much larger, trained many more apprentices, and were far more concentrated in industry than was the case in West Germany. Small firms engaged in craft and artisanal work were increasingly denied access to apprentices in the GDR. Thus while 80 percent of all East German apprentices were trained in small firms in 1950, in 1989 the figure was only 3 percent (Degen, Walden, and Becker 1995, 16). In the Federal Republic, by comparison, in 1989 35 percent of all apprentices in were trained in small craft enterprises. Moreover, while at the end of the 1980s, 80 percent of the East German apprentices were trained in industrial firms, only about 52 percent of the West German apprentices were. Finally, while 20 percent of the East German apprentices were trained in service occupations, 48 percent were trained in these occupations in the West (ibid., 36).

As in West Germany, curriculum changes were a major focus of training policies during the 1980s, and by 1989, 92 percent of youth were trained under revised curricula. As in the FRG, the reform process in the GDR brought about a dramatic decline in the number of vocations offered: from 922 in 1957 to 318 in 1984.[7] The training included both general knowledge and more specialized applications linked to particular occupations. Despite curriculum reforms, however, the prohibitive costs of technologically so-phisticated training equipment, especially following the microelectronics revolution, clearly affected the content of training in the GDR. Moreover, throughout the 1970s and 1980s, spending on vocational training actually represented a declining share of East German GDP (Burkhardt 1990, 9). As a result, only about 20 percent of the apprenticeships—according to offi-cial estimates—actually experienced a curriculum change in light of the "scientific-technological revolution" (Anweiler 1990). In the metalworking industry, for example, apprenticeships with training in CNC (computer nu-merically controlled) machinery and hydraulics were virtually nonexistent.

Thus, by the time of German unification, the essential differences between the West and East German vocational training systems lay first, in the

---

7. This number includes all the subspecialties in the twenty-eight broad occupational groups (Zimmerman et al. 1985, 330).

GDR's much higher concentration of training in large firms and its relative neglect of training in small artisanal and craft firms; second, in the GDR's focus on training for industry and not for service occupations; third, in the technological backwardness of much of the training; fourth, in the obligation by East German citizens to take up an apprenticeship (Cott 1991, 5); and finally in certain key structural differences: in the GDR employer associations were nonexistent, firms had little choice about whether or not to train, unions played no role in curricular reform, and local chambers, where they existed, played no appreciable role in "quality control," (See Table 2.1). These differences would later come to play a significant role in shaping the process of institutional transfer and reform in the years immediately following unification.

GERMAN UNIFICATION

Burdened by a growing external debt, economic stagnation, and declining support among its population, the East German state faced an immediate crisis in the autumn of 1989 when thousands of its citizens began seeking to leave the GDR by way of Hungary and Czechoslovakia. The subsequent

TABLE 2.1. Differences between the West and East German training systems

	FRG	GDR
Role of Social Partners	Actively involved in curriculum development, training, certification, and quality control	No appreciable role
Distribution of training by sector	52% industry 48% services	80% industry 20% services
Distribution of training by firm size	35% small firms 65% medium and large firms	3% small firms 97% large firms
Locus of training	Split between publicly funded schools and private firms	Primarily within conglomerate-based schools
Focus of training	On providing firms with skilled labor and youth with portable skills	On economic development: channeling youth into "targeted" industries
Freedom of choice	Firms chose whether or not to train; youth could choose occupations but firms selected apprentices based on performance.	Firms had no choice. Over time, youth could choose occupations but within highly structured state targets.

collapse of the Berlin Wall in early November led to a series of unsuccessful efforts by the Communist Party (SED) to retain its leading role in East German society. Meanwhile, East German citizens surged into West Germany. In February 1990, the West German government offered East Germany an "economic and monetary union," ostensibly to forestall political union; however, on March 18, 1990, national elections in the German Democratic Republic returned large pluralities for the Christian Democratic Union (CDU)-dominated "Democratic Alliances." The election results were widely interpreted as a mandate for reunification from the East German population. A partial step was taken with the Treaty for "German Economic, Monetary, and Social Union" (GEMSU), which was signed on May 18, 1990, and took effect on July 1, 1990. When the economic decline of East German firms and the migration of East German citizens continued more or less unabated, Bonn decided to move quickly toward full political union under Article 23 of the Federal Republic's "provisional" constitution of 1949, known as the "Basic Law." The choice of Article 23 reflected a fundamental commitment to remake Eastern Germany in the image of West Germany and represented a rejection of Article 146, which foresaw the dissolution of the Basic Law and the writing of a new, all-German constitution. The subsequent "Unification Treaty," negotiated between representatives of the FRG and GDR, was signed on August 31, 1990, and took effect on October 3, 1990.[8]

Between the currency union in July 1990 and April 1991, East German production collapsed to less than one-third of 1989 levels. Parts of the East are now slowly recovering, but economic stagnation continues to characterize most sectors of the economy. As a result of this collapse, employment has fallen dramatically. The number of persons in paid employment dropped from just under 10 million in 1990 to around 5.5 million in 1995.[9] Registered unemployment has risen to 1.2 million, although the actual unemployment rate is twice the official rate of 15 percent with the undercounting of unemployment in the new federal states caused by the massive deployment of labor market policies. A significant volume of labor migration (including commuting) to the West has also eased the pressure on Eastern German labor markets. Moreover, by the end of 1992, as a result of short-time work arrangements, a reduction of overtime, and cuts in work hours, those people still employed in the new federal states were working 56 percent less than in 1989. Had it not been for the huge transfer of funds

8. The Implementation Articles of the Unity Treaty were not actually signed until September 18; the Four Power Treaty on Germany was signed on September 12, 1990, and also took effect on October 3.

9. Labor market statistics are from the Federal Labor Office 1995.

from the West, estimated to have been about DM 166 billion in 1994 alone, the labor market situation in the East would have been even more dramatic (Commission of the European Communities 1994, 3).

The implications of this economic situation for the process of institutional transfer have been enormous. Certainly, the collapse of major industrial sectors and the ongoing difficulties facing both newly established and recently privatized enterprises in the new federal states have restricted the ability, let alone the willingness, of these enterprises to train new apprentices. Moreover, the various secondary associations and interest groups that play key roles in the dual system (e.g., the chambers of industry and commerce, local unions) have experienced tremendous difficulty in establishing themselves and thus are not always able to assist in the implementation of the new training arrangements.[10] As a result, West German-style "dual system" is still struggling to take root in the new federal states. New training arrangements are indeed being established in Eastern Germany but because of its weak economy and poorly developed social infrastructure, and despite the federal and state governments' strong financial and political commitment to replicating West German practices, these training arrangements are highly dependent on government funding, not well linked to private firms, and often train apprentices for occupations with weak prospects for long-term and stable employment.

EMULATING THE WEST: THE REMAKING OF EAST GERMAN VOCATIONAL TRAINING

Following the establishment of GEMSU in July 1990, the East German parliament adopted the West German *Berufsbildungsgesetz* (BBiG) of 1969, the West German *Handwerksordnung* (HwO), and the West German provisions for training in the professions and in agriculture. The BBiG provides the legal framework governing training in industry and commerce, while the HwO regulates training in the artisanal and craft occupations, which include most construction trades along with vocations such as baker, auto mechanic, and the skilled trades. These measures established legal basis for the harmonization of vocational training arrangements. The Federal Institute for Vocational Training (BiBB) took over much of the personnel from the GDR's *Zentralinstitut für Berufsbildung* and extended its responsibilities to Eastern Germany.

Following unification, this process of remaking vocational training arrangements in the image of the West continued. There was no effort to

10. For more on this see Boll 1994, Dininio 1994, Fichter 1994, Lehmbruch 1994, and Silvia 1997.

accommodate particular East German approaches to training or to address problems that had long vexed the West German training system. For example, the close cooperation between vocational school teachers and the in-firm trainers characteristic of the East German system was seen by West Germans as an outgrowth of centralized planning and thus incompatible with West German-style training. In reality, however, closer cooperation had long been a desired goal in the FRG but because so much training in West Germany takes place in small firms, coordination with schools was very difficult to achieve. The East German practice of allowing some youth to integrate academic and vocational credentials in one apprenticeship, a step that West German employers' associations have now publicly demanded, was then opposed by the West German chambers of commerce and damned as a political tool for privileging an SED elite. West German training authorities did initially agree to recognize some thirty East German vocational profiles, although in most cases this process stalled before official regulations were ever written.[11] In short, the overwhelming thrust of the efforts to reform East German vocational training was geared toward reproducing West German structures and practices as closely as possible. East German practices were deemed unacceptable solutions to long-standing weaknesses in the West German system.

With the unification of the two Germanies on October 3, 1990, the five new federal states were established. Each state placed representatives on the expanded governing board of BiBB, while representatives of the unions and employers from the new states also took their places in BiBB's corporatist governing body. Authority for the vocational schools was transferred to the newly established state and municipal governments. In practice, this meant that physical facilities located inside the large East German conglomerates were handed over to the local authorities. In the first year of unification, over half of these schools were then reorganized as branches of larger community-run schools.[12]

While state and local authorities were acquiring control over the vocational schools, the municipalities began transferring their oversight responsibilities to the craft chambers and the chambers of industry and commerce.[13] The craft chambers had existed in the GDR but had overseen only the training of the master craftsmen, while the chambers of industry and commerce had been completely dismantled by 1990. An enormous cooperative effort on the part of West German chambers along with sub-

---

11. Interview with Dr. Günther Albrecht, BIFO, Berlin, April 1994. See also Johnson 1995.

12. *Gesetz über Berufsschulen.* For details see Bund-Länder-Kommission 1992, 8.

13. For sake of simplicity, the *Handwerkskammern* will be translated as "craft chambers" and the IHK as "chambers of industry and commerce."

stantial investment subsidies from the federal government led to the relatively rapid establishment of formal competence by these chambers (Johnson 1995, 137–39).

The governments of the FRG and the GDR had negotiated a number of special provisions aimed at officially recognizing East German certificates (important because of the system of prerequisites for further training in West Germany) and for the continuation of ongoing apprenticeships.[14] Youth who were already in training under contracts signed before August 13, 1990, were given a choice of continuing under East German curricula or switching to new curricula adopted from the West.[15] Much more important were a series of ad hoc programs designed to ease the transition toward a West German-style dual system. The programs were directed, first, at building training capacity in Eastern Germany and, second, at providing training for those for whom traditional in-firm training was not available. The ad hoc programs included the bundling of European Union, federal, and state monies to provide incentives for firms that already had training facilities to maintain and refurbish them. Total spending on physical infrastructure from the federal government alone equaled DM 450 million from 1990 to 1994.[16] In addition, a variety of programs were developed to encourage other firms to train apprentices. A high priority was assigned to training in the craft and professional areas (tax counseling, law, medical technology). Each state developed programs that provided between DM 4000 and 10,000 for each new apprenticeship offered by small firms, usually those with fewer than twenty-five employees. By contrast, industrial and commercial firms received relatively less public funding. For example, between 1991 and 1994, firms in industry and commerce received just over 10 percent of public subsidies in Saxony with the rest going to craft, artisanal, and white-collar employers.[17]

DEVELOPMENTS IN VOCATIONAL TRAINING SINCE UNIFICATION

A combination of economic crisis and targeted policies have fundamentally shifted the structure of training in Eastern Germany. The sheer volume of change in vocational training in the new federal states since unification

---

14. See IG Metall 1991, which lists seven minor rule changes designed to effect the transition to a single national apprenticeship system.

15. Several interviewees suggested that the apprentices overwhelmingly chose to switch to the West German curriculums offered for their occupations.

16. These figures represent combined spending from the ministries of education and economics. In some cases, these facilities could also be used for further training of adults. See Degen, Walden, and Becker 1995, p. 136.

17. Interview with Dr. Hans-Peter Schmidt, Chamber of Industry and Commerce, Leipzig.

is striking. A massive reduction of industrial training in large firms has been accompanied by vigorous efforts to promote training both in small and medium-sized firms in a variety of industries and in the public sector in administrative and service occupations. Whereas in 1989 only 3 percent of the East German youth cohort were trained in craft firms and over 80 percent in industrial firms, by 1993 49 percent of the youth in the new federal states were being trained for careers in industry and commerce, 38 percent in crafts, 5 percent in professional occupations, and 2 percent in agriculture. When one disregards extra-firm training, the shifts appear even more stark: 50 percent in crafts, 18 percent in industry, 12 percent in commerce, 11 percent in the public sector, and 5 percent in the professions (Schober 1994, 5).

Carsten Johnson has attributed the increase in craft-based training to three factors. First, there was pent-up demand in East Germany for craft and artisanal work—demand that had never been accommodated because of the shortage of craftsmen. Second, the boom in craft training has continued in part because the boom in the craft economy has continued. The rebuilding of Eastern German cities, housing stock, commercial properties, and transportation networks has resulted in a demand for skilled labor in the construction trades. Finally, targeted programs by both the federal and state governments have favored the creation of new apprenticeships in the smallest firms (Johnson 1995).

Along with the substantial shift away from training for industrial occupations and toward crafts, a significant number of non-firm-based apprenticeships have been created in Eastern Germany. The original unification statutes foresaw both the use of the standard West German provisions for the training of educationally disadvantaged youth at "extra-firm" sites along with the creation of a special program aimed at promoting extra-firm training through the 1992–93 school year. The original hopes of Germany's policymakers that substantial extra-firm training would be limited to the first three years have now been shattered. Extra-firm training did decline from 37,000 slots in 1990, to 20,700 in 1991, to only 13,200 in 1992, but as these special provisions neared their expiration dates, it became clear that extra-firm training was still needed, especially to cope with larger cohorts in the near future as a result of both strong birth rates in the mid-1970s and the appearance of youth who had earlier stayed in school in part because of the lack of training opportunities.

Each spring, German newspapers have trumpeted the huge gaps between the number of youth seeking apprenticeships and the number of apprenticeships advertised by firms at the local labor offices. As the figures in Table 2.2 demonstrate, extra-firm training made a substantial contribution to total training in each of the first five years of unification. Further, the demo-

TABLE 2.2. The Composition of Apprenticeships in Eastern Germany

Year	1990–91	1991–92	1992–93	1993–94	1994–95
Applicants	145,700	138,300	145,600	171,100	203,000
Total apprenticeships	99,700	95,800	97,200	114,600	n.a.
Extra-firm slots	37,000	20,700	13,200	27,100	n.a.
Firm-based slots	62,700	75,100	84,000	87,500	n.a.
Ratio of firm-based slots to applicants	.43	.54	.58	.51	n.a.

Source: Schober 1994, 4; BiBB, *Berufsbildungsbericht,* various years.

graphic figures suggest that youth cohorts, after rising from an average of about 175,000 per year during the first four years of unification, will from 1994 through 2000 average 210,000 per year (Johnson 1995, 142). In other words, state efforts to retreat from financing the non-school portion of vocational training is colliding head-on with recalcitrant firms and with demographic developments that have exacerbated the shortage of apprenticeships.

Thus despite the substantial efforts of a number of political and social actors, dualist firm-based vocational training has not yet been firmly established in Eastern Germany—at least, not in ways that reconcile firm financing of their own labor market needs with the aspirations of Eastern German youth.[18]

Compounding the challenge to the dual system that arises from the expiration of special transitional programs and a growth in demand for apprenticeships is the much greater danger that firms in the new federal states are collectively unenthusiastic about training. Systematic data is hard to find, but Eastern German chambers of commerce and industry routinely cite figures suggesting that only 5 to 10 percent of their member firms are engaged in vocational training.[19] More worrisome still, the firms that currently train appear ambivalent about continuing this activity. A 1994 survey of 1575 Eastern German firms that trained apprentices revealed that in the

18. Interestingly, it appears as if the new federal states now suffer from particularly acute versions of the ills that had plagued the West German training system. Firms increasingly view training as a cost to be controlled while youth increasingly see higher education as necessary insurance against unpredictable labor markets. The fundamental dilemma is that policies designed to make training more attractive for firms almost invariably make it less attractive for Eastern German youth. To the extent that the federal and state governments try to resolve this dilemma with financial incentives, they run the risk of being forced to assume permanent financial responsibility for a sizable portion of vocational training.

19. Statements of IHK officials at the Second South Thuringen Workshop on Vocational Training, December 1994. The 5 to 10 percent figure applies to all firms; the proportion of training firms to those firms large enough to be listed in the *Handelsregister* appears to be around 20 percent.

next three years far more were planning to reduce their training efforts than to expand them (Degen and Walden 1994, 2063–64). Another study of approximately 100 Eastern German firms that did not currently train youth revealed that they had quite varied reasons for not training. The firms, nearly three-fourths of which were, by their own judgment, either fairly modern or in the process of becoming so, and of which 55 percent claimed that their economic health was "very good" or "excellent," claimed that they did not train because of the time and resources required for training, no need for new apprentices, the lack of training personnel, and the uncertain future of the firm (Degen 1993).

Confronted with this reluctance to train, the federal government has stepped in. The heavy reliance on public funding to support training in the new federal states has become a contentious issue. In order to prevent a "training catastrophe," the government has heavily subsidized training in many firms and has also established large numbers of extra-firm training slots. Whereas public funding for extra-firm training in the old federal states amounts to a mere 7000 spaces annually, various reports from the East suggest that between 60 and 80 percent of all apprenticeships in the new federal states are either partially or fully funded by the government.[20] Many firms in the East have come to expect financial assistance from the state, and it appears that without such financing, there will be a substantial drop in the provision of vocational training.[21]

According to the *Frankfurter Rundschau* (January 9, 1995), even in Saxony, the most prosperous of the new federal states, Ministry of Economics and Labor officials claim that 47 percent of all training slots receive partial or complete funding from the government. In short, labor market developments in Eastern Germany have stubbornly refused to conform to the West German practice of private-sector funding for apprenticeship training. Whereas German policymakers envisioned a rapid phasing out of state subsidies for both in-firm and extra-firm training, the need for such funding has remained steady. For the 1994–95 school year, approximately 35,000 in-firm slots were being subsidized by the federal and state governments at a total cost of DM 400–500 million.

20. Degen and Walden's data show that about 70 percent of firms presently training say they would continue to train even without financial support. Thirty percent say they would cease training. Among firms that appear "dependent" on state subsidies for their willingness to train, small firms with under twenty employees and firms belonging to the crafts chambers (as opposed to industry and commerce or the professions) are strongly overrepresented; see Degen and Walden 1994, 2072–73.

21. *Frankfurter Rundschau*, February 18, 1995, reported 60 percent. In a *Landtag* speech in Potsdam on March 23, 1995, Brandenburg's minister of Labor, Regina Hildebrandt, claimed the figure was about 80 percent. In 1994–95, Brandenburg will spend about 84 million DM to promote vocational training.

Beyond the inability and/or reluctance of private firms to train apprentices and the heavy reliance on government funding for much of the training actually taking place in Eastern Germany, another major obstacle to the development of dualistic training is the poorly developed social infrastructure of the new federal states. A number of authors[22] have argued that a vibrant and well-developed network of secondary associations is important for economic development and institutional performance. According to these authors, contexts with greater numbers of associations or at least with associations with particular qualitative features and patterns of interaction (such as leadership accountability, inclusiveness of group membership, cooperative modes of interaction with other groups) will be more "civic" and their political and economic institutions will perform better than settings with fewer associations and less-engaged inhabitants.

This represents a major problem for Eastern Germany, where the former regime sought to either control or eliminate all intermediary organizations. As a result, several scholars have argued that civil society was virtually destroyed in the GDR,[23] and thus, the various secondary associations that normally participate in Germany's numerous corporatist decision-making processes are either absent or very weak.[24] This poses a particular problem for training, given the important role various associations and groups play in the dual system. In fact, the capacity of local actors to gather information, persuade reluctant actors, and monitor training—tasks integral to the functioning of the dual system—and to make optimal use of various public and private resources to promote training is, in turn, dependent on the underlying sociopolitical structure and pattern of associationalism of the localities in which they are embedded.

STRUGGLING TO CHANGE: A TALE OF TWO SAXON CITIES

In many ways Saxony represents a "best case" scenario for the successful diffusion of vocational training practices. Dual vocational training depends on a healthy underlying economy, and Saxony is, by all accounts, the new federal state with the highest levels of absolute and per capita economic activity in all of Eastern Germany. Leipzig and Chemnitz, two of the largest

22. See Cohen and Rogers 1992, Coleman 1988, Locke 1995, and Putnam 1993.

23. See Bendix 1991 and Seibel 1992. For a somewhat dissenting view that not all forms of civil society were destroyed in the GDR but rather that in certain localities, various groups managed to survive, perhaps only in latent or subterranean forms, and are now reemerging and shaping the current transformation process in interesting ways, see Locke, "Rebirth."

24. For more on Germany's corporatist style of decision-/policy-making process, see Katzenstein 1987 and various chapters in Katzenstein 1989. For more on the problems these associations are facing in Eastern Germany, see Fichter 1994 and Silvia 1997.

centers of commercial activity in Saxony, have suffered from the reduction of industrial employment caused by severe post-unification deindustrialization but not to the truly insignificant levels found in many other parts of Eastern Germany. Our unit of analysis is the labor market district, which, in both Leipzig and Chemnitz, includes the entire city plus a small portion of the surrounding rural area.

Although the two cities were hardly socioeconomic peas in a pod in 1989, they were similar in terms of industry structure, demographics, and institutional supports, which recommends them as matched cases to compare and assess the viability of our argument concerning the importance of local sociopolitical relations for institutional transfer and development. The logic of comparison is to see if exceptional local outcomes can be distinguished from rather ordinary ones and explained by underlying sociopolitical relations. Using a range of quantitative and qualitative measures, Chemnitz appears to be more or less typical of Eastern German cities in terms of the development of dual-system training arrangements, but Leipzig has performed well above the norm. Closer examination of training practices in these two cities reveals the important role different patterns of associationalism and intergroup relations played in producing these divergent outcomes.

Leipzig, the tenth-largest city in Germany, is situated in the western part of Saxony. Its position at the intersection of important trade routes permitted the city to become one of Europe's leading commercial and cultural centers by the fifteenth century. By the nineteenth century, trade in books, yarns, furs, and textiles dominated the local economy but with the opening of the Leipzig-Dresden railroad in 1839 (the first in Germany), the city's banking, textile, and metalworking industries began to develop. Industrialization in Leipzig was extraordinarily rapid, and the city's population rose from 106,925 in 1871 to 589,850 in 1910 (Usbeck 1991). By the turn of the century, Leipzig was a major industrial city and a leading center of the German labor movement. In the last years of World War II, major areas of Leipzig were destroyed. Yet after the war the city was rebuilt and once again emerged as a major industrial center. The city's principal industries included book publishing, large-scale engineering, electrical products, textiles and apparel, chemicals, and machine tools. The Leipzig Fair, held every spring, became one of the most important trade forums between Eastern and Western Europe.

Chemnitz, formerly Karl-Marx-Stadt (1953–90), is also located in Saxony and like Leipzig, its development was also triggered by its proximity to important trade routes. With its early monopoly in textile bleaching, Chemnitz emerged as a major textile and linen center. In fact, the first German spinning mill was in Chemnitz. In the nineteenth century, Chemnitz developed other industries as well. The first machine tools and the first German locomotive were built there. During the industrial revolution, factories were built at such a pace and pollution was so great that the city was nicknamed the "Manchester of Germany." In 1871, Chemnitz was the site of the first strikes for the ten-hour workday. The city was severely damaged in World War II, but it was largely rebuilt and held up by the East German regime as a showpiece of modern town planning. Under the GDR, Chemnitz was called Karl-Marx-Stadt and served as a major center for the production of textiles, automobiles, commercial vehicles, machine tools, and chemicals.

Prior to unification, Leipzig was substantially larger and somewhat less industrial than Chemnitz, although both cities have suffered population losses in recent years. The Leipzig population fell from 530,000 in 1989 to about 480,000 in 1994, Chemnitz's population, from 302,000 to 279,000 in the same years (*Statistisches Jahrbuch den deutschen Gemeinden* 1993, 107). Labor participation rates in both cities were comparable (59 percent in Chemnitz; 54 percent in Leipzig)(ibid., 153), the demographic profiles of the workforces of both cities were almost identical, and the composition of the two local economies in terms of employment were roughly similar as well. (See Table 2.3)

Following unification and the collapse of the GDR's major export markets in Eastern Europe, the local economies of both cities went into severe crisis, leading to massive unemployment and numerous plant closings. For example, in the all-important metalworking sector, Leipzig had about 79,000 jobs in 1989, Chemnitz about 80,000. By 1993, metalworking employment in Leipzig was reduced to around 5000 jobs; in Chemnitz it leveled off at about 15,000 (Karrasch 1995, 103). The current official unemployment rate in Leipzig is 12.4 percent; in Chemnitz it is 15.7 percent (the Eastern German average is 15.5 percent). Underemployment in the two cities is comparable, at about 33 percent (Federal Labor Office, 1995, 11).

These economic developments have posed dramatic challenges for both public and private officials as they seek to establish vocational training in both cities. As in other parts of Eastern Germany, previous conglomerate-based training centers have been converted into public-funded vocational

TABLE 2.3. Composition of Two Local Economies (1989)

	Industry	Crafts	Con-struction	Trans-portation	Trade	Other	E,C,H	Total
Leipzig	34%	4%	8%	9%	13%	6%	26%	100
Chemnitz	42%	3%	7%	8%	11%	7%	22%	100

Source: Statistisches Jahrbuch der deutschen Gemeinden 1990, 153; E,C,H = Education, Culture, and Health.

schools, and thus the school-based component of training is relatively well established in both cities. But the massive plant shutdowns and industrial bankruptcies that have taken place elsewhere in Eastern Germany have not spared Leipzig and Chemnitz, thus rendering the firm-based component of vocational training difficult to develop in these two cities as well.

As in other parts of Eastern Germany, efforts to establish dualistic training arrangements in Leipzig and Chemnitz have encountered serious difficulties. Private firms are reluctant to invest scarce resources in training youth, especially when their own economic viability is uncertain and there is already an abundance of underemployed skilled workers available in the local labor market. Youth are wary of committing themselves to three-year apprenticeship programs that may not result in stable employment. And the chambers, employers associations, local unions, and local labor offices are still struggling with their own, internal organizational issues and thus are often not yet up to the tasks assigned to them in the dual system. Notwithstanding these shared difficulties, interesting differences in training outcomes have emerged between Chemnitz and Leipzig. Closer examination of these divergent outcomes and their sources illuminates the important role sociopolitical relations play in facilitating the process of institutional development and performance.

RECENT DEVELOPMENTS IN LEIPZIG AND CHEMNITZ

Data sources on training are plentiful, but some are downright misleading. The indicators available to gauge the performance of the dual system in individual labor office districts in Eastern Germany are limited by the statistics collected by the Federal Employment Agency, the Federal Institute for Vocational Training (BiBB), and whatever data are collected by local actors for their own use. Given the volatility of this issue, the data must be used with caution. For example, the official ratio of supply (of apprenticeship slots) to demand (by youth for these places) in each local labor office district is virtually always reported to be about 1:1. But this is a statistical artifact that both inflates the number of adequate training slots and camouflages regional differences. As we saw earlier, since the government is committed to provide an apprenticeship for every youth desiring one, in-firm training slots have been supplemented by large numbers of extra-firm slots. Government funding is especially targeted to regions where the supply-demand ratio is particularly poor, thus further masking regional differences. Moreover, the official ratios reflect dampened demand by counting only those youth who have actually found an apprenticeship or are still searching for one at the *end* of the apprenticeship year. Youth who had originally sought apprenticeships but had then returned to school or taken jobs as unskilled workers are not counted as part of the demand. In 1992, for example, 27 percent of the original youth cohort who had expressed an interest in an apprenticeship, decided six months later to put off their training until a later date (Schober 1993).

Despite these limitations, a number of rough indicators exist which allow us to assess efforts to establish dualistic training in the new federal states. One measure of performance is the *absolute number* of youth whose efforts to find apprenticeships can be accommodated. In absolute terms, the Leipzig labor office district offers more apprenticeships than any other in Eastern Germany. The number of firm-based apprenticeships offered in Leipzig grew from 4,044 in 1991 to 6,364 in 1993 and rose again to 7,482 in 1994. By contrast, total supply in Chemnitz remained stagnant, 4,020 in 1991, 4,035 in 1993, and 4,564 in 1994. Thus, whereas total supply in Leipzig has increased 84 percent over the period for which data are available, supply in Chemnitz has grown less than 12 percent.[25]

A second indicator of the development of vocational training arrangements is the *range* of apprenticeships offered. The assumption underlying this measure is that youth who confront a broader range of career choices are better off than those who have fewer choices. As with supply-demand ratios, here too local differences are not easy to disentangle. Indeed, the official supply-demand statistics per occupational category suggest that this ratio is within a few decimal points of complete balance almost everywhere in Eastern Germany—a picture obviously belied by actual developments in labor office districts. Nevertheless, of the fifty occupations listed in the Federal Labor Office statistics for 1992 and 1993, Leipzig offered, after controlling for the size of the districts, substantially more opportunities than Chemnitz in fourteen occupations, whereas Chemnitz offered advantageous conditions in only four vis-à-vis Leipzig *(Ausbildungsstellenmarkt 1994)*. Leipzig's supply advantages thus come from a number of different sources in the economy. Service and construction apprenticeships make up more of these advantageous occupational groups than do industrial jobs, but Leipzig

25. Data provided by the Landesarbeitsamt Sachsen. We recognize that absolute numbers and changes in supply are very rough measures, especially given that the two cities differ in size and economic structure. But we still think it is interesting that the number of training slots grew by 84 percent in Leipzig but by only 12 percent in Chemnitz, 56 percent in Saxony, and 45 percent in the new federal states. Clearly something special is happening in Leipzig. The best way to compare these two cities would have been by comparing rates (number of slots per youth), but given that the number of youth actively searching for slots (the appropriate denominator) is itself a function of the number of training slots available (many youth stay in school if they think there are not enough training slots available in the local labor markets), this number too is very difficult to obtain. For more on these problems, see Schober 1993 and Arbeitsamt Chemnitz 1995, 3.

has expanded industrial apprenticeships as well. In fact, whereas in Chemnitz, the number of industry and commerce apprenticeships offered fell by 600 between 1992 and 1993, they rose by the equivalent amount in Leipzig during the same period. BiBB data from 1994 confirm this picture of an almost across-the-board advantage in the availability of training opportunities in Leipzig. Of the thirteen occupational categories listed, Chemnitz offered a better supply-demand ratio in only two (interestingly, both are service-sector occupations). Leipzig led in all other occupational groups. Leipzig's overall ratio was the best of any district in Eastern Germany, whereas that of Chemnitz was slightly above the average.[26]

A third measure of how well West German-style training practices are performing is the relative reliance on extra-firm training to accommodate the demand for training by local youth. The basic assumption underlying the German dual training system is that in-firm training is better than extra-firm training: better for youth, because it links them to potential employers; better for employers because it permits them to recruit, screen, and train future employees; and better for the government because it splits the costs of training with the private sector. Of course, there must be sufficient numbers of firms willing to train. Since this is not the case in Eastern Germany and since the labor offices have an immediate concern to place youth in *some* form of training program, extra-firm training in Eastern Germany has grown in recent years. Stories abound of youth being trained to be florists, auto mechanics, and hairstylists in numbers that the local labor markets will clearly be unable to absorb. Even the trade unions, which bitterly denounce what they perceive as employer efforts to shift the costs of skill formation from the private to the public sectors, have generally supported extra-firm training with the argument that "some training is better than none at all." Nonetheless, the danger is that youth are being trained for jobs that do not and perhaps will not exist. IAB data show that in November 1993, 62 percent of youth in in-firm apprenticeships gauged their prospects of employment after completion as "good" or "very good," whereas only about 47 percent of those in extra-firm training did so.

According to the BiBB's *Berufsbildungbericht* (Occupational training report) for 1993, Leipzig was, at one point, head and shoulders above other labor market districts in Eastern Germany in the percentage of total training slots that were firm-based. In 1992, 98 percent of Leipzig's apprenticeships were firm-based. The corresponding figure for Chemnitz was 88 percent and the Eastern German average was 81 percent. But in subsequent years, Leipzig's lead over Chemnitz on this dimension has disappeared. Yet Leipzig

26. *BiBB Erheburg*, September 30, 1994; Table 1.1.

TABLE 2.4. In-firm as Percentage of Total Supply

City	1992 (%)	1993 (%)	1994 (%)	Total supply growth, 1992–94 (%)	In-firm supply growth, 1992–94 (%)
Leipzig	98	90	87	59	41
Chemnitz	88	90	88	1	2
Eastern German average	81	n.a.	n.a.	6	16

Source: *Berufsbildungsbericht 1993*, 45; Johnson 1995, 143.

has still relied less than most other Eastern German districts on extra-firm training at a time when it has dramatically increased the number of apprenticeships available, whereas most other districts, including Chemnitz, have built up much more slowly. (See Table 2.4.)

Thus measured along several dimensions, the differences in vocational training outcomes in Chemnitz and Leipzig appear quite striking. Although both cities have, by Eastern German standards, an above-average percentage of in-firm training slots, the actual number and range of new training opportunities in Chemnitz is much more limited than what we observe for Leipzig. How do we explain these differences, especially given that both cities are embedded in the same institutional and cultural environment?

Given the importance of economic activity for the functioning of dualistic training and the fact that Eastern Germany has experienced a severe economic crisis since unification, one's first instinct is to attribute differences in the performance of training arrangements in Leipzig and Chemnitz to differences in either the overall levels of economic activity in the two cities or the composition of their local economies. Certainly economic differences exist between these two cities. As we saw earlier, in 1989 Chemnitz was a slightly more industrial city than Leipzig, and since unification, a combination of de-industrialization and new investment in banking and services has continued to make Leipzig less industrial than Chemnitz. The current unemployment rate in Chemnitz (15.7 percent) is also somewhat higher than in Leipzig (12.4 percent) (Federal Labor Office 1995, 11).

Yet these economic differences do not translate directly into different opportunity structures for training in the two cities. For example, if we use unemployment rates as rough indicators of the *level* of economic activity, it is not clear how a 3.3 percent difference between Leipzig and Chemnitz would by itself translate into a 72 percent difference in the growth of training opportunities. Moreover, a quick look at a breakdown of appren-

TABLE 2.5. Breakdown of Apprenticeship Slots by Sector

Major sector	Leipzig		Chemnitz	
	1992 (%)	1993 (%)	1992 (%)	1993 (%)
Industry and commerce	52	47	57	49
Crafts	33	42	28	39
Administrative/office work	3	4	3	5
Agriculture	2	5	2	3

Source: Our calculations based on Federal Labor Office statistics.

ticeship slots in Leipzig and Chemnitz reveals that despite underlying structural differences in their local economies, the composition of training opportunities is basically the same. (See Table 2.5) In other words, differences in the underlying economic profiles of these two cities did not translate into starkly different opportunity structures for youth in search of training. Thus economic vitality and/or structure, although certainly an important factor in accounting for the divergent patterns observed between these two cities, cannot alone explain the differences between Leipzig and Chemnitz.

A second possible explanation for these differences focuses on policy differences between the two cities. Perhaps Leipzig benefited more from particular public policies and subsidies than Chemnitz did. Yet the most important programs affecting vocational training promotion come from either the federal government or the individual states. And given that both Leipzig and Chemnitz are located in the same federal state (Saxony) and thus are eligible for the same programs and funds, policy differences between the two cities are also controlled for. Even if Leipzig *had* obtained more government funding than Chemnitz (we were unable to collect data on this question), the issue to be explained would not be the *amount* of funding received by each city but rather *why* Leipzig was more capable than Chemnitz of tapping into funds available to all cities in Eastern Germany and/or Saxony. In other words, closer examination of local politics and not federal and state level programs would be required.

A third possible explanation centers around the underlying sociopolitical relations of the two localities. Earlier we discussed how a vibrant and well-developed network of secondary associations is important for both economic development and institutional performance. As a result, we would expect that contexts with greater numbers of associations would possess more developed and effective political and economic institutions than settings with fewer secondary associations.

Yet a quick glance at the associational patterns of our two cities reveals some remarkable similarities. Since 1990, 2455 organizations and associations have registered in Leipzig's Landkreis.[27] Chemnitz registered about 1700 groups in those same years. Yet, when controlling for population differences, Chemnitz does not appear to suffer from a paucity of associational life, at least not in comparison to Leipzig.

Elsewhere Richard Locke (1995) has argued that the qualitative features and patterns of interaction among the different groups in civil society are as important (if not more) than their actual number. In other words, groups linked through multiple, horizontal ties are more likely to share information, pool scarce resources, and engage in collective efforts than groups situated in settings where relations were more polarized or hierarchical. Perhaps these qualitative features of civil society are also important in Eastern Germany, especially given that none of these groups is especially well developed. In fact, given their recent establishment and lack of organizational resources, one would expect that alternative modes of interaction (cooperative vs. competitive) and divergent patterns of interest representation and aggregation would have a tremendous impact on local patterns of political and economic behavior. This would be especially true in the case of the dual system of training, which as we saw earlier, relies heavily on an articulated network of organizations and secondary associations to function properly. Cooperation and coordination among these local associations are key in ensuring that there are sufficient numbers of apprenticeship slots for each year's youth cohort and that the training provided meets national standards. Given the reluctance of private firms to train in Eastern Germany and the diffidence with which Eastern German youth view this system, cooperation among these local groups is all the more important in the new federal states.

Indeed, our multiple interviews with key actors in both cities convinced us that it was precisely along this dimension that Leipzig and Chemnitz appeared most different. Although in both localities, secondary associations and interest groups were struggling simply to establish themselves, let alone build a dualistic training system, local groups in Leipzig had transcended both their own organizational concerns and, in a certain way, the minimalist institutional roles assigned to them and were beginning to cooperate with one another in new and important ways—ways that had a direct consequence for the development of vocational training. In contrast, local groups in Chemnitz, while diligent in performing the institutional duties required of them, did little to extend these roles or to cooperate with one another in order to facilitate the development of training institutions in their locality.

27. Vereinsregister, Leipzig, February 1995. The Landkreise include areas larger than the labor office districts, but as it turns out, about 90 percent of registered groups are located in the cities.

COOPERATIVE INSTITUTION-BUILDING IN LEIPZIG

Of the many labor market districts we visited in Eastern Germany, Leipzig clearly took the most comprehensive approach toward convincing youth to consider a training position and encouraging firms to train these youth. In every labor office district throughout the Federal Republic, the tripartite "vocational advising committee" discusses issues of supply and demand for apprenticeships in its district. But the main task of these organizations is to negotiate local interpretations of broader guidelines, and they actually have few levers for addressing the most pressing problems (such as creating in-firm training slots) in Eastern Germany. In Leipzig, however, local actors have begun experimenting with new forms of cooperation aimed at addressing these problems. For instance, the periodic meetings of the local "vocational advising committee" are augmented by a biweekly meeting of a "Coordination Round" that includes regular members of the committee but also more "practitioners." Together, members of this Coordination Round seek to encourage local firms to train by engaging in five intensive weeks of firm and school visits. Labor office officials and training specialists from the respective chambers visit local firms together, armed with information about state subsidies, sermons about the need for sound long-term personnel policies, and lists of local youth appropriate for the firms. They also visit local schools in order to stimulate demand among youth for available training opportunities. According to a member of the Leipzig labor office: "The motivation for the Coordination Round was that we were tired of wasteful duplication of efforts to match youth to apprenticeships they found desirable. For us in the labor office, the advantage is that we can visit firms with the training experts of the chambers—the people who really know the firms and their personnel plans."[28]

The composition of the Coordination Round includes representatives of the labor office advising staff, the chambers of industry and commerce, the crafts chamber, and the office of schools. The participation of the office of schools is interesting in two ways. First, the inclusion of school representatives is an attempt to recapture one of the strengths of the former East German training system, which included close communication between teachers and firm-based trainers. Although such communication is much more difficult to sustain in a network of smaller training sites than in a large industrial conglomerate with its own vocational school, virtually all vocational training personnel from the former GDR regret the incapacity of the West German system for such communication. Second, and perhaps

28. Interview with Mr. Kurt Dornberger, Vocational Training Advisor, Federal Labor Office, Leipzig, January 1994.

more important, the school officials in Leipzig are able to use their ties to the Ministry of Culture to fund worthy local projects.

Local actors in Leipzig have also undertaken extensive efforts to counter the messages that youth receive from parents and the media which suggest that industrial work has no future in Leipzig. For the last three years, the Leipzig chamber of industry and commerce has held a one-day event in which they have invited all of the youth who have sought apprenticeships through the local labor office but have yet to find one. Firms that have available apprenticeship slots are also invited to introduce their companies at this event. The chamber hopes to persuade the firms that they need to engage in public self-promotion as part of a long-term strategy for reproducing their own labor market needs. Thus the relentless flow of bad news from the industrial labor market is now being countered in small ways. In addition to the metalworking firms, which are strongly represented at these annual events, the chamber allows employers from outside its jurisdiction to compete for the attention of the youth still seeking apprenticeships. The police, for example, also use the event to recruit apprentices. During the 1994 event, about 800 Leipzig youth participated, and about 300 of them actually signed apprenticeship contracts.

Thus local actors in Leipzig have sought to compensate for their own organizational weaknesses by coming together to share information, pool resources, and organize a series of initiatives aimed at fostering dualistic training.[29]

"POLITICS AS USUAL" IN CHEMNITZ

Chemnitz has also experienced some interesting new forms of collaboration, yet these efforts have been notable for what they have left out as much as for what they have brought in. A few years ago, for instance, the local metalworkers' union (IG Metall) organized the *Interessenverband Chemnitzer Maschinenbau* (ICM), an association which brought together local unions and business interests in an effort to prevent the liquidation of the local machine tool industry.[30] Yet with the decision to exclude controversial issues like vocational training from the agenda of the ICM, local coordination of training has taken a somewhat different turn in this city. The main sustained effort has been the development of a "trainers working group," the *Ausbildungsleiterarbeitskreis* (ALAK). Begun in early 1992 by representatives of a training corporation run by employers in Saxony, the thrice-

29. The efforts by local actors in Leipzig to build new institutions resemble in interesting ways the mutual learning and monitoring processes described in Sabel 1994.

30. For more on this experience, see Bluhm 1995.

yearly meetings have been geared toward securing the continued participation of those firms already training. The ALAK has won the consistent cooperation of the chamber of commerce and industry in Chemnitz as well as of the state labor office for Saxony, which is located in Chemnitz. These connections, along with a series of visits to firms considered by the employers to be model trainers, has no doubt had some benefits for the twenty or so firms that have participated. But there is no evidence that the lessons learned by the participants have spilled over to affect the overwhelming majority of Chemnitz firms that are still not training. Moreover, the structure of the organization has been one in which union representatives have been excluded from the beginning. The ALAK has attempted to enlist the participation of the schools but has by its own admission not been notably successful.[31]

Local actors' own descriptions of negotiations over training in Chemnitz paint a very different picture from that of Leipzig. While the employers' representatives describe relations among the local actors in Chemnitz as "peaceful," the unions describe it as a "war of all against all." By all accounts, however, the tripartite advisory commission does nothing to increase the number of available apprenticeships; indeed, it only meets a few times per year. Chemnitz also has a "Coordination Round," but it meets only once a year, in February, as opposed to every two weeks as in Leipzig. If cooperative measures are not widespread, individual actors are also hard pressed to help increase the supply of training on their own. For example, this past spring the Chemnitz chamber of industry and commerce invited 120 firms to an event on vocational training. Only one company actually attended.[32] Of course, the Chemnitz chamber helps advise firms on state-level subsidy programs. But still, the local chamber's activities generally consist of rather isolated efforts to address supply and/or demand issues. In short, both the style and the outcomes present a striking contrast to Leipzig, where efforts to promote coordination appear to have helped generate a sizable growth in firm-based training.

The key point, we want to emphasize, is not so much that the Leipzig chamber and/or its local labor office is more capable or industrious than the local labor office or chamber in Chemnitz but rather that this process in Leipzig is better coordinated in the sense that the various local actors physically meet to do it. This coordination appears to correlate with the more positive training outcomes observed in Leipzig.

These findings, however, beg a further question: *Why* are local actors more able or willing to cooperate in Leipzig that in Chemnitz? Our inter-

31. See Schmidt and Günther 1993.
32. Interview with Ms. Zimmermann, DGB, Saxony, January 1994.

views with key actors in both localities suggest that these differences in behavior are themselves the product of the alternative patterns of intergroup relations manifest in the two cities. In Leipzig, the key actors involved in training—the chambers, schools, employer associations, and so on—are embedded in a dense network of secondary associations linked to one another through many horizontal ties. Communication among the different groups is frequent and relatively open. As a result, these intermediary organizations in Leipzig are not only well informed but also have come to depend upon, even trust, one another and other groups in the network. This clearly facilitates collective problem solving and the pooling of scarce resources in that locality.

In contrast, patterns of intergroup relations in Chemnitz are much more polarized. As we saw earlier Chemnitz does not suffer from any particular shortage of secondary associations or interest groups *per se,* but these groups are nevertheless clustered together into two opposing camps—one linked to organized labor, and the other to business interests. Ties linking the various groups within each camp are strong but linkages across the two clusters are few and tenuous. As a result, the flow of information among key intermediary organizations involved in training in Chemnitz is much more limited and, hence, their ability to engage in collective efforts is greatly reduced. In short, similar actors behave differently in Leipzig and Chemnitz, not out of whim, or ideological commitment, or even because they possessed unequal resources, but rather because they are embedded in different settings, which provide them with different levels (and quality) of information and different opportunities to collaborate with one another in the resolution of common problems. The source of these divergent networks is a very interesting and important issue but not one that can be taken up in here.[33] For our purposes, the point of the comparison is simply to illustrate the important role local sociopolitical relations play in the process of institution building and development in the new federal states.

CONCLUSION

Given that both Germanies now share the same institutions and well-endowed government, the reconfiguration of training practices in the new federal states presents itself as an interesting case through which to explore the politics of institutional transfer more generally. Despite massive govern-

---

33. These different patterns of associationalism and intergroup relations appear to be the result of divergent historical legacies in which local groups in Leipzig were able to maintain and develop their organizational capacities even during the previous regime. These organizational capacities have resurfaced in recent years and have influenced the current transformation process in interesting and unexpected ways. For more on this, see Locke, "Rebirth."

ment funding, the presence of various institutional supports, and the concerted efforts of the country's major social partners, this process of institutional transfer and change is experiencing significant difficulties. Although new training arrangements are indeed being established in the new federal states, they are often poorly linked to private firms, highly dependent on government funding, and at times, supporting training programs that will not necessarily translate into stable employment opportunities in the future.

The current difficulties confronting this process of institutional transfer in the new federal states as a whole as well as in Chemnitz and Leipzig in particular, are the product of three factors: first, the general politics of unification and institutional transfer which led to the wholesale transfer of West German arrangements, regardless of the problems these same institutions were facing in their established setting and/or whether they were appropriate to Eastern Germany; second, to the paucity of dynamic private firms willing and able to train in the new federal states; and finally, and perhaps most important, to the weaknesses of the underlying sociopolitical infrastructure on which institutions like the dual training system rest. In fact, as our analysis of recent developments in Leipzig made clear, despite a variety of economic difficulties it shares with other localities in Eastern Germany, the city's vibrant network of local interest groups and secondary associations played a major role in facilitating the development of the new training institutions. In other words, cooperative efforts by local sociopolitical groups were able to compensate for a variety of economic and organizational shortcomings and thus successfully promote dualistic training arrangements in Leipzig.

This case study suggests that institutional transfer is certainly possible but that its success, will depend in large part on local sociopolitical relations.[34] Localities with rich patterns of associationalism and intergroup cooperation appear to provide more fertile soil for institutional transfer and development than do settings with fewer and/or more parochial secondary associations. This finding has important implications for both policymaking and future research.

Yet it also has implications for the way we think about institutions and their relationship to civil society. Traditionally, analyses of institutional arrangements like the German dual system of vocational training describe (in highly stylized terms) the way things are supposed to work, that is, the way the institutions are designed, as opposed to how they actually operate in the real world. As an academic convention, this style of presentation makes

---

34. See Jacoby 1996 for more on the relationship between groups in civil society and the process of institutional transfer.

sense. It is parsimonious and lends itself more easily to comparison. But as a way of enriching our knowledge and furthering a variety of policy-related debates concerning training, skill formation, work reorganization, and so on, this approach has some serious shortcomings. Often these highly stylized accounts take on an ahistorical and noncontextual quality by focusing primarily on the institutional design and structural features of the institutions themselves—frequently slighting or ignoring the broader social, political, and economic contexts in which they were developed and embedded.[35] As a result, this approach often jumps too quickly to normative and prescriptive analyses by concluding that certain institutional arrangements with particular organizational features are more "efficient" than others and either prescribes the active replication of these "best practices" or assumes their inevitable diffusion across national boundaries.

This essay has followed a somewhat different course by focusing instead on recent strains and difficulties encountered during the process of remaking the vocational training system in the former GDR in the image of the West German system. In pursuing this alternative strategy, we hoped to provide greater insight into how key features of this system interact with and depend on other local sociopolitical actors and resources. Bringing civil society back into our analyses of institutions is absolutely necessary if we are to fully grasp the nature of the changes and challenges many institutions currently face. Doing this, however, means that we have to be more nuanced in our treatment of civil society. We cannot simply treat it as a dichotomous variable—one either has a "good" civil society or a "bad" one, depending on rough indicators like numbers of associations. Instead, it requires that we examine more carefully the qualitative features of civil society (such as the organizational attributes of the different groups and the patterns of interaction among them) in order to better understand how these different patterns shape behavior in distinct ways. In addition, we must be careful not to treat civil society as if it exists in a vacuum or even in a zero-sum relationship with the institutions of the state. Relations between institutions and groups in civil society are complicated and highly interdependent. Understanding how these relations work and how they change over time is key to analyzing institutional behavior and institutional change.

APPENDIX: SELECTED LIST OF INTERVIEWEES

1. Dr. Günther Albrecht, BIFO, Berlin
2. Professor Martin Baethge, Sociologisches Seminar, Göttingen

---

35. For more on this, see Locke and Thelen 1995.

3. Ms. Heidi Becherer, DGB Chemnitz
4. Mr. Hans-Dieter Becker, Handwerkskammer, Leipzig-Bosdorf
5. Mr. Sieghard Bender, IG Metall, Chemnitz
6. Mr. Klaus Boldorf, Treuhandanstalt, Berlin
7. Dr. Gerhard Bosch, Institut für Arbeit und Technik, Gelsenkirchen
8. Mr. Kurt Bradatsch, IG Metall, Schwerin
9. Dr. Hans-Joachim Buggenhagen, Innovationstransfer-und Forschungstelle, Schwerin
10. Dr. Burkand, BiBB, Berlin
11. Dr. Ulrich Degen, BiBB, Berlin
12. Mr. Kurt Dornberger, Arbeitsamt (Berufsberatung), Leipzig
13. Dr. Helmut Ernst, Innovationstransfer-und Forschungstelle, Schwerin
14. Dr. Ulrich Göhler, Treuhandanstalt, Berlin
15. Mr. Wolfgang Handschuh, Arbeitsamt, Chemnitz
16. Mr. Klaus Hermann, IG Metall, Frankfurt
17. Mr. Stephan Ittner, Handwerkskammer, Chemnitz/Sachsen
18. Professor Horst Kern, Soziologisches Seminar, Göttingen
19. Mr. Eberhard Koch, Fahrzeugguß Leipzig GmbH, Leipzig
20. Dr. Gerhard Korb, Chamber of Industry and Commerce, Chemnitz
21. Mr. Harst Kowalak, DGB (Bildung), Dusseldorf
22. Ms. Eva Kuda, IG Metall (Bildung), Frankfurt
23. Dr. Gerhard Leminsky, Hans Böckler Stiftung, Dusseldorf
24. Mr. Steffan Lemme, IG Metall Youth Department, Erfurt
25. Mr. Manfred Melzer, Arbeitgeberverband der Metall-und Elektroberufe, Erfurt
26. Mr. Herbert Michel, Schwerinerausbildungszentrum, Schwerin
27. Mr. Klaus Müller, Verband der Wirtschaft Thuringen, Erfurt
28. Ms. Karla Nowak, ERFEGAU Entwicklungsgesellschaft Arbeit und Umwelt, Erfurt
29. Dr. Henrich Lehmann-Grube, Bürgermeister, Leipzig
30. Professor Martin Osterland, Universität Bremen, Bremen
31. Ms. Katharina Pistor, Harvard University and Chamber of Industry and Commerce, Dresden
32. Mr. Rackow, Association of Construction Employees of Mecklenburg-Vorpommern, Schwerin
33. Dr. Rolf Raddatz, German Chamber of Industry and Commerce (DIHT), Bonn
34. Mr. Bernd Repke, Niles Werkzeugmaschinen GmbH, Berlin
35. Dr. Jurgen Riedel, Aufbauwerk im Freistaat Sachsen, GmbH, Dresden
36. Professor Hedwig Rudolf, WZB, Berlin
37. Dr. Axel Sanne, Dresdner Bank Gruppe, Dresden

38. Dr. Johannes Sauer, Ministerium für Bildung und Wissenschaft, Bonn
39. Mr. Bernd Schlichting, Chamber of Industry and Commerce, Chemnitz
40. Dr. Hans-Peter Schmidt, Chamber of Industry and Commerce, Leipzig
41. Mr. Klaus Schmidt, Bildungswerk der Sächischen Wirtschaft
42. Dr. Wolfgang Schroeder, IG Metall, Frankfurt
43. Dr. Wolfgang Schwegler-Rohmeis, LASA Brandenburg, Potsdam
44. Karen Schober, Institut für Arbeitsmarkt-und Berufsforschung, Nürnberg
45. Mr. Gerhard Sonntag, Betriebsrat, Heckert Werkzeugmachinen GmbH, Chemnitz
46. Mr. Andreas Streitberger, IG Metall, Jugend, Chemnitz
47. Dr. Manfred Tessaring, Institut für Arbeitsmarkt-und Berufsforschung, Nürnberg
48. Mr. Tuschke, Ministerium für Bildung und Wissenschaft, Bonn
49. Mr. Richard von Bardeleben, BiBB, Bonn
50. Dr. Reinhold Weiss, Institut der deutschen Wirtschaft, Köln
51. Mr. Günther Willfgang, Handwerkskammer, Vocational Education, Leipzig-Bosdorf
52. Ms. Claudia Wolfinger, Institut für Arbeitsmarkt-und Berufsforschung, Nürnberg
53. Mr. Klaus Wünderlich, Geschäftsführer der IHK Bildungszentrum, Schwerin
54. Ms. Sabine Zimmerman, DGB, Sachsen

REFERENCES

Anweiler, Oskar, ed., 1990. *Vergleich von Bildung und Erziehung in der Bundesrepublik Deutschland und in der Deutschen Demokratischen Republik.* Bonn: BiBB.

Arbeitsamt, Chemnitz. 1995. "Kritische Entwicklung auf dem Ausbildungsmarkt." April 6, p. 3. *Ausbildungstellenmarkt 1994.* 1995. Nuremberg: Bundesanstalt für Arbeit.

Baethge, Martin. 1995. "Technology, Public Policy, and Employment Relations in Germany." Paper presented at the International Industrial Relations Association World Congress, Washington, D.C., May 31.

Baethge, Martin, Volker Baethe-Kinsley, and Robert Hendrich. 1995. "Die Zukunft des Facharbeiters—im Kontext neuer betrieblicher Produktions-und Ausbildungskonzepte, veränderter beruflicher Ansprüche und neugeordneter Ausbildungsberufe." Göttingen, June 15.

Bendix, Reinhard. 1991. "Staat, Legitimierung und 'Zivilgesellschaaft.' " *Berliner Journal für Soziologie* 1: 3–11.

Berggren, Christian. 1992. *Alternatives to Lean Production: Work Organization in the Swedish Automobile Industry.* Ithaca ILR Press.

Bluhm, Katharina. 1995. "Regionale Unterstützungsnetzwerke in der ostdeutschen industrie: Der Interessenverband Chemnitzer Maschinenbau." In Helmut Wiesenthal, ed., *Einheit als Interessenpolitik: Studien zur sektoralen Transformation Ostdeutschlands.* Frankfurt: Campus-Verlag.

Boll, Bernard. 1994. "Interest Organization and Intermediation in the New Ländern,"*German Politics* 3, no. 1: 114–28.

Bosch, Gerhard. 1992. "Vocational Training and Change in Patterns of Labour Relations in Germany." Unpublished manuscript, Institut Arbeit und Technik, Gelsenkirchen.

Bund-Länder-Kommission für Bildungsplanung. 1992. *Forschungs fürderung und Entwicklung der Berufsausbildung in den neuen Ländern* (draft), February.

Burkhardt, Dieter. 1990. "Aspekte zur Finanzierung und Förderung der Berufsausbildung in den neuen Bundesländern." *Gewerschaftliche Bildungspolitik*, January, pp. 7–10.

Camuffo, Arnaldo, and Stefano Micelli. 1995. "Mediterranean Lean Production?" Unpublished manuscript, University of Venice, Italy, May.

Casey, Bernard. 1991. "Recent Developments in the German Apprenticeship System." *British Journal of Industrial Relations* 29, no. 2: 205–22.

Cohen, Joshua, and Joel Rogers. 1992. "Secondary Associations and Democratic Governance." *Politics and Society* 20, no. 4: 393–472.

Coleman, James. 1988. "Social Capital Is the Creation of Human Capital." *American Journal of Sociology* 94 (supplement): s95-s120.

Commission of the European Communities. 1994. *Employment Observatory,* no. 10, February.

Cott, Hans-Jürgen. 1991. "Berfusbildung im Umbruch." *Wirtschaft und Berufserziehung*, January, pp. 5–9.

Degen, Ulrich, 1993. "Was könnte die nicht-ausbildenden Betriebe in den neuen Ländern zur Ausbildung motivieren?" *BWP Nachrichten* 22, no. 4: 30–31.

Degen, Ulrich, and Günther Walden. 1994. "Situation, Organisation und Gestaltung der betrieblichen Berufsausbildung in den neuen Bundesländern," *Information für die Beratungs- und Vermittlungsdienst des IAB,* June 8, p. 2073.

Degen, Ulrich, Günther Walden, and Klaus Becker. 1995. *Berufsbildung in den neuen Bundesländern. Berlin: BiBB.*

Dininio, Phyllis. 1994. "Transferring the German Model to Eastern Germany: Old Institutions Faltering in a New Economic Environment." Paper presented at the Northeastern Political Science Association Annual Meeting, November 10–12.

Dore, Ronald. 1973. *British Factory—Japanese Faculty,* Berkelely: University of California Press.

Federal Labor Office (Nürnberg). 1995. *IAB Werkstattbericht,* no. 13, March 15.

Fichter, Michael. 1994. "Remolding Union Structures: Does Eastern Germany Count?" Paper presented at the Ninth International Conference of Europeanists, Chicago, Ill., March 31-April 2.

Hamilton, Stephen. 1990. *Apprenticeship for Adulthood.* New York: Basic Books.

Harhoff, Dietmar, and Thomas J. Kane. 1993. "Financing Apprenticeship Training: Evidence from Germany." Unpublished manuscript, Cambridge, Mass., October.

Herrigel, Gary, and Charles Sabel. 1994 "Craft Production in Crisis: Industrial Restructuring in Germany during the 1990s." Paper presented at the Conference on "Globalization and Regionalization: Implications for the Asian NIES," East-West Center, Honolulu, Hawaii, August 15–17.

IG Metall. 1991. "Informationen zum jetzt geltenden Recht der beruflicher Bildung in den neuen Bundesländern." January.

Jacoby, Wade. 1996. "The Politics of Institutional Transfer: Two Postwar Reconstructions in Germany, 1945–1995." Ph.D. diss., Department of Political Science, MIT.

Jeong, Jooyeon. 1995. "The Failure of Recent State Vocational Training Policies in Korea from a Comparative Perspective." *British Journal of Industrial Relations* 33, no. 2: 237–52.

Johnson, Carsten. 1995. "Die Rolle intermediärer Organisationen beim Wandel des Berufsbildungssystems." In Helmut Wiesenthal, ed., *Einheit als Interessenpolitik: Studien zur sektoralen Transformation Ostdeutschlands.* Frankfurt: Campus-Verlag.

Karrasch, Petra. 1995. "Gewerkschaftliche und gewerkschaftsnahe Politikformen in und mit der Kommune: Leipziger Erfahrungen." In Susanne Benzler, Udo Bullmann, and Dieter Eißel, eds., *Deutschland-Ost vor Ort.* Opladen: Leske & Budrich.

Katzenstein, Peter J. 1987. *Policy and Politics in West Germany: The Growth of a Semi-Sovereign State?* Philadelphia: Temple University Press.

——, ed. 1989. *Industry and Politics in West Germany: Toward the Third Republic.* Ithaca: Cornell University Press.

Kochan, Thomas A., and Paul Osterman. 1994. *The Mutual Gains Enterprise.* Boston: Harvard Business School Press.

Lehmbruch, Gerhard. 1994. "Dilemmata verbandlicher Einflußlogik im Prozess der deutschen Vereinigung." In *Staat und Verbände,* special issue of *Politische Vierteljahresschrift* 25: 370–92.

Locke, Richard M. "The Rebirth of Civil Society?: Historical Legacies and

Local Politics in Eastern Germany." Unpublished manuscript, MIT, August 1996.

———. 1995. *Remaking the Italian Economy.* Ithaca: Cornell University Press.

Locke, Richard M., and Kathleen Thelen. 1995. "Apples and Oranges Revisited: Contextualized Comparisons and the Study of Comparative Labor Politics." *Politics and Society* 23, no. 3: 337–67.

Lynch, Lisa. 1992. "A National Training Agenda: Lessons from Abroad." Report to the Economic Policy Institute, Washington, D.C., July.

MacDuffie, John Paul. 1995. "Human Resource Bundles and Manufacturing Performance: Organizational Logic and Flexible Production Systems in the World Auto Industry." *Industrial and Labor Relations Review* 48, no. 2: 197–221.

Milgram, Paul, and John Roberts. 1990. "The Economics of Modern Manufacturing: Technology, Strategy, and Organization." *American Economic Review* 80, no. 3: 511–28.

Offe, Claus. 1992. "German Reunification as a 'Natural Experiment.' " *German Politics* 1, no. 1: 1–12.

Osterman, Paul. 1988. *Employment Futures.* New York: Oxford University Press.

Putnam, Robert. 1993. *Making Democracy Work.* Princeton: Princeton University Press.

Rogers, Joel, and Wolfgang Streeck. 1994. "Workplace Representation Overseas: The Works Council Story." In Richard B. Freeman, ed., *Working Under Different Rules.* New York: Russell Sage Foundation.

Sabel, Charles F. 1994. "Learning by Monitoring: The Institutions of Economic Development." In Neil J. Smelser and Richard Swedberg, eds., *The Handbook of Economic Sociology,* 137–65. Princeton: Princeton University Press.

Sabel, Charles F., and Gary Herrigel. 1994. "A Sudden Crisis in Craft Production in Germany." Unpublished manuscript, MIT.

Schober, Karen. 1993. "Aufgeschoben ist nicht aufgehoben." *IAB Kurzbericht,* February 1, pp. 1–4.

———. 1994. "Der schwierige Weg zum dualen System." *Materialien aus der Arbeitsmarkt-und Berufsforschung* 3: 3–27.

Schmidt, Klaus, and Ulrich Günther. 1993. "Aufbau und Arbeitsweise eines regionalen Ausbildungsleiter-Arbeitskreises: Schaffung wirkungsvoller regionaler Strukturen und Kooperationen." *Ausbildungs-Entwicklung* 5: 17–27.

Seibel, Wolfgang. 1992. "Necessary Illusions: The Transformation of Governance Structures in the New Germany." *The Tocqueville Review* 13, no. 1: 190.

Silvia, Stephen J. 1994. "A House Divided: German Employers' Associations after Unification." Paper presented at the MIT Industrial Relations Research Seminar, Cambridge, Mass., October 25.

——. 1997. "A House Divided: Employers and the Challenges to Pattern Bargaining in the United States." *Comparative Politics* 29: 187–207.

Soskice, David. 1994. "Reconciling Markets and Institutions: The German Apprenticeship System." In Lisa Lynch, ed., *Training and the Private Sector: International Comparisons,* 25–60. Chicago: University of Chicago Press.

Streeck, Wolfgang, Josef Hilbert, Karl-Heinz van Kevelaer, Friederike Maier, and Hajo Weber. 1987. *The Role of the Social Partners in Vocational Training and Further Training in the Federal Republic.* Berlin: CEDEFOP.

Trades Union Congress. 1995. "Your Rights at Work: TUC Proposals for Rights to Representation." July.

Usbeck, Hartmut. 1991. "Leipzig und seine Region." In Deutsches Institut für Urbanistik, ed., *Urbanität in Deutschland.* Stuttgart: Deutscher Gemeindeverlag, 1991.

Weiler, Paul. 1990. *Governing the Work Place: The Future of Labor and Employment Law.* Cambridge: Harvard University Press.

Westney, D. Eleanor. 1987. *Imitation and Innovation: The Transfer of Western Organizational Patterns in Meiji Japan.* Cambridge: Harvard University Press.

Wever, Kirsten, Peter Berg, and Thomas Kochan. 1994. "The Role of Labor Market Institutions in Employee Training: Comparing the United States and Germany." Economic Policy Institute Working Paper, no. 114, December, Washington, D.C.

Womack, James P., Daniel T. Jones, and Daniel Roos. 1990. *The Machine That Changed the World.* New York: Rawson Associates.

Zimmerman, Hartmut, et. al. 1985. *DDR Handbuch.* 3d edition. Cologne: Verlag Wissenschaft und Politik.

3 • Active Labor Market Policy and German Unification: The Role of Employment and Training Companies

Matthias Knuth

THE TRANQUIL CATACLYSM

Among the countries of the former Soviet sphere, the case of East Germany is unique insofar as one can hardly speak of a process of transformation. What we witnessed in the former German Democratic Republic was an almost instant and wholesale imposition of West German regulations and institutions and the mechanisms of the capitalist world order of which they are a part. Because of the imbalance of size and strength, both economic and political, between the two Germanys, the five newly formed Eastern Länder had no alternative but to join the existing federation and constitution. Calls for a new German state in which some Eastern traditions and social rights would have been preserved remained unheard.

But in terms of the impact on economic and social life, the monetary and economic union that preceded political unification was the more decisive step, just as the currency reform of 1948 was more important than the Parliamentary Convention of 1949 to the early postwar history of the Federal Republic of Germany. Given the early currency union, German unification took the form of a benevolent and costly conquest undertaken by the West on the urgent request of the people of the East—nonviolent in appearance, yet brutal in its consequences. For East German industry, monetary union resulted in an immediate loss of markets and a plummeting of production by 1993 to about 30 percent of 1989 levels. Severe drops in employment levels followed: between 1989 and 1993, dependent employment decreased by 40 percent, with only marginal compensation through an increase in self-employment.

Reasons for this massive job destruction, and possible alternatives, are discussed elsewhere (see Hall and Ludwig 1993, Rothschild 1993, and Bosch and Knuth 1993). The outcome, however, was a marked change not only in the level of employment but in the sectoral structure of the East German economy as well. East German industrial density (jobs in industry per 1,000 population) has declined to 58 percent of the West German index. In 1993, only 15 percent of East Germany value-added was produced in industry (as compared to 28 percent in the West), and at the end of the year, only 20 percent of Eastern jobs were in industry—as compared to 34 percent in the West. Within four years, East Germany moved from overindustrialization to underindustrialization.

Individual mobility on the labor market was higher still than these dramatic aggregate shifts suggest. According to a representative panel study, in November 1993, only 29 percent of the working population were still—and without interruption—employed in the same establishment or public body as four years before (Bielenski, Brinkmann, and Kohler 1994).

These changes would have been even more disruptive had structural adaptation been left entirely to private decisions based on market conditions. But even though the incumbent Christian-Liberal coalition might have preferred such a strategy, it was first necessary to privatize the state-run economy of the East. The last government of the GDR had placed the legacy of the socialist economy in the hands of the Treuhand Agency, which on being founded in 1990, became responsible for 40 percent of East German jobs. After unification, the Treuhand became an agency of the Federal Treasury. Its mission was ambivalent from the beginning: instant privatization, or active restructuring as a precondition of privatization? The Treuhand vacillated between these two strategies (Nolte 1995), and in many cases, preoccupation with rapid privatization hindered the sort of restructuring that would have made the companies more attractive for investors (Knuth 1993a).

When the thin stratum of "cream" companies had been sold, it became clear that further privatization was impossible without first reducing company payrolls to numbers compatible with their medium-term viability. The downsizing of workforces and the managing of closures where privatization was regarded hopeless turned out to be just as important a job for the Treuhand as privatization itself. Three-quarters of Eastern Germany's total job destruction took place in the sector of the economy for which the Treuhand was responsible. Not counting jobs destroyed or externalized either before the Treuhand became operational or after units had been privatized, the Treuhand was immediately involved in the elimination of 1.75 million jobs, 45 percent of the total East German job loss. Thus East Germany's shock therapy could not pose as the regretable result of the working of the "invisible hand" but had to be administered under conditions of visible political responsibility.

In this chapter, I argue that such a dramatic reduction and reallocation of employment, compressed into a mere four years without an explosion of social and political unrest, would have been impossible without the massive implementation of an active labor market policy which, to a large extent, served to outplace workers from Treuhand companies. The implementation of direct job creation programs on such a scale and in close coordination with the Treuhand companies' outplacement policies was mediated by a new type of agent in the field of active labor market policy, the so-called employment and training companies (ETCs). Acting as temporary substitute employers and financed through public labor market programs, they can be analyzed as an extension of the employment relations systems of dwindling Treuhand companies. The Treuhand's contribution to direct job creation programs and to their implementation in ETCs became one of the prominent coins of exchange in a specific type of Treuhand corporatism, which evolved both at the level of the plant or enterprise between Treuhand company managements and works councils and at the level of the Treuhand Agency and the federal and regional trade union leadership.

ACTIVE LABOR MARKET POLICY IN THE EAST GERMAN CRASH

Cushioning the Job Loss

Although 3.9 million jobs were eliminated between 1990 and 19; ' registered unemployment in 1993 averaged 1.15 million, or less than on third of the net job loss. In other words, for two-thirds of the net total of redundancies, individual workers either were given an alternative to registered unemployment or found it on their own. The most important individual solution was working in the West. At the end of 1993, net migration and commuting accounted for slightly over one million members of the former East German labor force. These numbers must be read against the backdrop of an active labor force of 9.8 million persons in 1989. While the proportions of the population of working age (from fifteen to sixty-five) were rather similar in East and West Germany (69.7 and 67.2 percent), participation rates were widely different (87 percent in East Germany vs. 69 percent in West Germany within the population of working age). The main reason for this difference was that in East German there were almost as many women in the workforce as men.

All the other major alternatives to unemployment were related to labor market policy:

1. Almost one million workers had left the labor market by the end of 1992 through a special early retirement program. Since then, the numerical impact of this program has declined as participants enter the regular pension system.

2. A peak of more than two million persons worked short-time (working-time reductions were subsidized through government unemployment funds) in spring 1991. Short-time working—often at zero hours—was used to dam up underemployment and to slow its transformation into unemployment. It was also used to buy time until active labor market policy projects could be organized or until individuals had reached their age of eligibility for early retirement.

3. Up to 450,000 persons participated in programs of further training and retraining, not counting training for those still formally employed but put on short time.

4. Up to 400,000 persons were temporarily employed on fixed-term contracts in programs of direct job creation.

5. At the end of 1994, the total volume of relief through labor market policy instruments was still slightly above the level of registered unemployment.

These aggregate numbers do not sufficiently reveal the personal incidence of labor market policy. Until November 1993, almost half of the working population had participated in a labor market program at least once, whereas "only" one-third had experienced periods of unemployment (Bielenski, Brinkmann, and Kohler 1994). The first element of an explanation of the relative social and political stability during Eastern German economic collapse is labor market policy; alternatives to unemployment were offered on a large scale, and even those who became unemployed could still hope to have access to such a program later.

The Proactive Implementation of Labor Market Policy in East Germany

The traditional crux of active labor market policy in West Germany has been its tendency to react, with some time lag, to rising unemployment in a pro-cyclical rather than an anti-cyclical manner (Reissert 1994a). "Passive" spending for unemployment benefits and short-time allowances are financed from the same unemployment insurance contributions as "active" spending for training, direct job creation programs, and the rehabilitation of handicapped persons. Budget deficits are covered by the federal budget, but with budget supervision on the one hand and frequent amendments to the Employment Promotion Act on the other, the federal government controls these budgets through executive as well as legislative mechanisms. In times of economic crisis, the number of benefit claimants rises, whereas the number of contributors declines. Raising the rate of contributions (paid by employers and employees at par) would be unpopular and economically unwise, and the Federal Treasury would be unwilling to accept rising deficits. In the resulting squeeze, active measures, because they are optional, are typically crowded out by passive spending, to which claimants have an entitlement right.

In the regionally split labor market emerging after the unification, these mechanisms worked the opposite way, allowing an anti-cyclical active labor market policy. Given the "national challenge" posed by unification and in the wake of the West German boom of 1991, the rate of unemployment insurance contributions was set at a record high level. In 1992, employment offices in the East spent DM 46 billion (for active as well as passive purposes) but only 7.5 billion were collected in Eastern contributions. The remainder of the 38.5 billion was covered by the West German contribution surplus (64 percent) and from the federal budget (36 percent). The spending of the Federal Employment Agency, always an important but inconspicuous mechanism of interregional redistribution (Reissert 1994b), now became the largest single element of the huge financial transfers flowing from West to East.

Bolstered by these transfers, East German labor market policy took on a markedly active profile, whereas the activity rate in the West fell when the unification boom came to an end. In 1991, when underemployment was still to a large extent contained within firms through short-time working, participation in job creation and training rose faster than unemployment. Contrary to the pro-cyclical tradition in West Germany, active labor market policy in the East was used in an anti-cyclical, proactive manner to head off rising unemployment. Direct creation of highly subsidized temporary jobs took the form of a public employment program designed to curb the level of unemployment. The East German ratio of job creation participants per 100 persons remaining unemployed ran above 30, a remarkably high level, from September 1991 to the end of 1992, whereas the West German peak record had been a ratio of 6 in 1979, a year of relatively low unemployment. For a short time job creation became the principal means of job placement. In 1991, 63 percent of job placements by employment offices were in subsidized jobs created by the Federal Employment Agency itself; in 1992, this number was still 45 percent.

Direct Job Creation as a Public Employment Program

In the context of proactive labor market policy, direct job creation assumed a function completely different from the West German tradition. After the tacit abandonment of the full-employment policy (Webber 1982), job creation became an instrument of individual promotion for target groups disadvantaged on the labor market. With few exceptions, the programs were accessible only to the already unemployed, for the most part the long-term unemployed. In contrast, job creation in the East was primarily aimed at the level rather than the structure of unemployment. Long-term unemployment was still almost absent when the implementation of job creation programs gained momentum in the spring of 1991. In order to contain unemployment, job creation had to intervene into the very process of redundancy, accepting a seamless transition from "regular" but economically obsolete employment to subsidized temporary employment. Here, then, is part of the explanation for why mass dismissals from Treuhand establishments did not meet with more opposition: not only did labor market policy offer alternatives to unemployment, but for many individuals, it made redundancy appear less threatening by preventing unemployment altogether, at least for the time being.

The high human resource potential of participants not yet degraded by long-term unemployment and the close connection to abandoned sites and resources of Treuhand companies account for another difference between programs of direct job creation in the East and in the West: the different profiles of the work performed. Whereas in West Germany, direct job creation over the years has been more and more concentrated in public and social services, more than half of the jobs created in East Germany through labor market programs are of a "value-adding" nature, yielding results that may contribute to future economic development by removing industrial pollution or improving the infrastructure.

EMPLOYMENT AND TRAINING COMPANIES AS AGENTS OF OUTPLACEMENT

The Need for a New Type of Employment Agent

In order to implement programs of direct job creation, someone must be willing to employ the participants, to design a project that qualifies for subsidy, and to file an application for a subsidy with the employment office. Since an important criterion of eligibility is the "public interest," private enterprises usually have neither the desire nor much of an opportunity to be agents of direct job creation. In West Germany, job creation employers were local authorities, churches, charitable organizations, and nonprofit initiatives of all sorts but rarely private companies (Spitznagel 1989). In East Germany, too, public authorities used job creation programs extensively. But the intermediate nonprofit sector based on civil self-organization in charities, social work, environmental protection, and the like was almost completely lacking in East Germany. The churches had been marginalized in the old system and were not prepared to assume a role in labor market policy. There was a void to be filled.

Early on, the Federal Employment Agency accepted the notion that Treuhand companies themselves, because they were not yet pursuing private profit interests, could use job creation as a wage subsidy. Participants could dismantle abandoned machinery, remove industrial waste, and demolish derelict buildings. This solution relieved the companies of labor costs and enhanced the value of their real estate but did not solve the Treuhand's main problem: how to get redundant workers permanently off the payrolls. According to German law, any buyer of an enterprise automatically takes on existing labor contracts, and exit costs (severance payments, negotiations with the works council, possibly lawsuits) are high. It was only under the Treuhand administration that it was possible, through central guidelines, to limit average severance payments to a small fraction of what they would have been in the West. For these reasons, the severing of labor contracts was seen as necessary to make companies lean and attractive for acquisition; in case of liquidation, there was no alternative to dismissals anyway. Rather than use direct job creation as a wage subsidy within Treuhand establishments, the Treuhand realized that there was a need to use these programs to outplace workers. In order to do this, a separate legal entity was needed to implement the measures and to act as a temporary substitute employer for the participants. Albeit external, such an outplacement agency should cooperate closely with the respective Treuhand firm. ETCs were the solution that came to be widely accepted in this situation.

The concept of employment and training companies was developed in West Germany by the trade unions, namely IG Metall, as a means to avoid mass dismissals, to create new jobs through product innovation and restructuring, and to retrain redundant workers for new employment. The concept had, in most cases, been opposed by employers and found little support from the Federal Employment Agency. By the second half of the 1980s, therefore, there had been only a few cases in which parts of the concept—mostly training—had been implemented. The establishment of a separate legal entity to carry out active labor market policy was very rare (Bosch 1992).

In East Germany, by contrast, from 1991 through 1993, the interests of the relevant actors converged, despite constant struggle over details, in the new ETCs:

1. The Treuhand needed substitute employers to facilitate outplacement, and it came to benefit from the work performed by ETCs on its sites.
2. What appeared as outplacement to the firm appeared as a proactive intervention into the process of redundancy from the side of labor

market policy. The Federal Employment Agency was willing to have its instruments of active labor market policy utilized in such a way and soon came to support ETCs that could organize this.

3. Works councils had little room to maneuver when they had to negotiate about mass dismissals because, through Treuhand guidelines, there was a very low ceiling on severance payments. But pushing to set up an employment and training company was an option they could pursue, and in cases of closures, it was the last thing they could do for their constituencies. Besides, some works councils survived for some time as works councils of the newly founded ETCs; in other cases, works council members became managers of the ETCs.

4. The governments of the new *Länder* had to assume political responsibility for processes they could hardly influence. Since they could not stop the destruction of jobs in Treuhand firms and since policies aimed at the creation of new regular jobs have only long-term effects at best, they developed a strong interest in local direct job creation. In order to facilitate this, state and local governments stabilized ETCs through complementary financing of projects and management overhead and by providing an infrastructure of information and counseling.

ETCs in Practice

The ETCs are firms set up for the primary purpose of acting as employers for direct job creation participants. Beyond pursuing the objectives of social and labor market policy, their mission and claim is to organize public employment projects in such a way that the work performed will foster structural development and the creation of new permanent jobs. The "value-adding" profile of job creation projects organized by ETCs stands out even more clearly than that of job creation in East Germany in general. At the end of 1993, 41 percent of ETC jobs were in clearing up old industrial sites to make them available for new productive activities. Another 34 percent were in the "green" area, enhancing "soft" factors of industrial location or the development of tourism, and 12 percent were directly involved with city and regional development or with the provision of facilities and services for recreation, physical exercise or cultural activities (Knuth 1993 b and 1996).

At the end of 1993, roughly 400 ETCs were operating in East Germany. They employed around 90,000 persons in direct job creation projects, a "market share" of almost 40 percent of the total volume of direct job creation (Brinkmann, Hiller, and Otto 1994). As far as formal training is concerned, their role is minor; training in ETCs has been mostly on-the-job, with some accompanying course work. Employment based on gainful market transactions of the ETCs themselves—that is, "regular" employment outside the subsidized job creation schemes—made up only 2 percent of the ETC workforces; but ETCs claimed to have fostered spin-offs that created new jobs at a magnitude of about 5 percent of the total volume of subsidized employment (Knuth 1996).

ETCs are companies of private law; they usually take the legal form of a limited company with a capital stock near the statutory minimum of DM 50,000. Their stakeholders are local authorities, private enterprises, individuals, trade unions, and nonprofit organizations. Fifty-five percent of the ETCs claim to have roots in Treuhand companies and because they are larger than the other ETCs, are responsible for 74 percent of ETC employment. At the end of 1993, 47 percent of the ETCs still had cooperation contracts with Treuhand companies which guaranteed them some overhead financing and the use of Treuhand facilities in return for their outplacement services (Knuth 1996).

A panel study of the employment policies of Treuhand enterprises (Wahse, Dahms, and Schaefer 1994) illustrates the significance of active labor market policy instruments as a means of outplacement and the role of ETCs. More than one-third of the employees displaced at Treuhand firms were accommodated in some labor market program, two-thirds of these in active programs. The ETCs have directly absorbed 8 percent, mostly into projects based on direct job creation.

ETCs as an Extension of Employment Relations

If we take active labor market policy as the first element of the explanation for the peaceful character of the East German transition, and its proactive implementation with the possibility of seamless transition into direct job creation programs as the second element, then the ETCs can be seen as the third element. Without their mediating role as outplacement agents, the transition from Treuhand companies into direct job creation programs would hardly have been possible. This was not only a question of coordinating personnel policy with project planning but also a question of social closeness and trust. Since ETC employees found themselves in familiar environments among familiar people, they had an easier time accepting the ETCs as substitute employers than would have been the case with anonymous and more distant organizations.

Even though ETCs were legally separate from Treuhand firms, they were tied into the regulatory framework of the social plans negotiated in cases of mass dismissals between works councils and employers. For example, in some social plans, workers were guaranteed temporary employment in the ETC if they voluntarily severed their labor contracts before a dismissal could take effect (thus allowing the firm to side-step advance-notice requirements). Some of the labor cost thus saved was handed over to the respective

ETC for start-up funding, and the workers had to entrust their severance payments as a free loan to the ETC until their employment relationship with the ETC ended. Interest yielded by the severance payment fund would be used by the ETC to finance overhead costs. Another example of the extended relations is that works councils in Treuhand firms remained responsible for "their" ETCs until the employees of the ETCs elected their own works councils.

ETCs also remained part of the larger industrial relations system. At first, they continued to be covered by collective agreements of the parent firm's industry. Unions continued to organize job creation participants. As a consequence, industrial unions found themselves in the novel situation of lobbying and organizing demonstrations against cuts in labor market policy spending. Active labor market policy became a direct part of the industrial relations system.

NEGOTIATED ADJUSTMENT IN EAST GERMANY: TREUHAND CORPORATISM

After German unification, the Treuhand became the only public administration responsible both for the whole of East Germany and only for East Germany. If the GDR as an administration had any successor, it was the Treuhand. It is natural, then, that the Treuhand became the focal point of what can be conceived of as a special type of East German corporatism, more intense and concerted than West German corporatism had ever been. But since the contribution of the Treuhand empire to the national product was negative, the shares to be distributed consisted mainly of funding for active labor market policy.

Direct Job Creation and ETCs as Catalysts of Treuhand Corporatism

Though set up in July 1990, the Treuhand did not become operational until early 1991. Until then, considerable workforce reductions at Treuhand firms had been perceived mostly as a result of migration to the West and decisions of local managements. After unification and the first all-German elections, the Treuhand suddenly found itself in the midst of criticism from the new *Länder* governments and protests from the shop floors.

The extraordinary and proactive labor market policy approach described above was launched by the federal government in March 1991 under the title "Gemeinschaftswerk Aufschwung Ost" (joint operation Eastern upswing). In the context of privatization policy, this initiative must be seen not only as an attack on unemployment but also as a program aimed at taking pressure off the Treuhand. It was also the beginning of tying the

Treuhand into labor market policy: only a few days after "Aufschwung Ost" went into effect, the federal government, the new *Länder* governments, and the Treuhand reached an agreement on "principles of cooperation," which included, in the case of mass dismissals, consultation regarding cushioning measures. Treuhand companies were required to draft concepts for direct job creation projects on their sites and to list items of property that could be used by the projects.

In April 1991, the Treuhand and the trade unions negotiated severance payments. This is normally a matter to be negotiated between the works council and the employer in the form of a social plan agreement. Since most companies in the East lacked the necessary financial resources, the Treuhand would have to foot the bill. The ceiling on Treuhand financing of social plans thus became a matter of centralized bargaining. In addition to the agreement on social plans, the Treuhand, in a joint declaration with the unions, pledged its commitment to an active approach that would give priority to direct job creation and training over dismissals and financial compensation. Treuhand firms, it was envisaged, would foster the founding of new enterprises and of ETCs.

Because the creation of outplacement agents was also in the interest of Treuhand company managers, many of these actively supported the founding of ETCs as subsidiaries. In June 1991, Treuhand headquarters prohibited this practice on the grounds that such subsidiaries might hamper privatization. The trade unions, on the other hand, favored Treuhand companies as majority shareholders in ETCs, in order to maintain the coverage of industrial collective agreements. The Treuhand's prohibition, therefore, aroused strong opposition from the unions in what became the sharpest confrontation with its immediate political environment (Seibel 1994, 14). The Treuhand was directly responsible for the elimination of 1.75 million jobs; but its hardest conflict was sparked by whether its companies should have shares in the approximately 200 ETCs that eventually originated from its establishments! The result of this conflict was a framework agreement negotiated in July 1991 among the Treuhand, trade unions, employers' organizations, and the new Länder, which regulated under what conditions and in what way Treuhand companies would support the ETCs. The trade unions had to accept severance of the ties between ETCs and Treuhand companies as shareholders in return for the guarantee that collective industry-level agreements would remain in effect for the ETCs. This agreement represents the maturation of a specific Treuhand corporatism, one that survived as long as the Treuhand operated.

The Increasing Weight of the Treuhand in Public Employment Programs

In 1991 and 1992, the labor market policy instruments used to effect outplacement from Treuhand firms were training offered by private institutions of continuing education and short-time and direct job creation organized in ETCs. At the end of 1992, several problems with direct job creation became clear:

1. The first generation of participants in the direct job creation program were approaching their personal maximum period of participation (two years), but regular jobs were not available for them.
2. The projects of industrial demolition and environmental restoration begun on the basis of direct job creation were not yet completed. It was only rational to let them be completed by those workers most experienced in this type of work.
3. With the end of the unification boom, the Federal Employment Agency budget deficit was rising, and it was considered impossible to continue financing direct job creation schemes at the previous level.
4. But the Treuhand still had workforces to downsize and establishments to liquidate. It wanted to continue outplacement into job creation projects.
5. Until then, the Treuhand profited considerably from the projects performed on its company sites but to which it had contributed relatively little financially. Labor costs in job creation projects were covered by the Federal Employment Agency, which also covered the bulk of the expenditures for new machinery and materials. The new *Länder,* as well, were seen to gain indirectly if industrial pollution was removed and if industrial sites within their territory were prepared for new uses.

In this situation, a new and supplementary instrument of direct job creation was introduced in East Germany in 1993. Whereas in traditional direct job creation the Federal Employment Agency subsidizes a certain percentage of labor costs (under the exceptional conditions of the East, 100 percent in most cases), a fixed per capita subsidy is granted per month of employment under the new program. Since this fixed rate is determined according to the average expenditure for unemployment benefits, the new instrument of active policy does not put an additional burden on the budget of the Federal Employment Agency. The money that would otherwise have to be spent to pay unemployment benefits is activated to finance employment instead. This fixed-rate subsidy, however, does not cover total labor costs, not to mention total project costs, which include, among other items, the leasing of equipment and subcontracts for special jobs the project participants cannot perform. As a consequence, the costs exceeding the subsidy from the Federal Employment Agency have to be covered by whoever is interested in the project. For the improvement of Treuhand sites, complementary financing was shared between the Treuhand (75 percent) and the *Land* in which the site was located (25 percent). The new instrument also contains a sting for the collective bargaining system: on the grounds that incentives for mobility into nonsubsidized jobs were needed, participants must be paid less than regular workers, either through working 80 percent part-time at standard hourly rates or through special collective agreements setting the hourly rates at no more than 90 percent of comparable jobs.

This new instrument of direct job creation by a fixed-rate subsidy was, in the larger part of its implementation (55 percent of the participants), utilized by the Treuhand to complete outplacement from its firms in 1993 and 1994. Its prominent role in financing the projects gave the Treuhand control over implementation of the new instrument. And again, labor market measures became a coin of exchange in the system of Treuhand corporatism:

1. The outplacement of employees from Treuhand companies into ETCs using the new instrument was, at the Treuhand's request, regulated by sectoral framework agreements between the Treuhand and the respective union.
2. Of the two alternatives for legally mandated income differentiation, part-time work or lowered wage rates, the Treuhand favored the second, which led to special collective agreements between unions and ETCs. To this purpose, ETCs from the chemical and mining industries set up an employers' association of their own, thus becoming a collective player in the industrial relations arena.

The Treuhand's Need for a Corporatist Consensus

The Treuhand suffered from its unpopular role as a "terminator" of industry as well as from a "legitimacy gap." The Treuhand had been set up by the East German *Volkskammer,* in early 1990, a legislative body that soon after ceased to exist. The Treuhand began its work with expectations of a net return from privatization sales, an assumption that soon turned out to be completely wrong. An analysis of the Treuhand's privatization policy, of its blunders, incompetence, and spectacular cases of corruption, are beyond the scope of this paper. It should be acknowledged, however, that despite justified criticism, the larger part of the Treuhand's negative employment record seems to have been inevitable, given monetary union as a starting point. While Chancellor Kohl promised "blossoming landscapes," it was the Treuhand's unpleasant job to convey to East Germans that what they for so long had toiled to keep running was, in effect, less than worthless. While Kohl promised that nobody would be worse off, it was up to the Treuhand to tell people the truth about downsizing and layoffs.

The agency stood quite alone in discharging this duty. Anxious to avoid an escalation of conflicts, it went to great lengths to negotiate decisions with the various parties in firms, Länder, and unions, spending considerable financial resources to gain consent and legitimacy for its decisions. The political value of each mark spent to cushion job loss was multiplied when the allocation for the expenditure was the result of an agreement between Treuhand and the trade unions and works councils. If the Treuhand's record of salvaging and privatizing jobs is not very impressive, its record of containing and dispersing conflict certainly is. Around the Treuhand, there was a continuous struggle on all fronts. There were marches on its headquarters, the managements of its companies were locked out when workers occupied plants, and there were continuous complaints and interventions. But none of this led to crisis or to a cessation of continuing negotiation.

The Treuhand's empire was highly centralized. Although the legal mechanisms of governance and participation at the enterprise level were in operation, in practice relevant decisions concerning the future of an enterprise and its workforce could not be made without the Treuhand's consent, leading to intense lobbying by managements, works councils, and union officers. Supervisory boards with workforce and union representation played an important role in getting unions involved and in building alliances between representatives of capital and labor against the Treuhand bureaucracy. This intensive interaction, in a continuous succession of conflict and compromise, in fact produced the grudging consent that accompanied the process of deindustrialization in East Germany. In comparison to these manifold forms of informal and formal participation, minority representation of the trade unions on the Treuhand's Board of Governors was of little immediate impact, serving nonetheless as a guarantee of legitimacy for what was happening informally.

The Treuhand never gave in to union demands for broader industrial and structural policy. The unions were kept in their traditional arena, dealing with the social consequences of Treuhand decisions. In this field, the Treuhand utilized the expertise and credibility of trade unions and union-affiliated experts to draw up and implement the intricate schemes of outplacement into ETCs. Only through close though often conflictive cooperation between unions, works councils, and the Treuhand was it possible to orchestrate massive layoffs and restructuring in post-unification East Germany.

Trade Unions, Deindustrialization and Proactive Labor Market Policy

What was the trade unions' rationale for supportive participation in a process of deindustrialization and, as a consequence, the loss of a large part of the newly acquired membership? Why did unions accept their assigned role as negotiatiors for outplacement and the implementation of labor market programs?

1. It seems that the unions, in the East, have taken an even more "realistic" approach to mass layoffs and closures than in the West. There were few attempts from the shop floor to save jobs through militant action, and the unions usually refused to support, even symbolically, what few there were. The fact that the "dual system" of industrial relations has never worked the same way in the East as in the West has important implications. It means not only that unions cannot so readily rely on the loyalty of works councils but also that East German works council members, as newcomers, have less power in informal decision-making processes of the unions. Full-time officials (mostly fresh imports from the West), therefore, were under little moral or political pressure from works councils to organize spectacular actions of last resort.

2. In most cases, the moral resources for militant action were lacking. Under "normal" market conditions, even in a run-down enterprise with no alternative to dismissals, unions can still blame management for running the business down, demanding that they accept responsibility for their failure. In East Germany, those primarily responsible for the appalling state of industry were no longer in a position to be confronted with demands.

3. Trade unions had more to benefit from actively shaping outplacement schemes than from engaging in hopeless defensive struggles. By organizing direct job creation collectively, trade unions for some time retained membership they would otherwise have lost sooner. In this way, industrial unions came to represent participants of labor market policy programs who traditionally had been the responsibility of the public-sector unions. Local union officers could defend their own jobs as long as they had enough members at least in ETCs. And their influence on ETC managements, via board membership and sometimes even by holding ETC shares personally, formed some last resource of local power while industries were crumbling away and where newly founded enterprises were found hard to organize.

The conclusion then, is, that proactive labor market policy served not only to make workforces comply with outplacement schemes but was also a precondition for the cooperation of trade unions both in terms of organizational interest and by giving them something to "sell" to their members. Without the coordination of Treuhand personnel policies with active labor market policy, there would have been little to negotiate except severance payments. But with labor market policy and Treuhand resources combined, trade unions and works councils could negotiate temporary jobs, maintain hope for future prospects, and retain union membership along with resources for prolonged union influence. ETCs emerged as the focal point in which all these interests converged.

OUTLOOK

Treuhand corporatism was an episode that ended with the institution around which it evolved. It has not resulted in the West German industrial relations system taking deep root in East Germany. While unions were concentrating on dealing with the legacies of the past in Treuhand enterprises and ETCs, they failed to get a firm grasp on newly founded establishments (for more details, see Chapter 4).

But there is an effect that can be observed in German labor market policy as a whole. To a degree unknown before unification, active labor market policy has gained significance beyond the circle of experts formerly dealing with it. It has become part of the industrial relations system and of the daily debate about its future:

1. The rule that participants of direct job creation programs have to be paid at least 10 percent below the level of comparable regular work was extended to the West and tightened. This was endorsed by the employers' top organization as part of their deregulation program demanding lower-paid entrance rates for the newly hired unemployed (BDA 1993).
2. Through the East German experience, active labor market policy has gained in importance on the trade union agenda, in the public and private sectors alike. At union headquarters, the issue is no longer confined to social policy and vocational training departments but has become of concern to bargaining and economic departments as well. An expert working party, which drew up a "Memorandum for a New Employment Promotion Act" (Arbeitskreis 1994), was coordinated by IG Metall.
3. Early in 1995, top-level talks between Chancellor Kohl and representatives of the social partners about an "employment pact" ended with

the resumption of a special integration program for the long-term unemployed that had expired at the end of 1994. Both sides expressed satisfaction with this result.

In the West German recession that followed the unification boom, ETCs gained significance in the West where plants were closed or severely down-sized. In several locations of the West German steel industry, ETCs dismantle equipment no longer in use. In other locations with a more qualified workforce, attempts to let redundant employees set up new enterprises have gained momentum. One ETC is acting as an agency for temporary work.

Current proposals to reshape the Employment Promotion Act foresee closer coordination between active labor market policies and the downsizing policies of firms. One possible result would be new regulations by which the Federal Employment Agency lends a hand in workforce downsizing, while management and works council agree to "activate" severance payment funds. Part of the money usually consumed "passively" as compensation for the loss of a job would be used to co-finance vocational reorientation programs and projects of direct job creation for those threatened by unemployment. Lessons learned in East Germany's structural crash might well be transferred to situations of accelerated structural change now facing West Germany and unified Germany as a whole in the late 1990s and beyond. In periods of major readjustment, social and labor peace may well justify the costs of expanded active labor market policy.

Author's postscript: Such legislation has in fact now been passed and is scheduled to take full effect in 1998.

REFERENCES

Arbeitskreis AFG-Reform, ed. (1994). *Memorandum für ein neues Arbeits-förderunqsgesetz.* Frankfurt.

BDA Bundesvereinigung der Deutschen Arbeitgeberverbände. 1993. *Wege zu mehr Beschäftigung und zum Abbau von Arbeitslosigkeit.* Köln. Bielenski, Harald, Christian Brinkmann, and Bärbl Kohler. 1994. "Erwerbsverläufe und arbeitsmarktpolitische Maßnahmen in Ostdeutschland. Ergebnisse des Arbeitsmarkt-Monitors über berufliche Veränderungen 1989 bis 1993." *IAB-Werkstattbericht,* no. 12.

Bosch, Gerhard. 1992. *Retraining—Not Redundancy. Innovative Approaches to Industrial Restructuring in Germany and France.* Geneva: International Institute for Labour Studies.

Bosch, Gerhard, and Matthias Knuth. 1993. "The Labour Market in East Germany." *Cambridge Journal of Economics* 3, no. 93: 295–308.

86 • *Matthias Knuth*

Brinkmann, Christian, Karin Hiller, and Manfred Otto. 1994. "Auffang-
becken und Hoffnungsträger. Beschäftigungsgesellschaften (ABS) in den
Neuen Bundesländern." *IAB-Kurzbericht, no. 1.*
Hall, John, and Udo Ludwig. 1993. "Creating Germany's Mezzogiorno?"
Challenge 4, no. 93 :38–45.
Knuth, Matthias. 1993a. "Employment and Training Companies: Bridging
Unemployment in the East German Crash." Paper presented to the Con-
ference of the Society for the Advancement of Socio-Economics, New
York, March.
———. 1993b. "ABS Companies and the Potential of Labour Market Policy
to Promote Structural Development." *Employment Observatory East
Germany* 8/93: 3–6.
———. 1996. *Drehscheiben im Strukturwandel. Agenturen für Mobilitäts-,
Arbeits-und Strukturförderung.* Berlin: Edition sigma.
Nolte, Dirk. 1995. "Politik der Treuhandanstalt." In D. Nolte, R. Sitte,
and A. Wagner, *Wirtschaftliche und soziale Einheit Deutschlands,* 66–87
Köln: Bund.
Reissert, Bernd. 1994a. "Beitrags- oder Steuerfinanzierung der Arbeitsmarktpolitik? Rückblick und Ausblick auf eine Debatte." In H. Heinelt,
G. Bosch, and B. Reissert, eds., *Arbeitsmarktpolitik nach der Vereinigung,*
43–57. Berlin: edition sigma.
———. 1994b. "The Regional Impact of Unemployment Insurance and Active
Labor Market Policy—An International Comparison." In W. Sengen-
berger and D. Campbell, eds., *Creating Economic Opportunities.* Ge-
neva: International Institute for Labour Studies.
Rothschild, Kurt W. 1993. "Like a 'Lehrstück' by Brecht: Notes on the
German Reunification Drama." *Cambridge Journal of Economics* 3, no.
93: 259–66.
Seibel, Wolfgang. 1994. "Strategische Fehler oder erfolgreiches Scheitern?
Zur Entwicklungslogik der Treuhandanstalt, 1990–93." *Politische Vier-
teljahresschrift* 35: 3–39.
Spitznagel, Eugen. 1989. "Zielgruppenorientierung und Eingliederung-
serfolg bei Allgemeinen Maßnahmen zur Arbeitsbeschaffung (ABM)."
MittAB 4, no. 89: 523–39.
Wahse, Jürgen, Vera Dahms, and Reinhard Schaefer. 1994. *Beschäftigung-
sperspektiven von Treuhandunternehmen und Ex-Treuhandfirmen im
Vergleich. Befragung Oktober 1994.* Berlin and Nuremberg: SÖSTRA
Sozialökonomische Strukturanalysen, Treuhandanstalt und Institut für
Arbeitsmarkt-und Berufsforschung.
Webber, Douglas. 1982. "Zwischen programmatischem Anspruch und poli-
tischer Praxis: Die Entwicklung der Arbeitsmarktpolitik in der Bundes-
republik Deutschland von 1974 bis 1982." *MittAB* 3, no. 82: 261–75.

4 • Unions in the New *Länder:* Evidence for the Urgency of Reform

Michael Fichter

Trade unions in Germany, as in most other industrial countries, face an uncertain future. In the midst of post-unification economic strains with lasting structural repercussions such as the continuing high rate of long-term unemployment, the German Trade Union Federation (*Deutscher Gewerkschaftsbund*—DGB) and its member unions have been struggling for solutions to the greatest array of challenges they have faced since their reorganization immediately after World War II. Simultaneously they are trying to make a reasonable defense of the high level of benefits they have won over the years in the West, raise the income levels of their new members in eastern Germany to parity with those of their members in western Germany, formulate a new programmatic vision of union goals for the next decades and overhaul organizational structures to which they have grown accustomed over the past forty years in the former West Germany.

Indeed, the comparatively ordered and structured world of the cold war era has been unceremoniously swept away. The growing influence of the supranational European Union, a development already well advanced by the late 1980s, and the processes that have been transforming the Eastern European countries since 1990 are undermining yesterday's economic givens in Germany. As public enterprises are being privatized, the challenges of global production and marketing are forcing German companies, from the single workplace all the way up to the international level, to reassess their strengths and weaknesses in coping with new demands.

Such a redefinition of the basic parameters of the German regulatory framework of production, previously agreed upon and adhered to by all relevant parties, has certainly not left the unions unscathed. Add to the

87

global economic challenges the demise of the Soviet bloc and the state unification process in Germany, and it becomes evident that the unions are being tested to the very core to retain the high level of success they had become accustomed to in West Germany.

One measure of how well the unions are meeting these challenges is the status of their organizational and political efforts in eastern Germany since unification. Developments there not only reflect the progress of East-West integration in Germany, they also have considerable impact on the course of union policy and organizational stability in western Germany. Indeed, instead of incremental steps toward the high economic standards prevalent in western Germany, the new *Länder* are becoming the laboratory for a downward revision of union-won achievements throughout the country.

The unions are falling behind in their attempts to retain a decisive role in managing the political economy of the new Germany. While the across-the-board institutional transfer of the industrial relations system from West to East has been completed, its underpinnings in the political culture are weak, especially as far as the union organizational basis and the relationship between unions and works councils are concerned. In general, the crucial step from institutional transfer to institutionalization (Ettl and Wiesenthal 1994) has not been completed, and the difficulties being encountered raise questions about its possible outcome. Instead of the indigenous growth of participation and a conscious identification with the presence of unions, East-West animosities still abound and apathy and disenchantment are widespread.

To an extent, mistaken expectations held by East Germans are a contributing factor. But the core of responsibility lies with deficiencies in union decision making, organizational democracy, and strategic perspectives. In the transfer process, the West German unions chose to ignore the question of their own organizational reform and were not receptive to the necessity of the structural and political adaptation of their institutional structures to the new conditions in eastern Germany. By not reacting to reform initiatives or promoting more grassroots orientation, the unions have succeeded in establishing relatively stable organizational shells that conform to the "dictates of the treasurers" but are inadequate to promote strong unionism. Easing East-West tensions, fostering social learning, and advancing democratic participation are essential to the future effectiveness of union policy. Barring an intensified and fundamental effort for reform that would mobilize the dwindling membership in the new Länder, the unions are in danger of being unable to fulfill their role in the "partnership of conflict" (Müller-Jentsch 1991) central to the German system of industrial relations.

INDUSTRIAL RELATIONS AND
INSTITUTIONAL TRANSFER IN GERMANY

In the course of Germany's post-World War II rise to become a powerful factor in the world economy, it was generally acknowledged that the institutional arrangements governing industrial relations and providing labor with a major stake in directing the political economy were quite successful by international comparison (Katzenstein 1989). While the unsolved problem of structural unemployment and pressures generated by European unification and world market changes prior to the collapse of the Soviet bloc did raise some concern about the capacity of the West German system to adapt to new challenges, it was in fact that momentous occurrence that in opening the door to German unification created a wholly new political and socioeconomic environment in which existing and calculable institutional arrangements were subjected to new pressures to change. Although the German system of industrial relations has by and large shown considerable resilience in the past, the question must be raised whether it is now entering a period of fundamental restructuring and realignment.

In itself, German unification was a model reaffirmation of a wide variety of institutional arrangements as they existed in West Germany. Through an act of direct transfer, the basic structure of institutional networks, so crucial to the postwar success story of West Germany, has been anchored in the new *Länder* and has a secure foundation in the new Germany as a whole (Sally and Webber 1994; Czada 1994; Lehmbruch 1994).

In the case of labor relations, the key social partners in West Germany reached an early consensus that was designed to remove all doubt regarding the future of their established structures, norms, and institutional arrangements in a unified Germany (DGB and BDA 1990). With the ensuing institutional and organizational transfer completed and its functionality in an unprecedented phase of privatization and deindustrialization having been tested, there are indeed reasons to argue, as Lowell Turner does, that social partnership is alive and well in eastern Germany.

On the other hand, the uncertainty within the unions over their policy and organizational future in the new *Länder* has certainly contributed to launching (but not sustaining)(Fichter 1994) an overall organizational restructuring process. Since 1992, the DGB has made large budget cuts and moved toward redefining its organizational status as well as its programmatic goals and overarching tasks as a federation. Member unions are discussing cooperative schemes and are completing amalgamation processes that will absorb the smallest and weakest unions. To be sure, this is not the first such effort in the DGB's history, and the need for internal reform is in part a result of earlier failures to make changes. But this is a major overhauling process, and it does seem that the policy and organizational deficits that the unification process in Germany laid bare have added a new and qualitatively different dimension, namely, that of achieving a level of integration of East Germans into the (West) German model of industrial relations—however reformed—beyond that accomplished by the act of institutional transfer alone.

UNION EXPANSION TO THE EAST: PHASES AND TYPOLOGIES

The spreading of organizational structures to cover the new *Länder* proved to be a considerable burden on the financial and personnel resources of the unions. Indeed, they were totally unprepared for this task, not in the least because within the context of the Bonn government's *Ostpolitik,* union activities in East Germany never developed beyond a ritualized program of top-level meetings with leaders of the East German labor organization *Freier Deutscher Gewerkschaftsbund* (FDGB).

During the initial months of the *Wende*-period in the GDR, the DGB and its member unions (along with most other voices on the left) trapped themselves in a bystander role, arguing that the new experience of democracy in the GDR should not be subject to meddling, manipulation, or control by West German interests.[1] Following the decision of the FDGB at the end of January 1990 to create financially independent, autonomous branch industrial unions, it was expected that a thorough process of democratization and decentralization would ensue and in time, unions in West and East Germany would find a suitable basis for cooperative relations and possible amalgamation (Fichter 1991). In retrospect, the unions overestimated the political potential of the East German citizens' movement, which was rapidly overwhelmed by the popular demand to become part of West Germany and gain access to the *Deutschmark* realm.

After the landslide election victory of the CDU-led East German *Allianz für Deutschland* in March 1990, the takeover strategy with the goal of "incorporation" assumed top priority in Bonn. As the tempo of this undertaking rapidly accelerated the DGB unions faced the choice of either mounting a breakneck effort to extend their organizational jurisdiction into the GDR or leaving the eastern part of a united Germany virtually devoid of functioning unions. Within only a few months, essentially from March to September 1990, the unions threw an immense amount of resources into

1. Some of the DGB unions (most noticeably IG Chemie, IG Metall, and IG Medien), got involved with their branch-level counterpart organizations even before the extraordinary congress of the FDGB in January 1990.

creating an organizational basis that could fulfill the need of East German employees to have democratic unions represent their interests in the new system. Adequate office space had to be found and equipped to handle the heavy load of new administrative tasks. Personnel had to be trained on the job and in special courses to deal with every possible aspect of member representation. New problems, specific to the transformation process in eastern Germany and for which there was no West German experience to draw upon, had to be addressed. Job contracts as well as plant closure plans had to be negotiated and job training programs for the unemployed instituted (Fichter and Kurbjuhn 1993).

The basic strategy chosen by all the DGB unions—jurisdictional expansion to the East—represented a conservative approach[2] designed to ensure maximum control and organizational stability in the face of the many uncertainties ahead. Union structures as they had existed since the founding of the Federal Republic, along with works councils as the second pillar of the dual system of representation, were transferred directly to the GDR, now called the *Beitrittsgebiet*. In the process, union leaders ignored grassroots and shopfloor initiatives associated with the East German citizens movements[3] and rebuffed all efforts by critical voices within their own camps to promote the idea of coupling the expansion process to necessary internal organizational reforms. In their efforts to stay on top of the complex expansion process, they found no time for a comprehensive analysis of problems and prospects as a basis for strategy decisions, preferring instead to rely on tried policy options. The new members and the new territory were destined to become part of their own well-known sociopolitical environment and set of institutions and arrangements, and as such, institutional transfer to the East became the essential foundation for everything that followed.

The upshot of this approach was an evident disregard for the future importance of the very different history, cultural heritage, and socioeconomic characteristics of the former GDR. While union leaders did debate the question of what the end of socialism meant for the future of the labor movement, they failed to address the more immediate question of whether

2. Czada (1994, 248) calls this approach a "situative reaction" that appeared at various times in all sectors of political life: "In dieser Sicht eracheint Beharrungsverhalten als eine *rationale*, der besonderen Lage angepaßte Problemiösung. Die vorhandenen Leitbilder und Ressourcen der Bundesrepublik konnten in einer turbulenten Umbruchsituation den situativen Handlungsbedarf der relevanten Akteure rescher, verläßlicher und kostengünstiger befriedigen, als es eine umfasende Problemanalyse je vermocht hätte."

3. Research on this aspect of the *Wende* has documented numerous examples of rebellious actions at the workplace and described the ill-fated attempts of the *Initiative für Unabhängige Gewerkschaften* to build an indigenous union movement upon them. See Ansorg and Hürtgen 1992 and Jander 1996.

their approach to the expansion process would adequately serve members' needs and union effectiveness in the new all-German context. And instead of seeking common ground for dealing with the new German scenario, each union went its separate way, making misunderstandings, jurisdictional disputes, and outright membership raiding unavoidable.[4]

While a minority of the unions decided to forgo close organizational cooperation with their East German counterpart organizations within the FDGB, most unions took a pragmatic stance, arguing that it made sense to take advantage of existing FDGB infrastructures and resources (buildings, offices, vehicles, union schools, and so on). At the same time, organizational cooperation made the involvement of West German union officials in FDGB union personnel matters unavoidable. The pitfalls of cooperation with *Alt-funktionäre* or "red socks" were evident, even if one considers that by spring 1990, the dogmatic supporters of the FDGB as an instrument of the ruling SED had generally been voted out of office or forced to resign. Nevertheless, most of their replacements, both salaried and voluntary, had been part of the organizational hierarchy before 1989, even if not in prominent positions. A few of the new leaders, however, had held no official positions in the FDGB and only assumed leadership roles on the basis of their demands for reform. But since organizational renewal did not usually begin at the rank-and-file level, most of the first wave of reformers had only a limited basis of democratic legitimation. For the most part, their mandate came from a top-level executive committee of questionable representative legitimacy.

Most DGB unions chose to avoid making any occupational commitments to officials of their FDGB counterpart unions; however, they sought working agreements with selected staff members of the reformed FDGB unions in order to create functioning structures as quickly as possible. In all cases, the unions relied on two principle safeguards in their hiring practices. For one, they required new officials from the GDR to sign a "declaration of honor" stating that they had not worked for the *Stasi*.[5] Second, with few exceptions, the unions considered East Germans for employment only in elective positions, all of which were located in the new eastern districts. Applicants were required to stand for election usually more than once in

---

4. Among the most spectacular instances have been the ones involving the public service union ÖTV, which fought with the miners' union over employees in sewer maintenance and hydroelectric plants and with the commercial and retail clerks union over employees in savings and loans. Conflicts with non-DGB employee organizations such as the German Salaried Employees Union (DAG) or the German Civil Servants Federation (DBB) have also occurred, but had no marked effect on the organizational process.

5. Actual relevance of this declaration varied greatly from one union to another. Some have only kept it on file, others have had investigations conducted.

the course of the organizational process. It was believed that persons who had been officials in the FDGB could possibly cajole their constituency into electing them at the outset, but that they could only survive a second election after a year in office if they had the acceptance and recognition of the members.

The widespread popular rejection of the FDGB was crucial to the decision of several DGB unions to create an organizational base in the GDR independent of the FDGB as a nucleus for their own expansion. As a rule, that entailed signing up new members individually. For the majority of DGB unions, however, cooperation with their FDGB counterpart was given priority. Although each new member had to apply individually, recruitment in this group of unions generally had a strong resemblance to a simple mass transfer of members.

The organizational expansion of all DGB unions was completed by the fall of 1991 (Fichter 1993). The subsequent rounds of union conferences and leadership elections, works' council elections, and contract negotiations attest to the fact that the (West) German system of labor relations has been established and is functioning in the new *Länder*.

But beyond this general conclusion there are a number of trends and developments that lend credence to a less optimistic view regarding the present status of unions in eastern Germany than that taken elsewhere in this book. Some of these are the result of the immediate economic transformation and privatization process and could in time become less important or disappear altogether. Others seem to me to be problems of a more lasting nature.

THE PRESENT STATUS OF UNIONS IN EASTERN GERMANY

Membership

In the years immediately preceding unification, organized labor recorded steady gains in membership. By 1991, net gains were all a result of new enrollments in eastern Germany. Since then, membership has been declining throughout the country in the wake of economic recession and—especially in the new *Länder*—massive deindustrialization. As Table 4.1 shows, among the four labor federations, only the *Deutscher Beamtenbund* (DBB), which represents public service employees, has been able to hold its own, while membership losses of the DGB; the *Deutsche Angestellten Gewerkschaft* (DAG), a union of salaried employees; and the *Christlicher Gewerkschaftsbund Deutschlands* (CGB) have continued unabated.

For the DGB unions, increases and declines in membership in the new *Länder* have been extreme. Initially, membership grew far beyond expecta-

TABLE 4.1. Union Membership in Germany 1988–1995 (in 1,000)

	1988	1989	1990	1991	1992	1993	1994	1995
Labor Force*	25,765.0	25,794.7	35,365.0	35,677.8	35,225.1	34,982.9	34,907.3	34,689.2
DGB								
Total	7,797.1	7,861.1	11.564.9	11,800.4	11,015.6	10,290.2	9,768.4	9,354.7
West	7,797.1	7,861.1	7,937.9	7,642.6	7,623.9	7,383.5	7,179.1	6,994.3
East**			3,627.0	4,157.8	3,391.7	2,906.7	2,589.3	2,360.4
DAG								
Total	497.0	503.5	573.4	584.8	578.4	527.9	520.7	507.5
West	497.0	503.5	509.0	473.6	471.4	441.1	434.3	388.8
East			64.4	111.2	107.0	86.8	85.4	118.7
DBB								
Total	786.9	793.6	997.7	1.053.0	1.095.4	1.078.8	1.089.2	1,075.6
West	786.9	793.6	799.0	n.a.	n.a	n.a	n.a	n.a
East			198.7	n.a.	n.a.	n.a.	n.a.	n.a.
CGB								
Total	307.0	305.0	309.4	310.8	315.6	310.7	306.8	303.8
West	307.0	305.0	304.7	302.5	306.4	302.8	297.5	294.4
East			4.6	8.3	9.1	7.9	9.0	9.4

* Sum of all employed salary and wage workers, civil servants and all registered unemployed
** As of 1991, DBG East includes Berlin-West
n.a. = not available
Source: DBG, DAG, DBB, CGB, *Statistische Jahrbücher,* author's calculations

tions, the number of new members peaking at nearly 4.2 million by the end of 1991. This figure represented more than half as many members as in western Germany and an organizational density of approximately 42 percent; however, deindustrialization soon halted this growth trend and by the end of 1992, membership in the new *Länder* had dropped by over 18 percent to just under 3.4 million. In 1993, another 500,000 turned their backs on the unions, and by the end of 1995, the DGB unions could claim only 2.36 million members in eastern Germany. That is just over 25 percent of the DGB overall total, down from 35 percent in 1991. Seven unions still have more than 30 percent of their members in the new *Länder,* one of which (agriculture and forestry) even accounts for over half of its membership there (54.6 percent).[6]

Losses among members under twenty-five in eastern Germany have been particularly high, ranging between 20 and 25 percent a year since 1992. On the other hand, the ratio of female to male members in eastern Germany, while declining, is still almost twice as high as in western Germany (45.6

6. This union, the GGLF, amalgamated with the construction workers union at the end of 1995.

TABLE 4.2. Union Membership Density, 1988–1995 (membership in relation to labor force)

	1988	1989	1990	1991	1992	1993	1994	1995
Total all								
Unions	36.4%	36.7%	38.0%	38.5%	36.9%	34.9%	33.5%	32.4%
DGB Total	30.3%	30.5%	32.7%	33.1%	31.3%	29.4%	28.0%	27.0%
DGB West	30.3%	30.5%	30.4%	29.6%	28.9%	27.6%	26.8%	26.2%
DGB East **			39.4%	42.2%	38.2%	35.2%	32.0%	29.5%

** As of 1991, DGB East includes Berlin-West
n.a. = not available
Source: DGB, DAG, DBB, CGB, Statistische Jahrbücher, author's calculations

percent, as compared to 25.5 percent, in 1995). Had it not been for this large contingent of female members and the retention of membership by substantial numbers of unemployed (the majority of whom are women), overall membership losses in eastern Germany would have been even more extreme.

Before unification, only 23 percent of all DGB union members were salaried employees (1990). Gains made in the new *Länder* pushed this share to 28.3 percent for all of Germany by the end of 1995. While all DGB unions have benefited, the bulk of the growth has been in public service (ÖTV, DPG, GEW, GdED) and agriculture and forestry.[7]

Although the loss of members has slackened over the past two years in eastern Germany, there is still no certainty that a stable level of membership is within reach. For one, job market trends, while still quite unpredictable in most branches of the private sector, do not give any indication that a substantial growth in employment is in the offing. In public service, long-awaited payroll cuts are inevitable. Second, a very high percentage of present union members is unemployed and has been for some time. As Peter Scherer of IG Metall has pointed out, in 1994 his union had an enrollment of 600,000 in industrial sectors with a total of only 300,000 employees (Scherer 1995, 22). The nonemployed members include a large number of persons in retirement (over 65) as well as those 55 and older who were forced into early retirement by the mass layoffs of the last five years. In general, these members have shown a high level of involvement in union activities. Presumably, they will retain their membership status because they do not regard it as a function of being employed. In contrast, younger members hit by unemployment regard the loss of a job as a stigma, often

7. It should be pointed out, however, that with the exception of their police forces, the new *Länder* have been very slow in granting civil servant *(Beamte)* status, so that such increases may be merely the result of a peculiar (and temporary) shift in statistical categories.

shying away from union-initiated group activities. These members tend to drop out, and if they find new employment, they do not usually reactivate their union membership voluntarily.

Finally, it should be noted that the privatization policy of the *Treuhand* and the emergence of new companies have clearly led to a marked decentralization of the economic structures in eastern Germany. Gone are the combines and with them most of the large concentrations of an industrial workforce. Today, the unions must attempt to recruit new members (and retain present ones) within the vastly expanded category of small and medium-size enterprises, an area within which they have never been especially successful.

Organizational Structures and the Integration of East German Personnel

By the end of 1991, all of the DGB unions had completed their expansion to the East and were organizationally established. For all of them it represented a substantial drain on their resources, and their subsequent ability to cope with the heavy membership losses has depended much on how they carried out this process. Some unions, such as the union of commercial, banking, and insurance employees (HBV), counted on making strong gains in membership and had poured large amounts of money into opening and equipping new offices and hiring many new employees. But the majority of unions took a much more cautious approach, setting up relatively large administrative districts and holding down the ratio of union officials to members.[8]

The heavy membership losses of the past three years seem to have confirmed the wisdom of this kind of organizational restraint. Union offices in the new *Länder* continue to operate at a net loss. Lower income levels mean that per capita membership dues are correspondingly lower than those in the western part of the country. And with a large percentage of the members unemployed, the financial basis for funding essential services such as legal aid is woefully insufficient, requiring either a continuation of substantial transfer payments from the West or unavoidable cuts in services. Warnings from union officials in the new *Länder* concerning the potentially negative consequences of personnel shortages and inadequate funding are not being answered in the face of growing budgetary problems in western Germany.

8. IG Metall for example created only one new administrative district (in Saxony), incorporating the rest of eastern Germany into already existing union districts. As of April 1, 1995, it consolidated its organization even further by combining the Saxony district with the district of Berlin-Brandenburg. The DGB for its part created large administrative districts from the outset. It has 33 district offices in eastern Germany, compared to 36 in North Rhine-Westphalia, which has approximately the same population, but is geographically much smaller.

Union headquarters' argue that members in the West are already subsidizing union operations in the eastern districts and cannot afford to increase this burden.

Organizational reform and consolidation is undoubtedly a financial (and political) necessity, but if the union members take such steps to be an organizational retreat, then the consequences could be severe. The unions are certainly in a precarious bind. On the one hand, it is a favorable sign that the composition of their membership in the new *Länder* is much more representative of the labor force than in the old *Länder*. On the other hand, the unions seem unable to cope with the expectations and the service needs —legal aid, training, job protection and workplace consultation—of this clientele. Moreover, despite encouraging instances of collective action—as in the metalworkers strike of 1993—the daily experience is one of minimal identification with the union. This, and the insecure job situation, has led to widespread reluctance on the part of union members to take on volunteer work within the union.

Apart from the social-psychological arguments that may be advanced to explain such individual passivity, there are also causes rooted in union policy to be considered as well. Cuts in union resources in the East are more apt to leave the impression of abandonment than in the West because of the lingering tendency to view the unions as West German organizations. Union headquarters, where final decisions are made, are all in western Germany and are staffed by West Germans. Statements by union officials to the effect that for the time being, continued losses in membership are to be expected, are taken as a sign of fatalism and indifference.

Repeated cases of bureaucratic rigidity and noncooperation among DGB member unions, in some cases culminating in outright membership raiding, have been damaging to the unions' image in the new *Länder*. Many East German unionists regard such incidents as symtomatic of the lack of solidarity within the union movement, pointing as well to the apparent weakness of the DGB as a federation in this context. This is perhaps a result of East German inexperience with autonomous industrial unions. But while not denying the need for the competency of the individual union in dealing with specific job, professional, workplace, and industry-related problems, these critics are at a loss to explain such organizational jealousy, especially in light of the overriding and growing need to push for economic programs that go beyond the industrial branch level. With long-standing organizational boundaries becoming increasingly blurred as the pace of changes in production processes and company structures accelerates, new approaches to the organization of union services is viewed as being of vital importance to creating binding membership ties and maximizing the effectiveness of representation.

Such deficiencies suggest that a thriving union organizational culture in the new *Länder* is not yet at hand. Indeed, the western orientation and domination on which organizational expansion was based still seems to be in effect. Union headquarters in the West and union members as well as local officials in the East still have markedly different perspectives on goals, accomplishments, and union policy requirements. While both East and West Germans are now institutionally united, their understanding and perception of as well as their behavior within these structures still reflects substantial differences. In some areas, the East-West gap may even be expanding, thriving on animosities nurtured by post-unification economic strains. An example of this kind of situation exists in Berlin, where East and West Germans are organized within the same union local but are still very foreign to one another (Uhlig 1994). As the writer Peter Schneider first put it, "the wall in our heads" has replaced the wall of concrete and steel that once stood between West and East Germany.

Another measure for judging the internal East-West integration process within the DGB unions is the extent to which East Germans have assumed official positions. By the end of 1990, the unions had revised their statutes to reflect the new organizational structures and the expanded membership. Subsequently, elections were held for regional leadership positions in the new *Länder*. Positions on national executive boards also had to be filled, and most unions made an effort to bring in some East Germans. The only exception is at DGB federation headquarters, where even after the leadership elections at the national congress in June 1994 there is still not a single former East German to be found.

A survey of all DGB unions made in December 1992 showed that the proportion of East Germans in elected and appointed leadership positions at the national office level was below the proportion of members from eastern Germany. In seven of the sixteen member unions there has been a marked increase in the number of women in elected (but not in appointed) leadership positions; however, their share of leadership positions is still not proportional to their membership. The picture at the level of regional and local leadership in the new *Länder* was clearly better, with a number of unions reporting comparatively high levels of East German representation in elected positions, both paid and voluntary. Moreover, the number of women in leadership positions in the new *Länder* was considerably greater than in western Germany. Still, the general picture was one of underrepresentation (Fichter and Kurbjuhn 1993: 55–68).

According to a subsequent survey made in April 1995, few changes have occurred at the national level to modify these findings; however, about half of the DGB unions along with many of the DGB offices in the new *Länder* now report a majority of East Germans in staff leadership positions. Some of the district offices have no West Germans at all. At the other end of the spectrum there are unions such as IG Metall, which has only two East Germans heading local offices in the new *Länder.*

In interviews conducted during 1992 the East Germans who had become union officials emphasized the difficulty of having to deal both with the past and simultaneously with the necessity of learning to live in a completely new and much more complex environment. Many of their original assumptions and expectations had proven to be far too naive, and they often felt overwhelmed by the elbow-mentality of Western individualism. On the other hand, these officials recognized then—as they still do today—that they (and other East Germans) will never achieve a greater say in union politics unless they become more intensively involved. To be sure, as the GDR experience recedes into the background, room for learning, adjusting, and finding common ground based on shared experiences is growing. Still, such a process will not develop automatically on its own. Even today, informal discussions with both East and West German union officials repeatedly confirm our earlier conclusion that both sides—East and West—must recognize the depth and persistence of differing worlds of experience if a constructive dialogue is to evolve (Fichter and Kurbjuhn 1992).

Union Offices—Works Councils— Union Representatives at the Workplace

The dualistic system of labor representation in Germany is recognized as being a key factor in the success and stability of the German economy. On the one hand, unions bargain with employers at the industrial branch level and sign framework contracts with representatives of employer associations, setting minimum standards for wages, salaries, and working conditions. The second pillar of the system is based on the works council (*Betriebs-*or *Personalrat*), established and protected by law, which operates as a separate institution of company-level employee representation. Since the creation of the councils in 1920, the unions have made every effort to prevent them from turning into syndicalist bodies or simply becoming tools of company policy. While the unions have no direct legal control over works councils, the development of the dualistic system in West Germany shows that they have been largely successful in establishing an effective division of labor with these bodies and integrating them into their overall collective bargaining strategies.

Under the strains of privatization and deindustrialization, the forced pace of union expansion into the former territory of the GDR, and the ensuing East-West tensions, numerous problems have thwarted the attainment of the same high level of cooperation between unions and works councils that existed in the old Federal Republic.

East-West animosities and the lack of experience, especially on the part of the new works councillors, in making this essential link function, have exacerbated the situation. But the structural causes of this lack of cooperation are more important. One of these has to do with the founding history of works councils in eastern Germany. The elimination of the communist-controlled factory representation of the FDGB, the *Betriebsgewerkschaftsleitung,* and the creation of works councils during the *Wende* period in the GDR were regarded as a necessary process of depoliticizing workplace industrial relations and creating a truly representative body of employee interests. As a result, many works councils are almost zealous about protecting their independence from outside guidance or control, even when they accept the basic role of the union as the representative of employee wage interests (Mickler et al. 1994: 277).

Second, through the *Wende*-rebellion and in the context of the disastrous loss of markets and jobs, many works councils in the new *Länder* have developed a strong sense of being the executors of grassroots democracy, cultivating an attachment to their workplaces and an identification with the survival of "their" companies. Technicians, scientists, and engineers, highly qualified but previously thwarted in the productive application of their skills, played a leading role in the first wave of building works councils. Their intensive involvement in keeping their companies afloat has not only given them a degree of competency and insight that union officials usually cannot match, it has also created a strategic bond with management *(Existenzsicherungspartnerschaft)* that closer ties to the union could endanger (Ermischer and Preusche 1993). With the passing of the exceptional conditions that characterized the post-unification period of *Treuhand* privatization, union officials and works councillors find management increasingly reluctant to uphold cooperative structures deemed so essential until recently. Works councils that hold their unions at arm's length are becoming more vulnerable to employer demands and finding themselves being pressured into accepting reduced standards in the hope of saving jobs or even the company itself (Neubauer 1993; Daniels and Lamparter 1994).

Most unionists agree that their ability to represent member interests depends not only on bargaining successes at the industry level but also on affirming and strengthening the bond of cooperation between local union offices and works councils. Supporting services provided by the union are recognized to be an essential element in this equation, but here again, limits on resources often thwart effective measures. Another possible link—establishing a shop-level network of union stewards *(Vertrauensleute)*—has always been a complex and difficult task for the unions within the German system of dualistic representation. As a union-based structure, such networks must function independently of the works councils but with the goal of achieving their optimal cooperation. Besides the various problems of communication that already exist between union offices and works councils in the new *Länder,* experience has shown that the introduction of union stewards can give rise to competition detrimental to the functioning of both the union and the works council if it has not been done cooperatively (Duddek, Hindrichs, and Wassermann 1995). One possible approach would be a joint strategy by works councils and unions to negotiate plant agreements that would secure a regulated operating basis for shop stewards. Under such conditions it might then be possible to stimulate voluntary activities by union members, most of whom have shown little inclination to get involved.

Participation and Membership Identification

In the course of organizational expansion, many union officials realized that they could not fulfill all the hopes and expectations of their new members, not the least because they arose from a misconception of a union's standing in a market economy as well as from the legacy of the GDR experience. The FDGB had been a union in name only. As an important political instrument of the ruling Socialist Unity Party (SED) used to put planning decisions into practice and to ensure the full application of labor to the achievement of production goals, the FDGB held a pervasive political, cultural, and social position at the workplace that was further enhanced by its administration of both the social security and the health insurance programs. After the Berlin Wall was erected in 1961, the FDGB's control over reservations for the available vacation spots became an especially important instrument for distributing favors and placating the desire to leave the GDR. As part of the ruling hierarchy, the FDGB had played a paternalistic and authoritarian role for GDR citizens. Workers could not bargain or negotiate for better wages and working conditions but had to accept them as announced. The passivity that developed out of this controlled environment is not easily discarded, and there has been a tendency for many East Germans to transfer elements of this role pattern to their new union affiliation in united Germany. Unfortunately, many of them also took union demands for rapid attainment of wage parity to be promises and hoped that union membership would protect them from unemployment.

While reports of dissatisfaction with the unions are to be expected in such difficult times, representative surveys also show that the unions are widely recognized and given relatively high marks for what they have accomplished (IFEP 1994; SFZ 1994). For the unions to build on this strength and develop a healthy environment of unionism it is nevertheless essential for them to address certain structural and cultural deficits in their relationship to the new members in the East.

For the most part, the workings of the West German dualistic system of representation made organized union activity at the workplace the de facto prerogative of the works councils. And in the unification process, organizational and institutional transfer at the level of the workplace meant above all ensuring that operational works councils would be installed. Beyond that, very little else has taken place to anchor union presence. As reported by a study of changes taking place in several automobile plants in the new *Länder*, the employees regard "IG Metall as an effective and useful instrument for realizing wage demands but find no functional relationship between the union and their problems at work" (Mickler et al. 1994; 277).

Such a viewpoint, already exacerbated by worker disappointment, is also nurtured by cultural discrepancies. Studies of the transformation processes occurring at the level of the workplace point out that there is a high level of identity with the workplace and that whatever expectations employees have of union presence, they are nowhere near being fulfilled. Nor has voluntary participation in union activities, for example, in organizing union committees at the workplace, come anywhere close to reaching a satisfactory level in the eyes of union officials (Duddeck, Hindrichs, and Wassermann 1995; Hintz 1994; Kletzin 1994).

To what extent a measure of nostalgia for the social and cultural bonds of the bygone East German workplace figures into such expectations is difficult to determine (Müller 1993; Alt et al. 1994). To be sure, East Germans have no tradition of unionism as it has grown in West Germany, but at the same time, it is they who must create a stable basis of unionism in the new *Länder*.

Future policy orientation and membership development will also be determined by how the unions deal with issues beyond the workplace in general and with their unemployed and underemployed members in particular. At issue is the question of broadening the present union organizational focus on the workplace to include members no longer employed there. Such a shift will entail involving the union in community activities and addressing the overall problem of the distribution of jobs and the setting of priorities for essential infrastructural programs. But without a clear mandate or clearly defined goals, such a policy expansion will rapidly overtax union resources and dissipate union strength (Silvia and Markovits 1994).

Examples of substantial membership identification with their union are available in the new *Länder* wherever members have actively participated in defending union agreements in conflict situations. The most evident example of such a development occured among metalworkers involved in the strike of May 1993, as Lowell Turner demonstrates clearly in Chapter 5. But such incidents are exceptional and require continuing reinforcement in a participatory context to produce a durable identification with the union. As one prominant leader of that strike stated, "The memory of those intensive strike days is receding and what remains are the hard facts of unequal pay and an insecure job."[9]

Collective Bargaining and Wage Policies

The introduction of the Economic and Currency Union on July 1, 1990, laid the foundation for the union goal of wage parity, initially projected for attainment within a three-to-five-year period. From the outset, the unions argued that a labor market segmented along an East-West fault line would have disastrous economic, political, and social consequences for the prospects of stability in united Germany. Since the employers' associations agreed in principle to extending the West German wage and bargaining structure to cover East Germany, there was little initial conflict over the goal of raising pay and working conditions to equal West German standards. But most employers' associations were not willing to follow the lead of the social partners in the metalworking and electrical industries (IG Metall and Gesamtmetall) in signing a contract for the equalization of pay scales between East and West over a fixed time period *(Stufenplan)*.[10]

In the meantime, all employers' associations, including Gesamtmetall, are spotlighting such agreements as the major factor in inhibiting private investment and the long-promised economic upswing. Such contracts are also being labeled as detrimental to employment policies in light of mushrooming unemployment, because, it is argued, employers need to be competitive and thus, with productivity still much lower than in the West, they cannot afford the total wage bill being presented to them.

At issue for the employers' associations is not only the question of wage levels but also their reputation as stable bargaining partners for industry-wide contract agreements. They have not achieved a rate of acceptance among businesses in eastern Germany on a level equal to the West. In the wake of sweeping privatization and the founding of new firms, they have found that their conservative "business as usual" approach has not produced the expected results in recruiting and binding companies to the association (Henneberger 1993). At present, the effects of such problems on the employers' side are potentially disastrous for the system of industry-wide collective bargaining. According to IG Metall in Frankfurt an der Oder, only six hundred of its members are still covered by the framework contract

9. Interview with Wolfgang Orphal, IG Metall, Potsdam, May 16, 1995.

10. Base pay scales are only a part of total income. An inclusive East-West comparison shows that in 1990, average gross income in eastern Germany was only about 33 percent of earnings of employees in western Germany. In 1991, there was an increase up to 44 percent, and by the end of 1993, the relationship was 64 percent (*Handelsblatt*, January 4, 1994, p. 4).

for the metalworking and electrical industries. Throughout eastern Germany the percentage of employees covered is estimated at about 60 percent; in contrast, the figure is around 90 percent in western Germany. Studies also indicate not only a tendency for companies that are not members of an employers' association to pay lower than union wages but also for member companies to ignore the binding wage contract (Ettl 1995). As the administrative director of the Association of Metalworking Companies in Saxony recently claimed, "The industrial branch wage agreement is practically nonexistent" (Neubauer 1995, 27). As such, the relative weakness of the employers' bargaining unit bears the mark of East-West differences over wage policy, the inability of the leadership to deliver necessary services, and internal differences among members from large, medium-sized, and small businesses.

While wage parity is still a priority goal for the unions, they are under pressure to become more flexible and support lower-than-contract wages in new schemes for combating unemployment, which remains quite high in the new *Länder*. One of these is the 1993 revision to the *Arbeitsförderungsgesetz* (AFG), which allows employers to claim government wage subsidies for work in the fields of ecology, social services, and youth activities; however, the law applies only jobs that are either part-time, that is, up to 80 percent of the negotiated working hours or full-time but paying "an acceptably lower" wage. "Acceptably lower" has been determined to be no more than 90 percent. While a number of unions have campaigned openly against this provision because it undercuts the constitutionally guaranteed autonomy of the bargaining parties, others have negotiated and signed contracts based on this legal provision. (IG Metall, incidentally, has done both.) Those unions willing to accept this situation regard it as one way to overcome the excessively high rate of unemployment in eastern Germany. And a number of unionists, especially women, have pointed out that this and similar measures may be the only way East German women will be reintegrated into the labor market (Quack and Maier 1993).

Regional Economic and Industrial Branch Structures: Policy Influence of the Unions

The network of policy and advisory contacts, made up of government agencies, political parties, unions, employer associations, and management representatives, which in western Germany is highly refined, long-standing, and (still) largely predictable, is weak and even volatile in eastern Germany. Conventional strategies and avenues of negotiation are ineffective under such circumstances, and even where customary networking has been possible, the demands on it posed by the reality of the existing economic crisis seem overly taxing, often producing a fragile construction based solely on the "chemistry" and proximity of its leading participants (situative corporatism)(Krumbein 1992).

In West Germany, the unions have had close ties to the established political parties; their traditional alliance between labor and the Social Democratic Party is well documented. But in the new *Länder* the relationship is extraordinarily tenuous. One cause of this is the legacy of the SED's instrumentalization of the FDGB. As a result, unionists from eastern Germany have tended to be wary about entering into active and close relationships with any of the political parties and have been adamant about avoiding special relationships such as the one that exists in the West between the DGB and the SPD. The other cause is that with the exception of the SED-successor *Partei des Demokratischen Sozialismus* (PDS), the existing parties have weak organizational bases and membership profiles.[11] Nor have the special suborganizations of the SPD or the CDU for employees (SPD-AfA, CDU-CDA) developed into recognized lobbying bodies for employee interests in eastern Germany.

Before the elections of 1994 there was a broad consensus in union circles, at least in public, that the PDS was to be avoided. The strong showing of the PDS in those elections has not kindled an open debate on this issue in the unions, but a number of local and regional union leaders in eastern Germany have included the PDS in their normal political contacts with the political parties. Interestingly, this reservation is also present within the PDS, which is neither pursuing a union-oriented political course nor attaching particular importance to securing and increasing its influence in the unions (Neugebauer and Stöss 1996).

OUTLOOK

Five years after unification the unions are clearly on the defensive in eastern Germany. Membership losses and budget deficits have initiated an organizational retreat. Employers are finding ways to side-step their contracts that the unions cannot block. The privatization phase of the *Treuhand* has passed, and with it the readiness of employers and government officials to seek out union and works council representatives for partnership solutions. Despite signs of economic stabilization, union officials in the new *Länder* claim that the original expectation that eastern Germany would rise incrementally to parity with western Germany is unrealistic. Instead, eastern Germany has become the testing grounds for dismantling labor standards and contract benefits established in western Germany.

11. Of the 850,000 members reported by the SPD at the end of 1993, only 27,000 were in the new *Länder*.

To be sure, there is as yet no solid evidence to support or refute this claim. And yet its very mention does seem to indicate a measure of weakness and defensiveness within the union camp in eastern Germany. Despite the still sizable East German membership figures, these are western-oriented unions, run by West Germans. If true unification is to be achieved, then union leadership must recognize the existing differences between East and West and make every effort to overcome them. The present approach has not produced fertile ground for the DGB reform debate in the new *Länder*. The call for active participation in this process is certainly necessary, but it is quite unlikely that the new members in eastern Germany will respond accordingly unless their ideas and interests are fully integrated into the process. Indeed, the unions need to recognize this step as the ultimate key to the successful representation of their goals in the new *Länder*.

Among union members in eastern Germany there seems to be a potential for creating stronger organizational bonds and revitalizing union policy approaches. A 1994 survey indicated that there is a stable core of members (44 percent) unwilling to consider returning their union cards. But the proportion of members prepared to take an active part in union life—whether in the form of an elected position or only "action related"—was still significantly lower than in western Germany. Far more favor increased grassroots decision-making and greater union activity on behalf of the unemployed, the handicapped, and persons forced into early retirement. Over 60 percent of the respondees regarded political parties to be important cooperation partners for the unions (IFEP 1994).

To be sure, the need for overall organizational reform cannot be justified solely on the basis of the present difficulties facing the unions in eastern Germany or in regard to the evident deficits of the East-West integration process. Seen from an institutional perspective, the unions are faced with an especially difficult structural contradiction throughout Germany, being torn between the givens of increasing diversity in market structures and membership interests on the one hand and the needs of continued unity on the other (Schmid 1994). Nevertheless, the current reform debate, especially concerning the DGB federation, has simply avoided addressing the issues specific to eastern Germany. There are, I think, several reasons for this:

1. The reform debate is a West German product, dominated by West German activists and embedded in personnel and organizational structures that existed prior to unification. That may be understandable, given the history of the debate, but in this form it will never aim at the real goal, namely, to give the unions an all-German perspective.

2. The reform debate has remained primarily a matter of finances and budgetary policy, its main protagonists being unionists at the head-

quarters level. Attempts to mobilize a broader segment of unionists for a discussion of elementary issues regarding the future of organized labor have failed. Local federation officials in eastern Germany feel like outsiders and complain that their contributions have not been taken seriously. Under the dictates of budgetary cuts ordered by the federation's leadership and directed at the local level, many of them have lost interest in struggling for a creative process of renewal.

3. East Germans find it difficult to join this debate. Many of them still do not identify themselves to such an extent with the union that they feel confident about presenting—and defending—their own ideas and suggestions. Instead, union officials in the new *Länder* are inclined to emphasize the identical nature of their situation with that of their colleagues in the old *Länder*.

4. Partly as a result, the debate does not recognize the specific context of problems and deficits in eastern Germany. Instead, it follows the underlying assumption that uniform solutions, equally applicable to both East and West, will be found.

With the transfer of West German institutions and organizational structures to eastern Germany a historically proven foundation for integrating the new territory and providing its inhabitants with economic prosperity and a democratic political environment was erected. But the assumption that West German institutions will function in the East and will be accepted in the East as they were in the West demonstrates a western failure to take into account the role of social learning and cultural heritage.

For member organizations such as unions, which thrive on being embedded in the social environment, this deficit is potentially destructive. And it is here that the urgency of reform is most evident. To be sure, union leadership has begun to address many of the overall structural aspects of union organizational culture which have been bureaucratized or degenerated into uninspired rituals, unattractive to both existing and potential members. This is an involved process, and the success or failure of union revitalization will not be decided overnight or by a single measure. But without strengthening organizational ties in the new *Länder*, fostering the integration of East and West as well as investing in a greater degree of involvement and decision making on the part of the East German membership, the benefits of any reform will be negligible. Without a doubt, the challenges facing the unions are immense, and much will depend on the overall progress of political and socioeconomic integration and the ability of the unions to reach an all-German understanding of their role. Failure will certainly weaken the ability of the unions to retain, much less strengthen, their position in the industrial relations system and successfully meet the challenges they are facing in the new Germany. And in the end, the status of the unions will have a crucial influence on the future of the German system of industrial relations in the broader European context.

REFERENCES

Alt, Ramona, Hans-Joachim Althaus, Werner Schmidt, Christoph Deutsch-mann, and Bernd Jürgen Warneken. 1994. *Vom Werktätigen zum Arbeit-nehmer.* HBS-Manuskripte 142. Düsseldorf: Hans-Böckler-Stiftung.

Ansorg, Leonore, and Renate Hürtgen. 1992. " 'Aber jetzt gibt es Initiative Leute und die müßte man eigentlich alle an einen Tisch bringen.' Die 'Initiative für unabhängige Gewerkschaften' (IUG) 1989 bis 1990: Dars-tellung und Dokumente." Berliner Arbeitschefte und Berichte zur sozialwissenschaftlichen Forschung 73. Berlin: Zentralinstitut für sozialwissenschaftliche Forschung, FU Berlin.

Czada, Roland. 1994. "Schleichweg in die 'Dritte Republik'. Politik der Vereinigung und politischer Wandel in Deutschland." *Politische Viertel-jahresschrift* 35, no. 2: 245–70.

Daniels, Arne, and Dietmar Lamparter. 1994. " 'Wir können nicht warten.' Metallindustrie: Die Tarifpartner verhandeln, die Betriebe gehen eigene Wege. Aus Angst um die Jobs werden Lohneinbußen und neue Arbeits-zeiten akzeptiert." *Die Zeit,* February 11, pp. 19–20.

Deutscher Gewerkschaftsbund und Bundesvereinigung der Deutschen Ar-beitgeberverbände. 1990. "Gemeinsame Erklärung zu einer einheitlichen Wirtschafts-und Sozialordnung in beiden deutschen Staaten." *DGB In-formationsdienst,* ID 7, Düsseldorf.

Duddek, Hans-Jürgen, Wolfgang Hindrichs, and Wolfram Wassermann. 1995. *Handlungsfeld Betrieb. Zwei Studien über Verhältnisse und Perspektiven gewerkschaftlicher Betriebspolitik am Beispiel der Ge-werkschaft NGG.* Bremen: Akademie für Arbeit und Politik an der Uni-versität Bremen.

Eichener, Volker, Ralf Kleinfeld, Detlef Pollack, Josef Schmid, Klaus Schu-bert, and Helmut Voelzkow, eds. 1992. *Organisierte Interessen in Ost-deutschland.* Probleme der Einheit, vol. 12. Marburg: Metropolis-Verlag.

Ermischer, Irina, and Evelyn Preusche. 1993. "Betriebsräte zwischen Mit-bestimmung und Abwicklungs—Komanagement.' " In Schmidt 1993, 169–92.

Ettl, Wilfried. 1995. "Arbeitgeberverbände als Transformationsakteure: Or-ganisationsentwicklung und Tarifpolitik im Dilemma von Funktionalität und Repräsentativät." In Wiesenthal 1995, 70–77.

Ettl, Wilfried, and Helmut Wiesenthal. 1994. "Tarifautonomie in deindustrialisiertem Gelände: Report und Analyse eines Institutionentransfers im Prozeß der deutschen Einheit." *Kölner Zeitschrift für Soziologie und Sozialpsychologie* 46, no. 3: 425–52.

Fichter, Michael. 1991. "From Transmission Belt to Social Partnership? The Case of Organized Labor in Eastern Germany." *German Politics and Society* 23: 21–39.

———. 1993. "A House Divided: German Unification and Organised Labour." *German Politics* 2, no. 1: 21–39.

———. 1994. "Was ist/ist was im Osten los?" *Gewerkschaftliche Monatshefte* 45, no. 6: 374–81.

Fichter, Michael, and Maria Kurbjuhn. 1992. "Spurensicherung—und dann?" *Die Mitbestimmung* 38, no. 5: 23–25.

———. 1993. "Spurensicherung. Der DGB und seine Gewerkschaften in den neuen Ländern, 1989–1991. Ergebnisse eines Dokumentationsprojekts." HBS-Manuskripte 120. Düsseldorf: Hans-Böckler-Stiftung.

Henneberger, Fred. 1993. "Transferstart: Organisationsdynamik und Strukturkonservatismus westdeutscher Unternehmerverbände—Aktuelle Entwicklungen unter besonderer Berücksichtigung des Aufbauprozesses in Sachsen und Thüringen." *Politische Vierteljahresschrift* 34, no. 4: 640–73.

Hintz, Cornelia. 1994. "ÖTV in den neuen Ländern." In Schmid, Löbler, and Tieman 1994, 87–99.

Hoffmann, Reiner, Norbert Kluge, Gudrun Linne, und Erika Mezger, eds. 1994. *Problemstart: Politischer und sozialer Wandel in den neuen Bundesländern.* HBS-Forschung, vol. 15. Köln: Bund-Verlag.

IFEP (Institut für empirische Psychologie). 1994. "Trendbarometer '94. Zusammenfassende Trendanalyse." Unpublished report, Köln.

Jander, Martin. 1996. *Formierung und Krise der DDR-Opposition. Die "Initiative für unabhängige Gewerkschaften." Dissidenten zwischen Demokratie und Romantik.* Berlin: Akademie Verlag.

Katzenstein, Peter J., ed. 1989. *Industry and Politics in West Germany: Toward the Third Republic.* Ithaca: Cornell University Press.

Kletzin, Jochen. 1994. "Politik und Organisation der IG Metall." In Schmid, Löbler, and Tieman 1994, 75–86.

Krumbein, Wolfgang. 1992. "Situativer Korporatismus." In Eichener et al. 1992, 211–24.

Lehmbruch, Gerhard. 1994. "Institutionen, Interessen und sektorale Variationen in der Transformationsdynamik der politischen Ökonomie Ostdeutschlands." *Journal für Sozialforschung* 34, no. 1: 22.

Mickler, Otfried, Norbert Engelhardt, Ralph Lungwitz, and Bettina Walker. 1994. "Ein Aufstieg wie Phönix aus der Asche? Der Wiederaufbau der ostdeutschen Automobilindustrie und die Konflikte der Betriebsräte." In Hoffmann et al. 1994, 263–80.

Müller, Birgit. 1993. "Der Mythos vom faulen Ossi. Deutsch-deutsche Vorurteile und die Erfahrungen mit der Marktwirtschaft in drei Ostberliner Betrieben." *Prokla* 23, no. 2: 51–68.

Müller-Jentsch, Walther, ed. 1991. *Konfliktpartnerschaft: Akteure und Institutionen der industriellen Beziehungen.* Schriftenreihe Industrielle Beziehungen, vol. 1. Munich: Hampp.

Neubauer, Ralf. 1993. "Auf der Suche nach neuen Modellen." *Die Zeit,* December 10, p. 25.

——. 1995. "Zum Überleben zuviel." *Die Zeit,* March 31, p. 27.

Neugebauer, Gero, and Richard Stöss. 1996. *Die PDS.* Opladen: Leske Verlag + Budrich.

Quack, Sigrid, and Friederike Maier. 1993. "Verliererinnen der Vereinigung? Entwicklungen der Frauenbeschäftigung in Ostdeutschland." *Beschäftigungsobservatorium Ostdeutschland,* no. 9: 3–5.

Sally, Razeen, and Douglas Webber. 1994. "The German Solidarity Pact: A Case Study in the Politics of the Unified Germany." *German Politics* 3, no. 1: 18–46.

Scherer, Peter. 1995. "Aus Verlusten lernen?" *Sozialismus,* no. 1: 22.

Schmid, Josef. 1994. "Sozio-ökonomische Disparitäten als Organisationsproblem der Gewerkschaften. Zur Dialektik von Einheit und Vielfalt." *Deutschland Archiv* 27, no. 1: 58–63.

Schmid, Josef, Frank Löbler, and Heinrich Tieman, eds. 1994. *Organisationsstrukturen und Probleme von Parteien und Verbänden. Berichte aus den neuen Ländern.* Probleme der Einheit, vol. 14. Marburg: Metropolis-Verlag.

Schmidt, Rudi, ed. 1993. *Zwischenbilanz. Analysen zum Transformationsprozeß der ostdeutschen Industrie.* Berlin: Akademie Verlag.

Silvia, Stephen J., and Andrei S. Markovits. 1994. "Ein Plädoyer für die Konzentration auf das Wesentliche." *Gewerkschaftliche Monatshefte* 45, no. 2: 93–102.

Sozialwissenschaftliches Forschungszentrum Berlin-Brandenburg (SFZ). 1994. *Sozialreport,* no. 1.

Steinmo, Sven, and Kathleen Thelen. 1994. "Historical Institutionalism in Comparative Politics." In Steinmo, Thelen, and Longstreth 1994, 1–32.

Steinmo, Sven, Kathleen Thelen, and Frank Longstreth, eds. 1994. *Structuring Politics: Historical Institutionalism in Comparative Analysis.* Cambridge: Cambridge University Press.

Streeck, Wolfgang. 1992. *Social Institutions and Economic Performance: Industrial Relations in Advanced Capitalist Economies.* London: Sage.

Uhlig, Christa. 1994. "Schule in der DDR—zwischen Anspruch und Wirklichkeit." *blz,* no. 1: 5, 8.

Wiesenthal, Helmut, ed. 1995. *Einheit als Interessenpolitik: Studien zur sektoralen Transformation Ostdeutschlands.* Frankfurt: Campus Verlag.

5 • Unifying Germany: Crisis, Conflict, and Social Partnership in the East

Lowell Turner

What was earlier an open question has now been resolved. Social partnership, including comprehensive collective bargaining, codetermination, influential unions, and employer associations, has been successfully established on new foundations in eastern Germany. This remarkable outcome, and the revolution in social relations that it implies, occurred in an extraordinarily short period of historical time (1990–94).

Far from a foregone conclusion, the development of modern social partnership relations in eastern Germany was very much in doubt in the early years after unification. Intelligent and well-informed observers suggested that a transfer of institutions from the West would not be successful, that employers would take advantage of new labor markets and low wages in the East to undermine the strength of German unions and fundamentally alter the German system of industrial relations, pushing toward a so-called Americanization—namely, deregulation and weakly organized labor (see, for example, Armingeon 1991 and Mahnkopf 1991 and 1993).

I argue that social partnership is alive and well in eastern Germany. My evidence for this surprising outcome includes the IG Metall strike victory of 1993 and plant-level case studies of restructuring and industrial relations in the metal and electronics industries of eastern Germany. The success of social partnership in eastern Germany can be traced both to the flexible

Funding for this research was provided by the German Marshall Fund of the United States; the Institute of Collective Bargaining, the Institute of European Studies, and the Center for Advanced Human Resource Studies, all three at Cornell University; and the Wissenchaftszentrum in Berlin. Many thanks to Michael Fichter, Charles Heckscher, Richard Locke, and Kathleen Thelen for detailed comments on earlier drafts.

suitability of institutions transferred from the West and to the actor choices in the negotiations and conflicts that have made it possible to adapt these institutions to a new environment. Both the institutional and political aspects of the argument are necessary to explain the success of social partnership in eastern Germany.

This issue is important not only for what it tells us about the political economy of unified Germany but also for the theoretical and practical lessons we can draw about institutional transfer, adaptation, and reinvigoration. In spite of extraordinary dislocation and hardship among its population, eastern Germany now appears well on the road to economic prosperity and democratic stability. This outcome, however, can be explained neither by the coming of a market economy in itself nor by markets combined with institutional transfer from the former West Germany under the terms of the unification treaty. Markets always require appropriate institutional regulation (Polanyi 1957; Hall 1986); at the same time, it is quite clear that institutions cannot be directly transferred from one area or society to another without being modified to fit local circumstances. New institutions, whether imported or locally developed, must build on the legacies and remnants of existing institutions and practices (Stark 1992). Both the case studies and the strike story presented here demonstrate how the West German institutions of social partnership have built successfully on earlier and existing practices in eastern Germany.

When institutions adapt to new circumstances, both are changed. This mutual process of influence and change, even in the one-sided process of unification, points to a broader conclusion: institutional expansion, transfer, and adaptation to new circumstances leads to institutional change. Such a process of change, although painful, may result in institutional reinvigoration or even reinvention; if it does not, the alternative may well be stagnation and decline.

Institutional expansion and adaptation to new circumstances, although necessary, are also risky. While social partnership is now newly established in eastern Germany, the necessary adaptations (similar to what Stark 1994 calls "recombination") exert pressure for change within the broader western and all-German institutions. The contours of such change are only dimly apparent at present. Whether the pressure for change will result in institutional reinvigoration or institutional decline for German social partnership remains to be played out in political processes of conflict and negotiation.

THE STRIKE OF 1993

The first great watershed for German social partnership in the post-unification era came in the spring of 1993, when employers in the metal industries of eastern Germany unilaterally imposed a pay raise smaller than the one they had contractually agreed to pay. IG Metall responded by calling eastern workers out on strike in a high-stakes effort to beat back the employer offensive and demonstrate its influence in the new states of Germany. The ensuing conflict was to have major consequences for the future of industrial relations in eastern Germany.[1]

Background

In March 1991, Gesamtmetall (the metal industries employers' association) and IG Metall signed similar three-year contracts for each region of eastern Germany, establishing basic pay levels and terms of employment for blue-and white-collar workers in the metal industries, including automobile assembly and parts, machinery, steel, shipbuilding, and electronics. These contracts provided for the phasing in of nominal wage parity with western workers over a three-year period, from 65 percent on April 1, 1991, to 100 percent on April 1, 1994.[2] Widely praised at the time, this arrangement gave eastern workers hope for the future (and a reason not to move to the already crowded western labor market), social stability in a precarious economic situation, and an incentive for employers and investors to get in early while wage costs remained low.

The cosy relationships of 1991, however, had evaporated by 1992 in the face of economic collapse in eastern Germany. Although the wage raise of April 1, 1992, was paid on schedule, many employers, especially small-to-medium-sized ones, complained that the continuing phase-in of nominal wage parity would bring economic ruin. Gesamtmetall was worried about its membership density in the East, which was much lower than levels enjoyed in western Germany; many eastern firms were seeking to go it alone in hopes of working out better deals with their own threatened workforces (Silvia 1993, 22; Wever 1995).[3] Employer criticism focused increasingly on the 26 percent pay raise due on April 1, 1993.

1. Although published work is cited where appropriate, most of the facts and analysis in this section are based on interviews as well as participant observation conducted in eastern Germany in the spring of 1993.

2. Although contracts offered eastern workers nominal wage parity in the foreseeable future, real wage parity remained an elusive and distant goal. This was true because vacation and holiday schedules and other benefits were to be phased in over a longer period, because eastern workers were often grouped in lower pay categories than similarly employed western workers, and because contractual minimums negotiated in the West were typically supplemented by firm-level premiums unavailable in the East. In the metal industries, this meant that by April 1, 1993, when wage levels in the East were scheduled to reach 82 percent of levels in the West, real wages (all things considered) would reach only 56.5 percent (Bispinck 1993a, 315, 326).

3. Precise membership data for employer associations, including meaningful density figures, is well-guarded. For a useful discussion of the dissatisfaction of eastern association members (in the employer associations as well as other interest organizations), see Wiesenthal, Ettl, and Bialas 1992.

The pressure that Gesamtmetall now felt from many eastern member firms dovetailed with similar pressure that had been growing in the West in the 1980s and early 1990s (Silvia 1994). The *Mittelstand* (the vast medium-sized firm sector, which included many innovative companies using advanced technology and oriented toward export as well as domestic markets) had grown especially critical of Gesamtmetall (dominated by large firms such as Daimler-Benz and Siemens) and its bargaining agreements. *Mittelstand* firms claimed that regional agreements since 1984, which included wage increases, workforce protections, and a shorter work week, were raising costs beyond what they could afford. Some had gone so far as to threaten to withdraw from Gesamtmetall if the bargaining system was not considerably decentralized and deregulated.

In this context, facing pressure from its own membership in both West and East, fearing membership losses in the West as well as a permanently smaller base in the East, Gesamtmetall seized an opportunity to play hard-ball in what looked like a sure-win situation in the winter and spring of 1993. A hard-line view came to dominate within the employers' camp: with 40 percent real unemployment and massive job insecurity in the East, with no recent history of western-style collective bargaining and labor conflict, and with membership in IG Metall quite new for eastern workers, the chances for mass mobilization and a successful strike in the East looked slim. Here was the breakthrough opportunity that Gesamtmetall sought for reform of the collective bargaining system in unified Germany. If IG Metall could be forced to retreat or pushed into a losing conflict in circumstances favorable to employers, a precedent could be set for holding down labor costs, introducing greater flexibility for firm-level adjustments, and demonstrating a new aggresiveness and resolve on the part of Gesamtmetall in the service of member interests.

With these goals in mind, in November of 1992 Gesamtmetall called for a revision of the three-year contract. Under terms of the revision clause, either party to the agreement could open new negotiations after January 1, 1993, in light of changing economic and social circumstances. After much public posturing, negotiations began in Saxony on January 18, 1993. Employers demanded cancellation of the three-year contract and its *Stufenplan* (phased-in wage parity); a one-year contract that would raise wages 9 percent in eastern Germany on April 1, instead of the scheduled 26 percent; and a new "opening clause" *(Öffnungsklausel)* to allow renegotiation at the firm level for employers unable to pay scheduled wage increases (Bispinck 1993b, 471–75).

IG Metall rejected these demands and asked for evidence to show how many firms could not pay the scheduled increase. Refusing to provide such information, Gesamtmetall declared the negotiations at an impasse on January 25 and called for arbitration. At the same time, the employers made it clear they would not accept an arbitrated settlement that exceeded their proposed 9 percent pay raise revision for April 1.[4]

On February 15, arbitration proceedings ended in Saxony without a formal recommendation. The chief arbitrator cited irreconcilable differences caused by inadequate industrial and monetary policies and an economic transformation that had completely overtaxed the capabilities of the bargaining parties. Similar, patterned outcomes occurred in bargaining and arbitration proceedings in the other eastern German bargaining districts. On February 18, the employers' association in Saxony announced the cancellation of the contract and demanded new negotiations with the union, based on the employer demand for a 9 percent raise, with downward adjustments possible under an opening clause. In the event that no new agreement was reached, the employers announced their intention to proceed unilaterally with a 9 percent raise on April 1.

IG Metall denounced the employer action as illegal and without precedent in the postwar period. Filing a formal complaint with the labor court (which was not scheduled to be heard until May 14), the union began to prepare for a strike (Bispinck 1993b, 475–76).

With no agreement in sight, Gesamtmetall associations in each of the eastern bargaining regions announced their intention to raise wages by 9 percent on April 1; IG Metall announced warning strikes, marches, and demonstrations beginning that same day, to be upgraded to a full-fledged strike if no settlement was reached.[5] Employers denounced IG Metall as intransigent and out of touch with a membership in desperate economic straits; the union accused the employers of breaking the postwar social contract and undermining the foundations of free collective bargaining.[6] Employers, backed by the business press and the broader employer community (through the umbrella federation BDA), appeared unusually confident of victory. Eastern metalworking employees, for their part, obviously felt

---

4. Each party appointed three members of an arbitration panel; these six members then appointed a seventh neutral member and chair. Arbitration is generally nonbinding in German collective bargaining, which means the results can be rejected by either party. In this case, an arbitrated agreement would have been binding only if five of the seven panel members had agreed on the settlement (Silvia 1993, 11).

5. Unlike common practice in the United States, where strikes tend to be all or nothing, German unions typically build up to a strike gradually. Warning strikes can last anywhere from a few minutes to a full day or more and are intended to strengthen the union bargaining position by demonstrating strike readiness and solidarity. When warning strikes do occur, negotiations typically continue or resume, leading in most cases to a settlement prior to the onset of a full-blown strike.

6. For the employer perspective, see, for example, *Handelsblatt*, April 6, 1993, p. 3. For the union view, see *Der Gewerkschafter*, 41, no. 3 (March 1993). For a debate between the two viewpoints just prior to the first warning strikes, see *Tagesspiegel*, March 23, 1993, p. 21.

betrayed by the unilateral reduction of their scheduled pay increases; yet according to numerous journalistic accounts they also appeared wary about going out on strike in a period of massive layoffs and economic crisis. Union representatives spoke militantly in public of the need to defend collective bargaining and free trade unionism but more hesitantly in private of their uncertainty regarding the viability of a strike in eastern Germany. Press editorials called for reason on both sides, especially exhorting IG Metall to avoid leading its new eastern members into a labor-market disaster. In a front-page editorial cartoon, *Handelsblatt*, Germany's leading business daily, showed IG Metall president Franz Steinkühler sitting at the helm of a small boat, steering his eastern members over the crest of a great waterfall.[7] The *Economist* titled its article on the coming conflict "Mass Suicide."[8]

From Partnership to Open Conflict

Highly successful warning strikes throughout the new German states on April 1–2 and again on April 14–15 shattered both employer expectations and western preconceptions of eastern worker passivity. Even Michael Fichter, for example, a leading Berlin-based observer of eastern German industrial relations since 1989, had referred to "the widespread instance of lethargy and passive expectation . . . after years of being watched over, taken care of, and having favors and social improvements—when forth-coming—doled out to them, East Germans seem to be particularly prone to such behavior" (Fichter 1991, 35).[9] For Gesamtmetall, the comfortable illusion vanished that easterners, after sixty combined years of nazism and command communism, would no longer stand up for their own interests when forcefully challenged. For IG Metall, the demonstrative shattering of this same troubling preconception cast new light on the union's bargaining position in eastern Germany.

For a few days, an early settlement looked possible. Kurt Biedenkopf, prime minister of Saxony, offered his services as a mediator, leading to discussions between IG Metall and employers' association (VSME in Saxony) on April 4 and 5. An agreement was reached between the two sides, reinstating the scheduled April 1 pay raise but stretching out the timetable for full parity by one additional year. IG Metall headquarters in Frankfurt indicated its willingness to accept the compromise; Gesamtmetall headquarters in Cologne, however, turned it down, forcing the Saxon employers'

7. *Handelsblatt*, April 5, 1993, p. 1.
8. *The Economist*, April 24, 1993, pp. 71–72.
9. See also Mahnkopf 1991, 276–79, and Röbenack and Hartung 1992. As *Der Spiegel* put it on the eve of the strike: "In the workplace, employees are profoundly insecure; fear of losing their jobs is paralyzing their willingness to strike" (*Der Spiegel*, no. 13 [1993]: 122; author's translation).

association chairman to resign his position. IG Metall pointed to this failed effort at compromise as evidence that Gesamtmetall's hard-line position was unreasonable.[10]

Rumors of further behind-the-scenes discussions and possible compromise solutions circulated throughout the month of April and into May. Publicly, however, both sides hardened their positions. The first strike votes, held on April 26–28, were 85 percent in favor in Saxony and 90 percent in favor in Mecklenburg-Pomerania. A parallel vote in the eastern steel industry, also organized by IG Metall but negotiating separately, was 86 percent in favor (Bispinck 1993b, 477).

The strike began in Saxony on May 3, with 7,000 workers at twenty workplaces, and in Mecklenburg-Pomerania on May 4, with 12,500 workers from twenty-four workplaces. The union raised the numbers gradually, so that by the second week, 30,000 workers from seventy-five workplaces had joined the strike. Solidarity among the strikers, who received an average of DM 220–50 (about $150) per week in strike benefits from the union, appeared strong.[11] There were no signs at all of what the employers had expected: an early return to work by dispirited eastern workers.

On May 10–12, IG Metall escalated the stakes by holding strike votes in the rest of eastern Germany, with 81 percent in favor in Berlin-Brandenburg, 86 percent in Saxony-Anhalt, and 85 percent in Thuringia (Bispinck 1993b, 477). On May 12, 400,000 workers and their supporters demonstrated throughout Germany in support of the strikers, including over 50,000 western workers who briefly laid down their tools in solidarity.[12] On May 13, the IG Metall national executive board announced its decision to spread the strike to all of eastern Germany. By the end of the second week (May 14), 50,000 eastern metalworkers were on strike.[13]

Intensive negotiations resumed in Saxony, again with the mediation of Kurt Biedenkopf, finally yielding a settlement on May 14. The terms of this agreement served as a closely followed pattern for the other regions of eastern Germany and the eastern steel industry as well. The parties agreed to the principle of phased-in wage parity for eastern workers but established a new timetable. In a symbolic but important gesture for the union, the 26 percent raise was reinstated retroactively to April 1. Effective April 16, the

---

10. For an account of the early abortive settlement, see *Der Spiegel*, no. 19 (1993): 114–17.

11. See, for example, Andreas Oldag, "Metallerstreik in Ostdeutschland," *Süddeutsche Zeitung*, May 6, 1993, p. 3.

12. Reported by IG Metall in its newsletter "Metall Nachrichten für den Bezirk Küste," May 13, 1993.

13. Dagmar Deckstein, "Ein fast genialer Kompromiß," *Süddeutsche Zeitung*, May 15, 1993, p. 4.

raise was dropped to 9 percent (plus anything else that individual firms had agreed to), then raised again in June, September, and December, so that the 26 percent level was reached by the end of the year. Further raises in 1994–96 were scheduled to bring wage parity between East and West by July 1, 1996. The employers issued a statement conceding that the extraordinary contract cancellation, used in this case only, was not an appropriate solution to collective bargaining problems.[14]

The union thus secured its main demands: reinstatement of the 26 percent pay increase, an admission by the employers that the contract cancellation would set no precedent for future labor conflicts, and a defense of phased-in wage parity for eastern workers. In addition, the union resisted the introduction of an "opening clause." Most important, perhaps, the union discovered in its new eastern membership a highly mobilizable force capable of conflict, solidarity, and personal sacrifice.

Employers secured considerable total labor cost savings for the period 1993–96, during the lengthened phase-in of wage parity.[15] In addition, Gesamtmetall was able to demonstrate a new bargaining aggressiveness on behalf of its members, as well as provide support services during a strike, to help convince skeptical eastern employers to join or retain membership in the association. But the employers, in the end, were forced to give in to the central union demands, including the concept of phased-in eastern wage parity; and they were forced to back down in the face of unexpectedly determined employee militance.

Instead of an opening clause, Gesamtmetall settled for a new "hardship clause." While both allow for downward wage adjustment at designated firms, the distinction is critical. An opening clause would put the essential power in the hand of firms and their works councils to negotiate lower wage levels. In a period of economic crisis and mass unemployment, works councils would find themselves under great pressure to make substantial concessions. A hardship clause, on the other hand, puts the essential power of approval in the hands of a union-employer commission, giving IG Metall effective veto power. While the employers heralded this as a breakthrough in the direction of greater wage flexibility, the union vowed to use the new instrument selectively, to monitor and control carefully all temporary adjustments.

14. As reported in *IDS News:* "Under the settlement, the employers recognised that breaching the original agreement was an 'unavoidable emergency measure solely occasioned by the unique situation in the five new *Länder*. . . . Terminating collective agreements is not an appropriate means for resolving collective disputes' " (*IDS European Report*, no. 378, June 1993, p. 5).

15. The amount has been estimated to be as high as DM 6 billion (Silvia 1993, 13; *Süddeutsche Zeitung*, May 21, 1993, p. 1).

Striking workers clearly viewed the settlement as a victory. With only 25 percent required for ratification, votes in favor totaled 78 percent in Saxony; 61 percent in Mecklenburg-Pomerania, Thuringia, and Saxony-Anhalt; 46 percent in Berlin-Brandenburg; and 78 percent for the eastern steel industry.[16]

Explaining the Unexpected

Where did the eastern workers find such unexpected resolve? Why did they choose to go out on strike in large numbers in a high-risk situation? Their interest in higher pay was clearly an important factor. Expectations had risen dramatically after unification; living costs had also risen rapidly toward western levels. Only wages had not. For similar work, easterners were paid far less than western workers, and the 26 percent raise scheduled for April 1 was seen as a major step toward parity. Wage interests alone, however, are not sufficient to explain the high-risk choice to strike. Union and worker bargaining power is typically low and the strike threat is least credible during periods of mass unemployment; at such times, worker militance is typically restrained, in spite of interests in higher pay (Katz and Kochan 1992).

There are, therefore, two other necessary parts to the explanation for eastern militance. Worker mobilization in this case was fueled by extraordinary passion, a product of the combined frustrations and disillusionment that German unification had produced for eastern Germans.[17] In the rush to unification, easterners had been promised prosperity to go with their newfound freedoms. What they found instead was economic crisis, mass unemployment, rising costs, great job insecurity, and western employers and government officials taking over their land. For easterners in the metal industries, the unilateral employer cancellation of the scheduled pay raise was the last straw. The bitterness and rage of what was in some ways a colonized people (Knuth 1993; Baylis 1993, 87) was channeled into this strike, much to the benefit of IG Metall.

The final necessary condition to explain eastern mobilization, therefore,

16. The lower figure for the Berlin area reflects a market converging rapidly around West Berlin levels, with both higher living costs and greater pressure on employees to work at western standards. The last of the eastern regions to settle, Berlin-Brandenburg produced a strong union critique against the Saxon settlement, arguing for quicker wage parity in an area where social differences were most painfully visible (Bispinck 1993b, 477; *Süddeutsche Zeitung*, May 19, 1993, p. 2).

17. See, for example, Marc Fisher, "Many in East Germany Redirect Their Anger," *International Herald Tribune*, March 27–28, 1993, p. 6. See also the editorial "Politisches Warnsignal" in *Süddeutsche Zeitung*, May 18, 1993, p. 4; "Wir stehen unter Druck," *Der Spiegel*, no. 17 (1993): 124–25; and Ferdinand Protzman, "Strike in Eastern Germany: Economics and Anger," *New York Times*, May 5, 1993, p. A3.

was the existence of a framework of credible institutions into which the passion could be funneled with reasonable prospects of success. These institutions were largely imported from the West: codetermination based on elected works councillors who could, in their capacity as union members, provide strike leadership, and a system of comprehensive regional collective bargaining, which included the participation of a powerful, conflict-tested metalworkers' union. The presence of these proven institutions, and the reassuring words of IG Metall that strikes were appropriate, legal, and winnable, provided the structure necessary for easterners to channel their passion into appropriate action (as opposed to either passive disillusionment and withdrawal or inappropriate action such as attacks on foreigners or other scapegoats).

And most important, why did IG Metall and its eastern membership win? The employers were certainly confident of victory, and with good reason. The careful analyses of perceptive academics such as Birgit Mahnkopf (1991, 1993) and Klaus Armingeon (1991) pointed clearly toward declining union influence in unified Germany. If this were the case, it would hardly lead one to expect a major IG Metall victory in eastern Germany in 1993. The prevalent viewpoint, however, underestimated two important factors: the passion and potential militance of eastern workers, and the resilience and adaptability of the institutions of industrial relations in the Federal Republic, in particular codetermination and the system of regional collective bargaining.

Under adverse circumstances, IG Metall won this strike because (1) it made the strategic and rather risky decision to strike at a time when the most prudent course of action might have been some face-saving compromise; (2) eastern workers in large numbers made the courageous decision to risk future employment prospects for an issue in which they deeply believed (phased-in wage parity); and (3) western institutions of industrial relations, transplanted and adapted to conditions in the East, afforded a viable framework in which the strike could be fought and won. Codetermination law meant that most works councillors had received union training and could thus provide a union base in most plants; regional collective bargaining made it possible to mobilize widespread solidarity.

For other sectors of the eastern economy, the settlement in the metal industries set an important pattern. In interviews in eastern Germany in March and April of 1993, I heard time and again from representatives of non-metal sectors that they were waiting to see what happened in the metal industry conflict. Union representatives at ÖTV (the public sector) and DPG (postal and telecommunications workers), for example, said that if IG Metall lost the strike, their own bargaining partners (chiefly in the Federal Ministry of the Interior) could be expected to follow a similar hard-line, union-challenging strategy. For both of those unions, comprehensive collective bargaining contracts were set to expire within a few months of the metal conflict. The IG Metall victory, however, led to a soft-line government strategy and a peaceful settlement with ÖTV and DPG based on phased-in wage parity.

The conflict and settlement in the metal industries, in other words, were precedent-setting events that led to a widespread consolidation throughout the eastern economy of (1) nominal wage parity for eastern workers in the medium term, and (2) new institutions of industrial relations, including considerable union influence along with comprehensive, region-and sector-based collective bargaining.

Although the crisis of social partnership was far from over, this strike and its settlement greatly increased the prospects for continuing social partner-style relations between employers and unions in eastern Germany.[18] It was still possible, however, that the union victory was a Pyrrhic one, a possibility that cannot be discounted.[19] Much depends on economic and industrial development in eastern Germany as well as the outcome of future labor conflicts in both eastern and western Germany.

CASE STUDIES IN THE METAL AND ELECTRONICS INDUSTRIES

Evidence gathered from ten case studies in the metal and electronics industries in eastern Germany expands, updates, and largely confirms conclusions drawn from the strike of 1993.[20]

Case-study evidence shows first of all a wide range of plant-level diversity

18. In a perceptive analysis, Horst Kern (1994, 38–45) argues that what IG Metall gained above all from the eastern strike was credibility: a demonstration of the capacity to mobilize its membership that would greatly strengthen the political and economic role of the unions in the new German states.

19. Note the long history in the United States and elsewhere of great labor victories followed by prolonged periods of union decline. I am indebted both to Nick Salvatore and Jonas Pontusson, each of whom separately impressed upon me this point.

20. Case-study presentations are based on plant visits, interviews, and documents collected between 1990 and 1995. I first visited Hella in Meerane and VW-Chemnitz in 1994, the other eight firms at least three times each between 1990 and 1995. I conducted in-depth interviews ranging in length from one to four hours with works councillors, managers, and union representatives. Some of the plant visits and interviews in Berlin and Rostock I conducted alone, others were conducted together with Larissa Klinzing of Humboldt University. For the cases in Saxony, Ulrich Jürgens of the Wissenschaftszentrum and I made research trips together to those plants in 1991, 1992, and again in 1994. Additional interviews were also conducted at several of the plants by research associates Owen Darbishire and Aline Hoffmann. Detailed presentations of the cases are presented in Turner forthcoming, chap. 3. The case studies were selected from a broader original sample, to demonstrate the full range of outcomes along a continuum from successful to failed adjustment (Jürgens, Klinzing, and Turner 1993).

along a number of dimensions, including characteristics of the transformation, production organization, and industrial relations. For production organization, outcomes range from state-of-the-art lean production at Opel-Eisenach, to innovative group work at Knorr-Bremse (the former Berliner Bremsenwerk), to rather traditional ("extended assembly line") production at ABB Kraftwerke Berlin (the former Bergmann-Borsig). For industrial relations, outcomes range from plants with influential works councils backed up by strike-hardened, mobilizable workforces (Siemens in Rostock, VW in Mosel), to highly cooperative works councils whose workforces have as yet shown little interest in mobilization (Niles in Berlin, Opel in Eisenach), and from firms committed to the employers' association and comprehensive collective bargaining (VW in Mosel) to nonmember, weakly unionized firms (Hella in Meerane).

Although a similar range of diversity exists in western Germany, the diversity appears considerably more pronounced in the East. Cases that would be outliers in the West are less unusual in the East; it is, in fact, difficult to find a real mainstream in the new federal states. There are, nonetheless, observable patterns of economic development and industrial relations that can be clearly discerned in the case studies considered here.

Findings: Partnership and Modernization

The most important observation to emerge from the case studies is the following: in a very short period of time (five years), a solid base for long-term, stable relations of social partnership has developed in eastern Germany.

Employer associations, despite low membership density relative to the West and intensive internal debate regarding strategy, have established a base for future growth and negotiation. Almost all large, influential firms in the East are members, and the associations play the key role from the employer side in setting wage standards at both sector and regional levels. Most of the managers interviewed indicated that their firms were committed members of the appropriate association. Employer solidarity, they maintained, was especially important in the difficult circumstances of the East; they viewed comprehensive collective bargaining by strong employer associations as the best way to prevent cutthroat and self-defeating labor-market competition and to maintain the high standards, quality, and profits for which German industry in the West has been known. All managers interviewed, even at nonmember Hella, fully expected the associations to occupy the same prominent position in the East that they have occupied in recent decades in the West.

There also appeared to be a solid base for the continuing development of union influence in eastern Germany. At the case-study firms, union membership levels for the most part equaled or exceeded membership levels at comparable western firms. In some cases, membership density was considerably higher, as at the electronics firms Siemens and El Pro. The two low-density cases were Hella (a small firm, most of which are also low-density in the West) and Opel-Eisenach (a special case, at which unionization was nonetheless on the rise). In all of these cases except Hella, the works councils were dominated by members of IG Metall. At several of these companies, strike preparations (or the actual strike itself) had strengthened union influence among the workforce; even where this had not occurred (as at Niles and VW-Chemnitz), works councillors remained committed union members and promoted union membership among the rank and file. In almost every case, works councillors, unionists, and managers predicted future high rates of unionization at their firms.

These findings offer a quite different perspective when set against the many pessimistic speculations on the future of unions, employer associations, and social partnership in eastern Germany (Mahnkopf 1991; Armingeon 1991; Wiesenthal, Ettl, and Bialas 1992). In fact, the future does not look at all bad for unions and employer associations here, at least at the firm level. True, many small and medium-sized employers do not belong to the association and set their own pay levels. As the economy of the East improves and as firm earnings rise, however, there is little reason to think that these nonmember firms will forgo the considerable benefits of membership (including legal advice, strike support, market information, and business contacts). For employees, the strike of 1993 has ensured a strong base of union support among both rank and file and works councils in the metal and electronics industries.

Comprehensively organized collective bargaining remains the primary mechanism for wage setting in eastern Germany and shows no signs of losing this role. Since plant premiums are less in the economically backward East, regional contracts bear an even closer relation to actual pay and other standards than is typically the case in the West. Where employers undercut bargained wage levels (sometimes with works council consent), contractual standards remain the benchmark for downward adjustment as well as the stated goal of works councils for the coming years when the crisis passes and economic growth resumes.

Relations of social partnership are thus already strongly entrenched in negotiations between unions and employer associations. At the firm level, works councils are at least as likely (and in many cases more likely) than in the West to work cooperatively and flexibly with management in the interest of firm survival. Works councils at the case-study firms are highly unionized (and this is typical throughout the East among larger firms in the metal and electronics industries); the works council-union-management social partnership appears firmly established at the level of the individual employer.

A second critical finding apparent from the case studies is the existence in the mid-1990s of a strong base for the modernization of industry in eastern Germany. Innovations at eastern plants include group work; aspects of lean production, including just-in-time parts delivery; and the latest technology. In the fight for survival, works councils collaborate closely with management in the introduction of innovation; in many cases, the works councils have pushed management (the reverse of the more usual case) to invest in new methods and to remove or reeducate authoritarian-minded "old red socks" who stand in the way of modern, participatory relations. In eastern Germany, firms found greenfield and semi-greenfield opportunities to introduce innovations more easily than in the industrially established West. They also found skilled workforces eager to accept innovation in the drive to keep plants open and preserve jobs.

Whether the strong base for modernization in eastern Germany becomes the dominant economic reality there depends on many factors, ranging from world and European economic conditions, to German federal and regional economic policy, to the outcomes of future collective bargaining rounds. From the evidence presented here, however, a strong case can be made to support the predictions of eastern managers and works councillors that over the next ten to twenty years, the new federal states will become the most modern part of the German economy. The strong base for modernization developed in only five years offers evidence to contradict widely pessimistic predictions regarding economic development in eastern Germany (see, for example, Grabher 1992).

The third key finding from case-study evidence concerns the important role played in modernization and economic development by legacies of industrial and social organization from the former GDR. David Stark has shown how the inherited form of industrial organization begets contrasting, "path-dependent" processes of privatization in Poland, Czechoslovakia, Hungary, and eastern Germany (Stark 1992). Thus the Treuhand as a unique organizational form and approach to privatization has roots in the industrial structure (and concentration) of the GDR. In similar fashion, the evidence considered here demonstrates a clear relationship between older shopfloor practices and the potential for particular kinds of modern production organization. Modern shopfloor teamwork in eastern Germany, where management is astute enough to develop it, builds at least indirectly on former traditions of collective work and improvisation. Such innovation-suitable traditions arise not so much from formal brigade structures as from tacit opposition to (and in spite of) former authoritarian practices. As a response to the inefficiency of a state-run economy, for example, groups of workers met their norms by improvisation and collective effort in the face of persistent material shortages and obsolete equipment (Voskamp and Wittke 1991; Kern 1991). Habits bred by years of common effort and adaptation in difficult circumstances provide fertile ground in the 1990s for the introduction of modern group and teamwork. This potential is well illustrated by successful innovations in production organization at Knorr-Bremse, Opel-Eisenach, VW-Mosel, VW-Chemnitz, and Hella, among others.

"Old red socks" in management, on the other hand, are a human legacy that is more mixed in its blessing. Firms in the East have built on this legacy for want of a viable alternative. On the negative side, former communist managers need training in cost-benefit analysis, human resource management, and modern relations with employees. Works councillors at several firms complained about inherited authoritarian bosses and their inability to work in a spirit of cooperation and trust either with the works councils or with other employees. On the positive side, however, such individuals do have experience in leadership and organization, they often possess considerable shopfloor knowledge by virtue of past apprenticeships and other technical training and on-the-job experience, and most important, they are desperate to hang on to their jobs and thus will do just about anything top management asks. Where top management has related to the old red socks strategically, such individuals have been sifted through, the bad ones sorted out, and the remaining core retrained to work in a facilitating role (rather than a commanding one) for shopfloor and office teams. This takes a major effort on the part of management, but it can pay off, as for example at Knorr-Bremse, VW-Chemnitz, and Hella. In successful cases, retrained old red socks bring (1) a powerful desire to adapt; (2) technical and managerial skills; and (3) a past practice of collaboration with eastern shop and office employees. This is a legacy on which the best firms can build in the push toward modern work organization.

Another important legacy can be found in the employment and training companies (ETCs) that have been spun off from several of the case-study firms (Knuth 1993; Jürgens, Klinzing, and Turner 1993, 240–41). In these cases, displaced employees using available plant space and surplus equipment are combined in a government-subsidized nonprofit company that provides jobs and training while performing necessary infrastructure tasks such as demolition and environmental cleanup. In the best cases, led by "unleashed" ambitious and entrepreneurial former skilled workers, these companies have in turn spun off small private firms that have survived to provide permanent jobs and even production innovations in the new market economy. The jury is still out on the ETCs, and whether the latter successful cases are more than isolated exceptions. At the very least, the ETCs have provided one-to-three more years of employment for displaced workers who then enter the ranks of the unemployed; at best, ETCs, especially when adequately funded (the main struggle for these bodies), have afforded bridges to future skills, employment, and even new firms and product or process innovation.

In addition to the above findings, each of which offers some grounds for an optimistic assessment of developments in the eastern economy, the evidence examined also shows major problems and potential obstacles on the road to a modern social-partnership economy. Employer associations, as we have seen, are undersubscribed; unions are losing membership, largely as a result of unemployment but also in some cases as a product of disillusionment; and works councils in many cases, although working closely with management and gaining some input, are weak in the capacity to mobilize the workforce and develop independent negotiating positions. Pessimistic analysts take each of these problems as indicators of the demise of employer associations, unions, and social partnership. An alternative interpretation, however, more in line with the evidence presented here, views such problems as indicators of transformation and institutional adaptation, quite possibly on the road to a modern economy regulated by strong social partners.

Other problems, however, may well prove more intractable and potentially destabilizing for social partnership in the East. For one thing, although this was not the case at any of the case-study firms, managers and works councillors told us repeatedly of *other* firms in the area that were paying at below contractual levels, with the agreement of their own works councils. In some cases, firms had dropped out of the employers' association (or never joined) in order to do this; in other cases, firms were doing this illegally in spite of association membership. In the latter cases, the union was reluctant to take legal action, since the better political solution lay in developing a union-conscious works council rather than fighting against an agreement to which elected works councillors had consented.

There is no doubt that this practice is currently widespread throughout eastern Germany (and has also become a problem in western Germany). Possible interpretations, however, vary. Does this phenomenon represent the beginning of the end for comprehensive collective bargaining led by strong employer associations and unions—the pessimistic and perhaps prevalent view? Or does this subcontractual wage-setting reflect a temporary adaptation and informal flexibility in a period of crisis and transformation? Considerable evidence supports the latter view: the continuing unionization of works councils that make such agreements; the consistent claim on the part both of works councils and management that such "adjustments" are only temporary, to save jobs in desperate circumstances; and the willingness of union and employer association to look the other way. Sources within IG Metall, in fact (off the record), view such firms as potential sites for future union mobilization, if and when employers betray the promise and attempt to make these "temporary" adjustments permanent.

The most serious problem for social partnership and modernization in eastern Germany is clearly deindustrialization, and the possibility that industry in the East will never recover from its dramatic collapse of 1991–92. It is difficult to imagine strong unions and employer associations in the absence of a substantial industrial base. Deindustrialization, with its corresponding mass unemployment, has indeed been the primary source of union membership decline in eastern Germany since 1992. The cases we have looked at, on the other hand, show potentially successful and innovative firms that may well attract future investment and contribute to processes of industrial recovery. Much depends here on government economic policy, levels of public and private investment, and the capacity of the social partners to continue to negotiate compromise agreements that set the framework for stability and expansion.

A final problem, linked directly to the preceding one, is continuing and long-term mass unemployment. In every case study, people related wrenching stories of almost unbelievable downsizing and mass layoffs. The firms that survived sell-off by the Treuhand did so with a fraction of their previously employed workforce. It is no secret that many of the displaced have no hope of future employment. For older workers and for many women forced out of the workforce into early retirement or long-term unemployment, the injustice and trauma of dislocation are extreme. The instability of mass unemployment is thus a potentially dangerous cost of rising productivity in eastern Germany. Not only does mass unemployment result in heavy and long-term fiscal burdens on the welfare state, massive dislocation opens the door for demagogery and right-wing terrorism against foreign or domestic scapegoats. Mass unemployment, in other words, whether in the East or West, threatens the fabric of postwar German democratic stability.

Once again the question arises whether these problems pose a long-term danger or represent temporary outrageous behavior in a period of profound dislocation. The answer depends in part on the speed with which economic growth takes off in the East; to that extent, the evidence of modernization examined here offers grounds for hope. The answer also depends, however, on the ability of the social partners, and especially the unions, to channel frustration and protest in constructive directions. Here again, the strike of

1993 gives us reason to take an optimistic perspective. The danger of social instability in unified Germany, however, should not be underestimated.

SOCIAL PARTNERSHIP: RESILIENCE AND ADAPTATION IN EASTERN GERMANY

Evidence from other sectors supports conclusions drawn from the metal and electronics industries: social partnership is alive and well in eastern Germany; employer associations and unions have established comprehensive collective bargaining coverage that looks likely to endure; both employer associations and unions appear to have solid bases for present and future membership; eastern Germany appears well poised for future economic growth and modernization in both manufacturing and services.[21]

Although membership density is lower for employer associations in the East than in the West, most large firms belong. The associations have established offices and a network of services, and have taken an aggressive stance in pursuit of broadly acceptable collective bargaining agreements. Union membership density, by contrast, is higher in most sectors in the East than in the West and appears likely to remain so.[22] Unions across a range of sectors have established solid membership bases that include most elected works and personnel council (the public-sector equivalent of the works council) members, who have in turn been trained in codetermination rights by the unions. While the building of effective shop-steward-based, plant-level union organization proceeds slowly, some progress has been made, especially at large plants. Successful labor conflicts and bargaining outcomes, above all in the metal industry, have helped to establish a workplace base for union influence.

While economic collapse, deindustrialization, and mass unemployment have taken an enormous economic and personal toll, there is important evidence of modernization. Innovations in many cases surpass standard practice in the West, including new technology (new machinery in the factories; the installation of a state-of-the-art fiber optic network for eastern

---

21. See also Soskice and Schettkat 1993 and Wever 1995. For additional sector studies, see Silvia 1993 and Fichter 1991 and 1993. In addition to the case studies in metals and electronics, my associates and I also conducted interviews in 1993–94 in the chemical industry, the public sector, and postal services and telecommunications, which together reinforced findings from the pattern-setting metal industries. Particularly striking was the extent to which representatives on both sides of the labor-management divide in other sectors watched events in the metal industries, and especially the strike of 1993, for indications of their own future bargaining prospects.

22. As of December 31, 1992, eastern members accounted for 30.8 percent of the total membership of the DGB unions at a time when eastern population and workforce were about 20 percent of the German total (Kittner 1994, 85–86).

telecommunications); and innovative production organization (semiautonomous group work, just-in-time supplier relations). Sectoral evidence shows a potentially solid base for economic take-off in the East.

Although numerous small and medium-sized employers may be undercutting established bargaining standards, this is likely to be a temporary phenomenon in a very difficult period of adjustment, tolerated in the short run by both unions and employer associations. Collective bargaining coverage is well established throughout the eastern economy, setting standards that are widely followed or at the very least used as benchmarks. While employer association membership is lower in the East than in the West (and also appears set to remain so), most large firms and many medium-sized firms in eastern Germany belong to the associations and themselves engaged in ongoing recruiting efforts to expand membership.[23]

The most serious problem for modernization in eastern Germany is deindustrialization. The "industrial core" has dropped to a dangerously low level, beyond which the necessary networks and infrastructure for the expansion of modern industry may no longer be available. On the other hand, the skills base is substantial in eastern Germany, contributing to a steady rise in productivity. When viewed next to comparable areas such as Northern Ireland, where great effort has been expended to develop industry, "underlying productivity" has risen considerably more rapidly in eastern Germany (Hitchens, Wagner, and Birnie 1993). Given access to western capital, the transfer of an institututional framework from western Germany, and a solid human capital base in the East, the possibility is strong for rapid growth in spite of rising wages.[24] Major sources of rising productivity include new work organization, retraining, increased intensity of work, and new plant and technology (Wagner, Hitchens, and Birnie 1994). Although far from a foregone conclusion, there is still a very real possibility that the prediction of eastern managers and works councillors will come true: that the East will in time become the most modern part of Germany.[25]

23. Parallel to the sector-level evidence presented here, Razeen Sally and Douglas Webber (1994) present macro-level evidence on the Solidarity Pact negotiations of 1992–93, and Webber (1994) analyzes the policies of the Treuhand, both of which demonstrate a "resurgence of the German model," including an active political and economic role for unions and employer associations. See also Wever 1995 on the intensification of "negotiated adjustment" in eastern Germany.

24. At thirty-two case-study plants in eastern Germany, Hitchens, Wagner, and Birnie (1993, 79–82) found that underlying productivity rose 50 percent in a one-year period, from June 1990 to June 1991.

25. Kern (1994) argues that the unions are now in a position to play a major role in both eastern and western Germany in promoting industrial policy and the renewal of the German production model, as an important contribution toward future economic development in both East and West.

EXPLAINING RESILIENCE

Three factors in particular stand out as most persuasive in explaining the consolidation and resilience of social partnership in eastern Germany. First, the transfer of institutions from West to East has provided an important framework or superstructure for social partnership in the East. Employer associations, industrial unions, comprehensive collective bargaining, elected works councils, and legally mandated codetermination have all been transferred from western to eastern Germany. In the absence of this institutional apparatus, it is difficult to imagine the rapid consolidation of cohesive and encompassing interest groups that could engage in meaningful bargaining relationships (and indeed no such consolidation has occurred in other eastern European countries where institutional transfer is not the case). Works councils, unions, employer associations, individual employers—all have used collective bargaining or codetermination channels to promote their interests and negotiate settlements.

Second, this institutional apparatus has taken root in the remnants of the old system; the institutions, in other words, have proven compatible with and adaptable to the existing historical legacy. The combination of inherited skills and a tradition of informal, common workplace effort (itself in part a response to dysfunctional authoritarian relations in the old system), for example, has provided a base both for modern production innovations such as teamwork and for works council and union solidarity and activism. In the new soil, however, the institutions have changed. In the common struggle for survival and the protection of remaining jobs, for example, works councils cooperate closely with management—more so than in the West— while at the same time pursuing close union-works council relations. Unions collaborate with employers in the building of new institutions, such as the widespread Employment and Training Companies at the firm level (Knuth 1993) and broader industrial policy efforts at the *Land* level (such as Atlas in Saxony; Kern 1994). The extent to which such innovations indicate long-lasting institutional recombination or change remains an open question.

Finally, within the framework set by institutional transfer and historical legacy, actors have made choices that have promoted social partnership. At the plant and firm level, employees and elected works councillors have decided overwhelmingly to join unions, and in many cases to give active support to union-led campaigns when called upon to do so. At the industry level, metal and electronics workers quite surprisingly chose to back a risky strike that consolidated the position of pattern-setting IG Metall in eastern Germany. Large employers, for their part, have chosen to belong to appropriate employer associations and to give their backing to comprehensive collective bargaining. At the same time, the militance of small and medium-sized employers, many of them not members of the associations, has pushed employer associations to take the offensive in collective bargaining. This latter choice (one among a menu of possibilities) has in turn resulted in (1) contractual adjustments and innovations, including the lengthening of the time period for phased-in wage parity, that made social partnership more affordable in the East; and (2) a solidaristic labor response that has considerably strengthened the position of unions in the East.

Social partnership, in other words, has established itself in eastern Germany because of appropriate institutions (transferred in from the West), the flexible adaptation of these institutions to existing historical legacies, and the choices that individuals and organizations have made to support, stretch, and work within these given channels. The evidence points to each of these as necessary conditions for the consolidation and resilience of social partnership in the East.

For proponents of social partnership, however, the story does not necessarily have a happy ending. As an important component of market regulation in the new Germany, social partnership now finds itself saddled with the imperative to solve enormous problems and meet high expectations. Widespread and at this point inevitable dissatisfaction in the East, which in 1993 IG Metall was able to channel into a winning strike effort, could just as easily in the future take shape as dissatisfaction with the accomplishments of unions and employer associations, and the framework agreements they have negotiated. If the major economic and social problems facing unified Germany are not solved by existing actors operating withing the given institutional framework, the expansion of social partnership to eastern Germany could be the beginning of its end.

Institutional expansion, certainly in the contemporary German case, requires institutional change in order to solve new problems. Such change can be a source of institutional reinvigoration—as, for example, dissatisfied eastern members, with higher percentages of white-collar employees and women, push for organizational reform within the unions. If, on the other hand, change and reinvigoration are resisted or fail, expansion can lead to organizational decline. Although the extension of modern relations of social partnership into eastern Germany is no longer in question, the future success of this mode of market regulation remains unknown. The institutions of social partnership will either find new life, reinvigoration, and reform in the new Germany or, overtaxed and unable to make the necessary changes, they will stagnate and decline.

REFERENCES

Armingeon, Klaus. 1991. "Ende einer Erfolgsstory? Gewerkschaften und Arbeitsbeziehungen im Einingungsprozeß." *Gegenwartskunde* 1: 29–42.

Baylis, Thomas A. 1993. "Transforming the East German Economy: Shock without Therapy." In Huelshoff, Markovits, and Reich 1993, 77–92.

Bispinck, Reinhard. 1993a. "Collective Bargaining in East Germany: Between Economic Constraints and Political Regulations." *Cambridge Journal of Economics* 17: 309–31.

——. 1993b. "Der Tarifkonflikt um den Stufenplan in der ostdeutschen Metallindustrie." *WSI Mitteilungen* 46, no. 8: 469–81.

Fichter, Michael. 1991. "From Transmission Belt to Social Partnership? The Case of Organized Labor in Eastern Germany." *German Politics and Society* 23 (Summer): 21–39.

——. 1993. "A House Divided: A View of German Unification as It Has Affected Organised Labour." *German Politics* 2, no. 1: 21–39.

Grabher, Gernot. 1992. "Eastern Conquista: The 'Truncated Industrialization' of East European Regions by Large West European Corporations." In H. Ernste and V. Meier, eds., *Regional Development: A Contemporary Response*. London: Bellhaven.

Hall, Peter A. 1986. *Governing the Economy: The Politics of State Intervention in Britain and France*. New York: Oxford University Press.

Hitchens, D. M. W. N., K. Wagner, and J. E. Birnie. 1993. *East German Productivity and the Transition to the Market Economy*. Aldershot: Avebury.

Huelshoff, Michael G., Andrei S. Markovits, and Simon Reich, eds. 1993. *From Bundesrepublik to Deutschland: German Politics after Unification*. Ann Arbor: University of Michigan Press.

Jürgens, Ulrich, Larissa Klinzing, and Lowell Turner. 1993. "The Transformation of Industrial Relations in Eastern Germany." *Industrial and Labor Relations Review* 46, no. 2: 229–44.

Katz, Harry C., and Thomas A. Kochan. 1992. *An Introduction to Collective Bargaining and Industrial Relations*. New York: McGraw-Hill.

Kern, Horst. 1991. "Die Transformation der östlichen Industrien: Soziologische Reflexionen über die Ex-DDR." *Die Neue Gesellschaft: Frankfurter Hefte* 38: 2, 114–21.

——. 1994. "Intelligente Regulierung: Gewerkschaftliche Beiträge in Ost und West zur Erneuerung des deutschen Produktionsmodells." *Soziale Welt* 45, no. 1: 33–59.

Kittner, Michael, ed. 1991. *Gewerkschaftsjahrbuch 1991*. Cologne: Bund-Verlag.

——, ed. 1994. *Gewerkschaften Heute: Jahrbuch für Arbeitnehmerfragen, 1994.* Köln: Bund-Verlag.

Knuth, Matthias. 1993. "Employment and Training Companies: Bridging Unemployment in the East German Crash." Paper prepared for the Conference of the Society for the Advancement of Socio-Economics, New York, March 26–28.

Mahnkopf, Birgit. 1991. "Vorwärts in die Vergangenheit? Pessimistische Spekulationen über die Zukunft der Gewerkschaften in der neuen Bundesrepublik." In Westphal et al. 1991, 269–94.

——. 1993. "The Impact of Unification on the German System of Industrial Relations." Discussion Paper FS I 93–102, Wissenschaftszentrum Berlin für Sozialforschung.

Markovits, Andrei S. 1986. *The Politics of the West German Trade Unions.* Cambridge: Cambridge University Press.

Polanyi, Karl. 1957. *The Great Transformation: The Political and Economic Origins of Our Time.* Boston: Beacon Press.

Röbenack, Silke, and Gabriella Hartung. 1992. "Strukturwandel industrieller Beziehungen in Ostdeutschen Industriebetrieben." Monograph AG 3/3, for the Commission for Research in Social and Political Transformation in the New States, Berlin.

Sally, Razeen, and Douglas Webber. 1994. "The German Solidarity Pact: A Case Study in the Politics of the Unified Germany." *German Politics* 3, no. 1: 18–46.

Silvia, Stephen J. 1993. " 'Holding the Shop Together': Old and New Challenges to the German System of Industrial Relations in the mid 1990s." Berliner Arbeitshefte und Berichte zur sozialwissenschaftlichen Forschung, no. 83, Freie Universität Berlin, Zentralinstitut für sozialwissenschaftliche Forschung.

——. 1994. "A House Divided: Employers and the Challenge to Pattern Bargaining in a United Germany." Unpublished manuscript, American University.

Soskice, David, and Ronald Schettkat. 1993. "West German Labor Market Institutions and East German Transformation." In Ulman, Eichengreen, and Dickens 1993, 102–27.

Stark, David. 1992. "Path Dependency and Privatization Strategies in East-Central Europe." *East European Politics and Societies* 6, no. 1: 17–54.

——. 1994. "Recombinant Property in Eastern European Capitalism." Unpublished manuscript, Cornell University, Ithaca, N.Y.

Streeck, Wolfgang. 1991. "More Uncertainties: German Unions Facing 1992." *Industrial Relations* 30, no. 3: 317–49.

Turner, Lowell. 1998. *"Defending the High Road: Labor and Politics in Unified Germany."* Ithaca: Cornell University Press.

Ulman, Lloyd, Barry Eichengreen, and William T. Dickens, eds. 1993. *Labor and an Integrated Europe.* Washington, D.C.: Brookings Institution.

Voskamp, Ulrich, and Volker Wittke. 1991. "Aus Modernisierungsblockaden werden Abwärtsspiralen: Zur Reorganisation von Betrieben und Kombinaten der ehemaligen DDR." *Berliner Journal der Soziologie* 1: 17–39.

Webber, Douglas. 1994. "The Decline and Resurgence of the German Model: The Treuhandanstalt and Privatisation Politics in East Germany." *Journal of European Public Policy* 1, no. 2: 151–75.

Westphal, Andreas, Hansjörg Herr, Michael Heine, and Ulrich Busch, eds. 1991. *Wirtschaftspolitische Konsequenzen der deutschen Vereinigung.* Frankfurt: Campus Verlag.

Wever, Kirsten S. 1995. *Negotiating Competitiveness: Employment Relations and Organizational Innovation in Germany and the United States.* Boston: Harvard Business School Press.

Wiesenthal, Helmut, Wilfried Ettl, and Christiane Bialas. 1992. "Interessenverbände im Transformationsprozeß." Arbeitsgruppe Transformationsprozesse in den neuen Bundesländern, Humboldt Universität, Max-Planck-Gesellschaft, Working Paper AG TRAP, no. 92/10, Berlin.

Womack, James P., Daniel T. Jones, and Daniel Roos. 1990. *The Machine That Changed the World: The Story of Lean Production.* New York: Rawson Associates.

2 • The Political Economy of Crisis and Reform

6 • Institutions Challenged: German Unification, Policy Errors, and The "Siren Song" of Deregulation

Christopher S. Allen

The 1990s have witnessed a critical reexamination of the foundations of the German postwar political economy. An institutional pattern characterized by a financial system integrated with and supportive of export-oriented manufacturing, close coordination among private and public sectors, and a toleration and acceptance of highly skilled and highly paid workers with increasingly shorter work weeks is under intense strain. Despite generally superior economic performance from the mid-1980s to the early 1990s, the condition of the German model in the mid-1990s is not enviable.

Clearly, Chancellor Helmut Kohl's center-right CDU/FDP government misjudged greatly both the economic and the political costs of unification. Moreover, as impressive as German institutions have been for enhancing economic competitiveness and solidifying the social market economy, they assume—if not require—a relatively stable and predictable sociopolitical order. Here, the Kohl center-right government has generally failed to provide the kind of basic institutional infrastructure that its center-right predecessor did during an earlier period of major reconstruction, in the early 1950s (Allen 1989). What accounts for these policy missteps and why has there been a departure from the German pattern of economic and industrial policymaking of the past two decades?

To understand the German organized capitalist model of the 1990s, it is first necessary to situate the framework of Germany's political economy

Research support for this project was generously provided by the German Marshall Fund (Grant #3–53619).

during the late 1980s and early 1990s through descriptive analysis of the domestic institutional structure of the apparently successful social market economy, an institutional model that produced strong German economic performance and confounded those who had predicted its stagnation during the early 1980s. The critics' belief that Germany's "model" economy would falter was based on a misunderstanding of the specific structure of the German economy and institutions.

Appearances to the contrary, German organized capitalism is an effective, but poorly understood, response to the challenges of unification. Three adverse policy choices in the economic integration of the five new *Bundesländer* in the post-unification years deviated from expected patterns of industrial adjustment. Private and public sector actors have embraced policies that were not only unsuccessful but also departed from prevailing and successful German industrial practice. Apparently German policymakers turned away from well-internalized and successful patterns of adaptation to deal with three problems specific to unification. In essence, German policymakers seemed to have lost their "institutional memory" of how an economy was successfully rebuilt and effective economic policy was formulated in the ten years that came to be known as the *Wirtschaftswunder*. And because of this "amnesia," they found themselves open to Anglo-American policy options that have proven much less appropriate for Germany than for the United States and Britain.

German policymakers need to rediscover the nuanced institutional relationships that enhance and enable public policy to function in the Federal Republic. But they cannot do this unless they first have a clear and explicit conceptual model of the institutions that served Germany so well in the past.

THE INSTITUTIONS OF GERMAN ORGANIZED CAPITALISM

For much of the early to mid-1980s, conventional wisdom suggested that the era of the "German Model" was over.[1] The demise of the last Helmut Schmidt government in 1982 apparently heralded a turning point that was more than just a change in political direction from the SPD to the CDU. Many observers argued that German organized capitalism would have to take a more laissez-faire direction and that the entrenched institutions that gave the German model its identity were no longer effective (Nussbaum 1983; Olson 1982). These authors—and others—looked to the free market policies of the Reagan and Thatcher regimes for approaches more appropriate to the modern era. Critics argued that the problems besetting the

---

1. Portions of the following are based on Wever and Allen 1992 and 1993.

Federal Republic—bureaucratic institutions, oligopolistic industry, highly paid union workers, generous social spending—were amenable to the "solutions" offered by the market-oriented, privatized, deregulatory, anti-union policies of the United States and Britain (Wilkes 1984). By the mid-1980s, conventional wisdom suggested that a dramatic change in the Federal Republic was necessary.

The conventional wisdom proved wrong. Despite alleged institutional rigidities, the German economy proved capable of maintaining its export orientation, high wage levels, and high productivity into the early 1990s. While talk of a *Modell Deutschland* may have disappeared with the end of the center-left Schmidt government in 1982, there was a substance and durability to Germany's organized capitalism that was not easily perceived (Piore and Sabel 1984). Without understanding the specifics of Germany's framework regulations and networks of relationships, it was easy to view the German political economy as "sclerotic." This misunderstanding was rooting in flawed perceptions of how existing flexible institutions supported the Federal Republic's competitive economy.

What were the components of this institutional arrangement? First of all, it is a system and not just a collection of firms and/or discrete policies. It is a pattern of running a capitalist democracy in which business, labor, and government work together to develop consensual policy solutions to national, regional, state-level, and local issues. Germans speak of their "social" (not "free") market economy, reflecting a deeply entrenched belief that business must share the responsibility of providing a stable economic and social order.

German business, labor, and government embrace a conception of regulation different from that commonly used elsewhere. Rather than see regulation as a stark choice between laissez-faire and state control, Germany has created *Rahmenbedingungen* (framework regulations)—a loose framework that encompasses both public and private sectors. These *Rahmenbedingungen* have produced a system that is often called externally rigid but internally flexible (Hirschman 1970). In short, this system regulates not the details but the rules of the game all actors must play. To quote one of the founders of the social market economy, Wilhelm Röpke, concerning the economic system that was established in the late 1940s:

> [Our program] consists of measures and institution which impart to competition the framework, rules, and machinery of impartial supervision which a competitive system needs as much as any game or match if it is not to degenerate into a vulgar brawl. A genuine, equitable, and smoothly functioning competitive system can not in fact survive without a judicious moral and legal framework and without regular supervision of the conditions under

which competition can take place pursuant to real efficiency principles. This presupposes mature economic discernment on the part of all responsible bodies and individuals and a strong impartial state. (Röpke 1982)

Labor, business, and government at all levels support an elaborate vocational education and apprenticeship system. As the foundation for high-quality manufacturing, these skill systems have received increasing attention as a reason for the apparent anomaly of a high-wage—yet internationally competitive—economy. Clearly, the unions have been entrenched in the economic and political life of the nation, including (and especially) the vocational education and apprenticeship system. To be sure, industrial relations rhetoric can be as conflict-laden as in Britain and even as chaotic at times as in Italy or France. But political compromise has been far easier to achieve in Germany. Observers have associated the Federal Republic with industrial peace and social tranquility, in large measure reinforced by the emphasis on worker education and skills.

The German political economy has in fact required a fair measure of social consensus. Industry's responses to changes in markets have almost always been endorsed by labor—by workers, works councils, and unions. In highly visible public debates labor and business hammer out their differences about, for example, the length of the work week, the nature of codetermination, or the provision of both initial and ongoing training, as well as retraining for workers in declining or rapidly changing industries. Consensus at the national level has presupposed a certain level of agreement about local issues. This is achieved in Germany through plant-or workplace-level bargaining between local managers and works councils. The councils are nationally mandated, democratically elected bodies representing blue- and white-collar workers. They have broad rights to information about the economic situation of the plant or firm, to consultation about many types of organizational changes, and to codetermination regarding basic personnel decisions, to include hiring, transfers, layoffs, and overtime (see Chapter 1 in this book). The councils rely on union expertise about the implications for employees of organizational change and industrial adjustment (Wever and Allen 1993). Largely because of this union influence, local negotiation between labor and management can generally be brought into line with national developments (Thelen 1992). As a result, the national-local union fragmentation so common elsewhere has been avoided.

Labor influence in strategic matters such as investment decisions or the introduction of new technology is also considerable. In large firms strategic codetermination effectively allows for 49 percent labor representation on supervisory boards. As such, employees have "voice" that can sometimes influence management decisions; in any case they receive information about investment and other strategic plans early in the planning process.[2] In typical German annual reports, for instance, employees and the public at large are referred to as the major stakeholders in the company. Shareholders are rarely referred to at all.

The unions, their federation, and the industry and employer associations commonly hammer out private agreements or even public contracts regarding most major public policy questions. Not only are German unions integrally involved in the definition and administration of the apprenticeship training system from the national to the local levels, but they also play central roles in the development and implementation of various other labor market policies and institutions, such as the transition out of noncompetitive industries and the establishment of employment agencies in the former East Germany (Turner 1992).

Among employers, there is also a tight-knit sense of organization that is reinforced by national industry-wide institutions such as the Bundesverband der Deutschen Industrie (Federal Association of German Industry, or BDI) and by employer groups such as the Bundesvereinigung der deutschen Arbeitgeberverbände (Federal Association of German Employers, or BDA) and the Deutscher Industrie- und Handelstag (Chamber of Commerce, or DIHT) (Braunthal 1965).

These peak organizations are far more than just lobbying groups. Rather, they often frame issues for industries and individual firms via their research branches, as well as develop general strategies for international competitiveness and negotiate with government at all levels on industrial policies. Although private organizations, they are granted considerable power and responsibility to organize their members and shape public policy. They are more than simple interest groups in that they are explicitly chartered by the state to perform important public policy functions. As such, they also carry significant obligations to balance the priorities of international competitiveness against the need for social peace.

In part, these organizations also stand as a counterpoint to the highly organized unions, developing collective bargaining strategies for entire industries and regions of the country. Moreover, these employer groups include subnational member units that function at regional and local levels, further reinforcing the sense of an interpenetrated organized capitalism. These private-sector organizations have been augmented and reinforced by public-sector agencies that take a "framing" role (Katzenstein 1987) rather than a "dirigiste" one.

The function of the public sector at all levels is to frame, not direct,

---

2. The receipt of this early information makes it possible for works councils to develop proactive strategies to shape organizational change before it occurs.

Germany's organized capitalism. This is one of the duties of not only the federal government but the regional government as well. The regional governments are much more important in this area than is commonly realized. The economic problems that developed in Germany after the first oil shock in 1973 were much more sector-and region-specific than they had been during the postwar reconstruction period (Hueglin 1986). And the coming to power of the center-right Kohl government in 1982 meant that Bonn was less willing to intervene in economic affairs than the SPD-led governments of Willy Brandt and Helmut Schmidt had been. Regional governments in the 1980s began to take increasingly active steps on their own. They somewhat less successfully pressed the federal government for increased aid and coordination and implored the federal system to prevent the reductions of certain subsidies for hard-hit industries (Fach 1990). Taken together, these policies laid to rest the "Eurosclerosis" arguments of the early 1980s (Olson 1982), since in the 1990s the Federal Republic still had the world's third-highest GNP, surpassed only by the United States and Japan (with one-fourth the population of the former and one-half the population of the latter). These policies enabled the German economy to combine order and adaptation—a kind of "shared capitalism"—in ways that neither free market nor statist analyses can recognize.

The other key component of the German political economy—the financial system—has been dominated for years by a small number of huge universal banks, the three largest being Deutsche, Dresdner, and Commerz (universal banks are banks that perform all financial functions). In order to rebuild rapidly after World War II the policymakers in the new Bonn government established a banking system based on a nineteenth-century model that could allocate large amounts of capital quickly and effectively. Unlike the American system, the German banking system is not restricted by detailed regulations that separate financial functions. German banks are free to own stock, sit on boards of directors, vote large numbers of proxy shares, and make long-term loans to most firms, large and small. The link between great institutional power and the investment needs of individual firms has made the banks major actors in the maintenance of the country's overall economic health (Shonfield 1965). In general, the German banking system's postwar preference for monetary stability has greatly reduced the desire for speculation that has often characterized aspects of American finance. During the 1980s German industry evolved from the earlier "one firm-one bank" ("house bank") relationship toward a looser system of "organized finance capitalism" (Oberbeck and Baethge 1989; Esser 1989). Despite this move to "banking networks" (Deeg 1992), there still remains a German preference for long-term investment, the presence of the banks on company boards, and the interpenetration among leaders of industry and finance.

In short, German banks remain an integral component of economic growth.[3] The banks—at all levels—are still "universal" in that they can perform all banking functions, unlike American banks, which are limited to acting in relatively narrow realms, such as mortgages, commercial loans, and so on. Moreover, German banks have maintained a system of self-regulation and self-insurance that requires them to interact regularly and frequently and reflects their status and self-conception as major and responsible actors in a larger system. Taking on this responsibility has enabled them to develop a private self-insurance system that has suffered far fewer losses than the public F.D.I.C. in the United States.

Taken together, these institutional patterns have proved more encompassing, durable, and effective than many critics anticipated.[4] The combination of framing regulations, social partners, organized business (especially small business), and a strategic system of long-term finance represented values to which many countries aspire.

The success of this model of institutionalized adaptation raises some profound questions. Does this system remain durable in the wake of domestic and international challenges of the 1990s? If so, what explains the apparent departure from this pattern toward more deregulatory forms in three specific post-unification policy areas? And are the Germans still interested in—or capable of—rediscovering their organized capitalist pattern and challenging the laissez-faire models characteristic of industrialized countries in the 1990s?

GERMAN ECONOMIC POLICY AFTER UNIFICATION

Just as conventional wisdom was wrong to predict the demise of German industrial competitiveness in the early 1980s, the "new" conventional wisdom in the early 1990s was also wrong to predict the continuation of a smoothly functioning German economic juggernaut. The Kohl government badly misjudged the costs of unification and the institutional resources necessary to integrate the five new federal states into a unified Germany. The

---

3. The contrast to the U.S. and British equities trading systems is particularly sharp. For instance, in 1987 (the latest year for which comparable figures are currently available) shareholders' equity as a percentage of total equity in manufacturing companies was 43 percent in the United States, 46 percent in Britain, and 27 percent in Germany (O.E.C.D., *National Accounts*, 1990).

4. For an excellent theoretical treatment of dynamic institutions, see Steinmo, Thelen, and Longstreth 1992.

structural challenges the German economy faced in the mid-1990s were far more extensive than any that the Federal Republic had experienced since the 1950s; and the West German-specific nature of their institutions (even when working well) made it difficult to impose them on—or even transfer them as a model to—the new eastern regions.

By mid-1992, Kohl finally acknowledged the obvious: the successful integration of the eastern economy into the western one would cost much more and take far longer than originally predicted (Bering 1992). The costs of reconstruction in the early and mid-1990s regularly exceeded 20 percent of the entire budget. In addition, funds from private firms, regional governments, and other subsidies amounted to billions of DM more; all expenditures combined, however, were not enough to make the assimilation process go more smoothly (Neckermann 1992). There remained a large gap in the productivity levels between the two regions, and the Treuhand (the government reconstruction agency) quickly privatized some 7,000 of the total of 11,000 firms that it had taken over. One of the most significant of the costs of this transition was massive unemployment in the East.

Pessimistic observers began to suggest that these stresses had placed the German political economy in a precarious position. Germany's economic prowess has resided in certain manufacturing industries whose goods may be eminently exportable, but many of whose technologies are decidedly "low," and the costs of wages continued to rise. The costs of the "social" market economy, as witnessed by the costs of unification, pressed on the upper limits of Germany's capacity to pay. Massive budget cuts—far higher than even imagined in 1992—became imperative by the spring of 1993.

In addition, tensions arose between the former East and former West Germans. While easterners resented the slow pace of change and high unemployment, western Germans have been bitter about losing jobs to easterners and paying—through increased taxes—for the cleanup of the ecological and infrastructural disaster inherited from the former East German regime. Also, racism has returned, often in the form of violent attacks on Asians, Turks, and others who "look" foreign (Roberts 1992). The two major parties—Christian Democrats and Social Democrats, as well as the chancellor himself—have been strangely passive in the face of this upsurge of neo-Nazi groups and racial violence.

What surprised many observers sympathetic to the "organized adaptation" view of German patterns of adjustment was the apparent inability of German policymakers to "return to form." Neither the Kohl government nor the private sector acted to establish an investment-oriented economy supplemented by a "safety net" for those most hurt by the transition to German unity modeled after the Wirtschaftswunder and the Sozialemarktwirtschaft (Grande 1987). No one seriously asserts that either phenomenon should or could have been magically recreated forty years after their original appearance; they were products of their time and times have changed. However, private-and public-sector actors in the early 1990s in Germany seemed to have forgotten that they ever happened.

A deeper look at the reconstruction of the former GDR raises some interesting questions. First, why did neither the private nor the public sector place a greater emphasis on basic investment goods and infrastructural public sector investment? Given rapid German industrialization in the nineteenth century and the rapid German reindustrialization during the Wirtschaftswunder years of the 1950s, it is clear that private and public officials should known better how to lead the reconstruction of the new federal states (Wallich 1955; Erhard 1962). In fact, several retired banking officials from the three large German banks (Deutsche, Dresdner, and Commerz) were called out of retirement to serve as consultants to contemporary banking officials precisely because they had direct experience during the Wirtschaftswunder in introducing a new currency, handling massive amounts of industrial investment, and creating a network of business services. They embodied an institutional memory that should have stood the economic reconstruction process in good stead. In other words, this was not a new exercise. Since the economic problems remained daunting, the mystery is why more appropriate policies were not pursued.

PROPERTY OWNERSHIP

One of the first departures from "form" in the five new states was the basic issue of providing the foundations for fixed capital investment. Take the problem of personal property ownership. Before investment could take place in the former GDR, some clarity on title to property was needed. This was complicated by the fact that property had been confiscated without compensation by the Nazis (1933–45) and the Soviet occupation forces (1945–49), as well as during the years of the GDR (1949–90). With this basic issue unresolved, economic growth and investment remained stalled throughout the early 1990s. The most difficult aspect of this issue—at least for the Kohl government—was that of compensation. The unification treaty stated that any compensation for property taken had to be paid at "current market value." The problem with this formulation was that the new federal states were just establishing a market system and the value of particular properties varied widely in these states, depending on whether surrounding property had begun to be developed or not. The treaty also stated, however, that a slightly less difficult option might be available, namely, that confiscated property could be returned to its owners.

The situation for commercial property was a only a little less difficult.

While some private western German firms made major commitments to invest, substantial productive commitment of private resources remained low. The two industries that moved physical capital investment most quickly were the two mainstays of the western German economy: machine tools and industrial electronics. While massive reinvestment was necessary to make machine tools a profitable sector in the five new *Länder,* many observers felt that there was at least a solid foundation to build on. With respect to industrial electronics, the giant firm Siemens was the first to step forward. Siemens's primary strength is in telecommunications; and the need for creating a modern telephone and communications system in the East was daunting. In fact, a large amount of the funding for such investment was to come from the federal government. Siemens, a maker of electrical appliances and computer equipment, was also expected to find a large demand for its consumer goods in the East. Aside from initial interest in these two sectors, however, rapid growth did not follow because the property issue had not been settled. Why not? Basic investment in industry and infrastructure requires clear title to property; yet the Kohl government postponed the smooth resolution of this issue.

CURRENCY REFORM

A second basic policy departure concerned currency reform and "social market" policies. Massive investment was needed to restore such basic functions as telecommunications and transportation and to clean up the environment. Research institutes estimated that the total public sector investment needed to rebuild the new federal states would total in the hundreds of billions of DM during the early 1990s, with large portions of that sum going to the ministries of telecommunications, rail, and the environment. This investment was delayed because for most of the early 1990s Kohl had argued that new taxes would not be needed to pay for the costs of integrating the former GDR into the Federal Republic (Neckermann 1992). The realities of unification, however, left the government no choice.

When the old East German reichsmarks were exchanged for deudeutschmarks, policy was much more consumption-oriented than was the case in the 1948 currency reform. In 1948 the policy explicitly favored property-holders; the Kohl policy produced many more immediate consumer benefits and far fewer incentives for investment. Because of the human costs of economic inequality between the two regions, Kohl chose to embrace a policy that was painless in the short run but problematic for the long. Many of the subsidies that East German citizens had enjoyed were gone. Among these were housing allowances, low-cost health care, subsidized day care, and low costs for such basic services as public transportation. While wages had been low in the former GDR, costs had also been low, and workers had not had to face unemployment in the western sense. There was considerable overstaffing at many firms, for which east Germans paid dearly, but there were no destitute individuals roaming the streets as is the case in affluent western societies. When the eastern Germans voted in 1990 to give up the meager certainty of the East for the greater freedom and opportunity of the West, the costs for basic services such as housing and health rose rapidly to market levels, but their wages did not.

To be sure, immediate pressure for providing a close-to-parity exchange rate was powerful. The mystery here was why the currency reform had not been designed to promote investment-enhancing choices. Such a policy choice should have been combined with a "new social market economy" based on a realistic estimate of how long it would take for the former GDR to "catch up" with the West. After all, the Wirtschaftswunder itself had taken the better part of a decade to come to fruition.

THE TREUHAND

A third set of policy choices was also a departure from form, namely the formation of the Treuhandanstalt (Trusteeship Agency). While it was part of the institutional legacy of the GDR, the Kohl government did nothing to harmonize the Treuhand's "mission" with the prevailing institutional norms of FRG economic policymaking. The Treuhand took a different philosophical position on the relationship between state and market than was the norm in Germany. Most economic policies in Germany—the most notable and egregious exception being those of the Nazi period—tried to avoid sharp choices between "state" and "market." In fact, the precondition of the German political economy since the late nineteenth century was the sense of "framework regulations" *(Rahmenbedingungen)* in which the state created a stable outer boundary—within which all actors had to play— but then allowed large amounts of flexibility and freedom "within" the framework. We can contrast this model with that of the United States (and other laissez-faire-oriented polities), where the opposite vision prevails: an assumption of "limitless opportunity" in the market, and a state that steps in only to regulate specific "market irregularities."

The Treuhand's operational philosophy seemed much more akin to the "state versus market" philosophy of regulation than it did to the more "normal" German pattern. Rather than carefully evaluate which firms— and their supplier networks—might serve as a foundation for new growth, the Treuhand took a "scorched earth" approach (Kern and Sabel 1991). Its operational assumption was that few, if any, of the former firms were worth saving. The only option that logically followed was the "scorched earth" rapid privatization of as many firms as possible. The effect of this policy was to undercut the potential formation in the five new federal states of the kind of institutional pattern upon which the former West Germany had relied.

Moreover, the Treuhand's hegemony distorted and undercut the coordination among the governing coalition partners necessary to produce effective, specific policies. The FDP, the party most sympathetic to Laissez-faire ideas, wanted to make the former GDR a "low-tax area," somewhat similar to the demands in the United States by some free markets for "enterprise zones." The CDU preferred to give targeted tax concessions to those firms and individuals that would commit to investing in the eastern states. While the goals were similar, the debate bespoke a more philosophical disagreement about whether laissez faire conditions should be created (FDP) or whether the state should maintain a more guiding hand in the transition to capitalism in the form of specific tax breaks for specific types of investment (CDU). There was also a dispute between the CSU on the one hand and the CDU/FDP on the other on the issue of rent subsidies. The CSU wanted to guarantee that rents in the eastern states would rise no more than 15 percent over three years while the CDU and FDP wanted the figure set at 20 percent. On both questions the CDU position prevailed.

With these basic policy choices made, a significant departure from the pattern of basic German foundational principles became evident. Kohl had sold unification well, and many former East German citizens wanted to look forward not backward, which explains their general indifference to the parties of the left. But this "selling" of unification took place at tremendous cost. Kohl's plan was a clear departure from policy options that had proven themselves over time. Consequently, it is not surprising to see the low ebb of political support for the center-right government in the face of the economic and political dislocation that followed. The question here is why this very "un-German" state versus market set of choices was made rather than the more expected "quasi-public" one?

GERMANY AND THE "SIREN SONG" OF DEREGULATION

Do these three departures from form suggest that Germany's system of organized capitalism is fundamentally changing? Is it moving toward a more Anglo-American deregulatory model? These are the kinds of policy suggestions that are currently emerging as the Federal Republic faces its severest economic challenge since its first decade of existence. One of the most effective responses that Germans, from both the private and public sectors, have made in the past in response to the siren songs of laissez faire, privatization, and deregulation was that those options were not needed because the German system "worked." This assessment now seems vulnerable.

Does this mean then that the unique form of Germany's political economy (organized, flexible capitalism with an active but non-dirigiste state presence) has had its day?

CORE FOUNDATIONS FOR ECONOMIC GROWTH

Several authors argue that the specific characteristics of German organized capitalism—patient, long-term capital investment; the emphasis on producing goods and not just services; and a highly skilled workforce—are a necessity for any internationally competitive economy. These components of the German system are most definitely still present. It remains for political and economic actors to realize where their strengths are and to resist the lure of policies that promise much but have proved questionable even in the countries where they have been most enthusiastically embraced.

For example, Lowell Turner offers an overview of the challenges that face Germany in the labor market arena and suggests that there are explicit choices that can produce adaptation along recognizably German lines (Turner 1992). Adjustment challenges are more sharply defined in the eastern part of Germany than in the western. Turner suggests that local diversity may be nowhere more critical to successful restructuring than in the East, and his research indicates that local "outcomes" are indeed varied. He describes a continuum from a "polarization" to a "modernization" scenario and argues that both are equally possible at this historical moment. "Polarization" occurs where management tries to profit at the expense of high labor standards. Modernization occurs where labor is integrated into a productive and flexible partnership that takes advantage of the latest organizational and production innovations and new technologies. Interviews with management and with union and works council representatives in former East Germany leads him to find no reason why unions should not be able to influence employers to embrace modernization; however, mobilizing the German institutional capacity to address these changes will require supportive policies in other areas as well.

In addition, the production of high-quality manufactures for export depends on a highly skilled workforce. (Sandholtz and Zysman 1989) such a workforce cannot exist without extensive apprenticeship, retraining, and further training mechanisms. These in turn function only on the basis of close consensus among the "social partners" who shape and administer these programs. That consensus hinges on the strong position of the unions in both regional and industry-level bargaining and in joint business-labor decision-making forums at the federal, state, and local levels. This coordinated and centralized approach to policymaking is not possible in the absence of powerful and pervasive employer and industry associations capable of negotiating with the unions and government on all important matters of public policy. Centralized industry associations are able to act cohesively in part because of the banks' detailed involvement in strategic management decisions about long-term investments, which enables firms to focus on the long-term collective good of the economy (Lazonick 1991). Despite all its apparent deficiencies—as current conventional wisdom would have it—German economic policy still addresses the core functions that any competitive economy must perform.

Ultimately, however, the key to any future success of the German political economy is that its structure remain flexible enough to accommodate significant changes in its politics and strategies. This political and social flexibility only works under circumstances where all major societal stakeholders—including employees and their representatives—are guaranteed a central role in carrying out the processes of social and economic change (Deeg 1994). Only under these circumstances can the main social "actors"—business, labor, and state, from the local level to the national—work together to develop and implement solutions that support the common good.

SOCIALLY CONSTRUCTED INSTITUTIONS

The essence of the German organized capitalist model is that socially constructed institutions of the political economy are interposed between the free market and the parties interacting within it.[5] These institutions foster relationships rather than deals. Deals cannot tolerate changes in the environmental circumstances in which they are made. That is why they must be subordinated to legally enforceable rules. Relationships, on the other hand, can be sustained by what Kathleen Thelen calls "negotiated adjustment" (Thelen 1992), which requires a coherent framework that recognizes and supports distinct and frequently conflicting social and economic interests. While many countries stress the need for adaptive institutions, effective ones are not created easily. Other countries that try to emulate competitive institutional patterns from Germany—at the public, private, local, state, regional, or national levels—may have to create new institutions (Soskice 1991). But the German patterns of framework regulation and organized capitalism, including institutionalized worker participation, comprehensive vocational education, and a long-term investment orientation, took decades

---

5. I thank Peter Katzenstein for suggestions that have helped refine the exposition of this concept.

to develop. Actors in eastern Germany who see the value of emulating West German institutions require not just strategies but also the means to implement them. The lack of a cohesive institutional framework would severely hinder efforts to meet the domestic and international challenges facing the new federal states. Actors in the eastern states know the goals to which they must aspire, namely, a highly skilled workforce able to compete in international markets on some basis other than a combination of low labor costs and high technology production strategies (Streeck and Schmitter 1991). But whether they can or want to emulate the western German model remains to be seen. I have argued that the departure from expected policy in three areas has robbed German policymakers of their most durable and successful tools for rapid and successful economic growth. Specifically, the Kohl government made key policy choices in the early 1990s that violated the fundamental assumptions of the institutional structure that has incorporated capital, labor, and the state in a broad regulatory framework that "bounds rationality," minimizes exit, and maximizes voice.

The mystery is whether or not this departure from expected action was deliberate. If it was deliberate, perhaps we can infer that the Kohl government—like many western European governments who embraced mixed economies throughout the postwar period—was seduced by the siren song of deregulation and concluded that the old German system was no longer applicable. If it was not, German policymakers in the Kohl regime may have lost their "institutional memory." If so, these "grandchildren" of the Adenauer-Erhard regime have now made their ancestors rest much less easily than they once did.

There are at least two plausible arguments that might account for the inability or unwillingness of German policymakers to articulate and promote a renewed form of German organized capitalism for a unified Germany. One might be a legacy of the "economic giant/political dwarf" phenomenon of the 1960s-1980s period. During that time, Germany (like Japan) could pursue economic growth without having to worry about international political responsibilities. Yet in the 1990s, with Germany unified and the cold war at an end, Germany found itself unprepared to advance an explicit and specific "model" for the transformation of formerly communist regimes. There were many Europeans who might have looked askance at such an enterprise. In other words, perhaps the Germans avoided talking about a model themselves because of the historical baggage that such a discussion would generate. Maybe they thought it would be much easier to "sell" the German pattern of industrial adaptation if it was not perceived as a new form of German hegemony. In other words, pragmatism may have won out over an explicit discussion of ideological forms of economic adaptation.

There is also a second plausible argument: that many German policymakers have indeed been heavily influenced by Anglo-American patterns of domestic policymaking. These patterns have been reinforced by the increasing internationalization of domestic economies. A more likely explanation, however, suggests an unintentional "departure from form." As the best of the new institutionalist literature (Steinmo, Thelen, and Longstreth 1992) has argued, institutions are not just fixed structures. They are dynamic entities that—at their best—are embodied in purposeful policymakers and patterns of understood responses to a wide range of policy outcomes. Yet these responses are not spontaneously occurring phenomena. Institutional responses need to be understood, reinforced, and continually tested against new challenges if they are to retain the capacity to produce suitable economic strategies. Because German organized capitalism has seldom been touted as an explicit model, German policymakers who have internalized such patterns of behavior, with little explicit discussion, may not be able to articulate its merits when attacked by adherents of deregulation and laissez-faire. In numerous interviews with German officials in both private and public sectors, researchers have reported that patterns of response are often more intuitively understood than explicitly discussed. In one sense, this might suggest a beneficial shared understanding of a range of suitable responses; however, it also might indicate an actual lack of understanding of how to use past and prevailing institutional patterns to solve contemporary problems. For Germany to build—or rebuild—institutional coherence in response to contemporary policy challenges, the precise role of these institutions must be discussed and understood, not just intuited.

REFERENCES

Allen, Christopher S. 1989. "The Underdevelopment of Keynesianism in the Federal Republic of Germany." In Peter A. Hall, ed., *The Political Power of Economic Ideas: Keynesianism across Nations,* 263–89. Princeton: Princeton University Press.

Bering, Klaus. 1992. "Economic Recovery in E. Germany Set to Take Longer, Cost More." DPA News Service, July 2.

Braunthal, Gerard. 1965. *The Federation of German Industry in Politics.* Ithaca: Cornell University Press.

Deeg, Richard. 1992. "Banking, the State, and the Small Firm in West Germany." Ph.D. diss., MIT.

——. 1994. "Institutional Transfer, Social Learning and Economic Policy in Eastern Germany." Unpublished manuscript.

Erhard, Ludwig. 1962. *Deutsche Wirtschaftspolitik: Der Weg der sozialen Marktwirtschaft.* Düsseldorf: Econ.

Esser, Josef. 1989. "Bank Power in West Germany Revisited." *West European Politics* 13: 17–32.

Fach, Wolfgang. 1990. "Industrial Modernization and the Federal System: A Comparative Study on Decentralization of Innovation Policies." In Ulrich Hilpert, ed., *Regional Innovation and Decentralization,* 151–76. London: Routledge, 1991.

Grande, Edgar. 1987. "Neoconservatism and Conservative-Liberal Economic Policy in West Germany." *European Journal of Political Research* 15: 281–96.

Hirschman, Albert O. 1970. *Exit, Voice, and Loyalty.* New Haven: Yale University Press.

Hueglin, Thomas O. 1986. "Regionalism in Western Europe: Conceptual Problems of a New Political Perspective." *Comparative Politics* 18, no. 4: 439–58.

Jacoby, Wade. 1995. "Two Postwar Reconstructions: Institutional Transfer in Germany, 1945–94." Ph.D. diss., MIT.

Katzenstein, Peter J. 1987. *Politics and Policy in West Germany: The Growth of a Semi-Sovereign State.* Philadelphia: Temple University Press.

Kern, Horst, and Charles F. Sabel. 1991. "Trade Unions and Decentralized Production: A Sketch of Strategic Problems in the West German Labor Movement." *Politics and Society* 194 (December): 373–402.

Lazonick, William. 1991. *Business Organization and the Myth of the Market Economy.* New York: Cambridge University Press.

Neckermann, Peter. 1992. "What Went Wrong in Germany after the Unification?" *East European Quarterly* 26, no. 4: 447–70.

Nussbaum, Bruce. 1983. *The World after Oil.* New York: Simon & Schuster.

Oberbeck, Herbert, and Martin Baethge. 1989. "Computers and Pinstripes: German Financial Institutions between Dominant Market Control and Conservative Business Policy." In Peter J. Katzenstein, ed., *Industry and Political Change: Toward the Third West German Republic,* 275–303. Ithaca: Cornell University Press.

Olson, Mancur. 1982. *The Rise and Decline of Nations: Economic Growth, Stagflation, and Social Rigidities.* New Haven: Yale University Press.

Piore, Michael, and Charles Sabel. 1984. *The Second Industrial Divide.* New York: Basic Books.

Roberts, Geoffrey K. 1992. "Right-wing Radicalism in the New Germany." *Parliamentary Affairs* 45, no. 3: 327–45.

Röpke, Wilhelm. 1982. "The Guiding Principles of the Liberal Programme." In Horst Friedrich Wünche, ed., *Standard Texts on the Social Market Economy,* 188. Stuttgart and New York: Gustav Fischer Verlag.

Sandholtz, Wayne, and John Zysman. 1989. "1992: Recasting the European Bargain." *World Politics* 42 (October): 95–128.

Shonfield, Andrew. 1965. *Modern Capitalism*. New York: Harper.

Silvia, Stephen J. 1994. "A House Divided: German Employers' Associations after Unification;" Paper presented at the Ninth International Conference of Europeanists, March 31-April 2.

Soskice, David. 1991. "The Institutional Infrastructure for International Competitiveness: A Comparative Analysis of the U.K. and Germany." In A. B. Atkinson, and R. Brunetta, eds., *The Economics of the New Europe*. London: Macmillan.

Steinmo, Sven, Kathleen Thelen, and Frank Longstreth. 1992. *Structuring Politics: Historical Institutionalism in Comparative Analysis*. New York: Cambridge University Press.

Streeck, Wolfgang, and Philippe C. Schmitter. 1991. "From National Corporatism to Transnational Pluralism: Organized Interests in the Single European Market." *Politics and Society* 19, no. 2: 133–64.

Thelen, Kathleen. 1992. *A Union of Parts: Labor Politics in Postwar Germany*. Ithaca: Cornell University Press.

Turner, Lowell. 1992. "German Unions in the 1990s: Between Unification and Europe." Paper delivered at the Industrial Relations Research Association Annual Meeting, New Orleans, January 3–5.

Wallich, Henry C. 1955. *Mainsprings of the German Revival*. New Haven: Yale University Press.

Wever, Kirsten S., and Christopher S. Allen. 1992. "Is Germany a Model for Managers?" *Harvard Business Review* 5 (September-October): 36–43.

——. 1993. "The Financial System and Corporate Governance in Germany: Institutions and the Diffusion of Innovations." *Journal of Public Policy* 13, no. 2: 183–202.

Wilkes, Stephen. 1984. "The Practice and Theory of Industrial Adaptation in Britain and West Germany." *Government and Opposition* 19, no. 4: 451–70.

7 • Political Adaptation to Growing Labor Market Segmentation

Stephen J. Silvia

Two distinguishing characteristics of West Germany[1] for the majority of its relatively brief history were the remarkably high quality of most jobs and the relative evenness of income distribution (Strauss-Kahn 1979; Wolff 1995). This is not to say that the West German labor market always performed flawlessly or that there was never a gap between rich and poor. Still, in comparison to many other affluent countries, the distribution of West German incomes was notably more even (especially within individual sectors), and the labor market was largely able to meet the demand for good jobs at good wages (Vitols 1994, 3–4). Arrangements within the German system of "social partnership," such as the "coordinated" collective bargaining regime, the "dual" educational system that prepares students either for university studies or skilled employment, and revenue sharing among the German states *(Länderausgleich),* all contributed to producing this favorable outcome.

Starting in the mid-1970s, however, some observers began to predict that the arrangements promoting income equity in the Federal Republic would not be able to withstand the upsurge in economic turbulence besetting the global economy (e.g., Altvater, Hoffmann, and Semmler 1979 and Henschel

1. This chapter refers to the united nation after 3 October 1990 as "Germany." It calls the western portion of Germany in the time before unification "West Germany" and the eastern segment either "East Germany" or "the German Democratic Republic," depending on the context of the discussion. It designates the territories of the two formerly independent German states after unification as "eastern" and "western" Germany, and uses the name "the Federal Republic of Germany" to refer to West Germany until unification, and unified Germany thereafter.

1980, 206–16). Their forecasts proved wrong. Although unemployment did expand substantially, particularly during the early 1980s, West Germany's economic architecture held firm, real wages continued to rise, and income differentials remained comparatively moderate. The vast majority of the jobless received unemployment insurance, which prevented them from sliding into poverty, and until the mid-1980s the spells of unemployment remained relatively brief for most who had lost their jobs (Reissert 1985, 3).

In the 1990s, German unification, the opening of central and eastern Europe, the completion of the single European market, and a massive net outflow of business investment all posed formidable challenges to Germany's economic and social fabric that have proved to be far more intractable than any faced previously in the postwar era. These developments have produced a new generation of pessimists that has begun to argue that this rapidly deteriorating economic environment is rendering nonviable the dense network of economic institutions that has been crucial for producing widespread domestic affluence in the Federal Republic (e.g., Mahnkopf 1991, and Streeck 1994). Is the new group of skeptics right this time? Is the postwar German social market economy no longer viable in the post-cold war era?

This chapter addresses that question by examining the impact of the German post-unification employment crisis on a central pillar of the institutional edifice that helped to promote income equality in the Federal Republic, namely, the collective bargaining order. It demonstrates that the government and the collective bargaining partners—despite sharp ideological and political differences and a vocal minority of dissidents within the ranks of the employers—have cooperated to a modest degree to preserve the status quo. This made it possible to manage, but not resolve, the employment crises of the 1990s. Still, shifts in the environment have attenuated the economic and social efficacy of the collective bargaining regime. The postwar German collective bargaining order still delivers affluence to the majority of German employees. Nonetheless, over the past fifteen years an increasing share of employees have found themselves on the economic periphery, which now encompasses a far wider spectrum of social groups, including for the first time skilled blue-collar native-born male workers.

Representatives from the three guarantors of collective bargaining—employers' associations, organized labor, and the state—have all acknowledged that the complex series of interwoven statutes, alliances, and compromises, which developed over the past five decades, produced an industrial relations regime that greatly restricts the room for unilateral action. Consequently, deadlock often prevails. Nonetheless, the representatives of labor, management, and the state have all begun to experiment within the limited realm of possibilities available to each in the current system to adjust the collective bargaining regime in accordance with their own preferences (which often work at cross-purposes). Moreover, growing numbers of the social partners' rank and file have also started leaving their associations (e.g., Silvia 1997).

Despite dissatisfaction and flight, the German collective bargaining order will persist largely as it now stands and will remain the primary means through which Germans set wages and distribute income for the foreseeable future because those who are clamoring for change have yet to propose an alternative that large numbers consider superior to the current regime. Yet the persistence of long-term unemployment concentrated in specific regions and industries, the expansion of the service sector (where both trade unions and employers' associations have a markedly weaker presence), and rank-and-file flight from associations will erode the influence of the current collective bargaining regime over wage determination, increase the cost of sustaining the industrial relations order for its remaining participants, and diminish the order's effectiveness and legitimacy.

THE INSTITUTIONAL CONTOURS OF THE GERMAN LABOR MARKET

As mentioned at the outset, a distinctive attribute of the West German economy was a relatively even distribution of income, which was primarily the product of an exceptionally unitary labor market. Two social and institutional arrangements have largely accounted for the structure of the German labor market: the collective bargaining regime and the educational system.

In practice, collective bargaining in the Federal Republic has typically produced highly uniform results nationwide. Collective bargaining occurs primarily at the sectoral level between the representatives of an employers' association and a trade union. This creates what the Germans call a *flächendeckender Tarifvertrag* (comprehensive collective bargaining contract covering in practice all of the employers in a sector and region), which sets a uniform minimum for wages, hours, and other terms and conditions of employment. Although annual wage negotiations for most sectors take place at the regional level, one district typically sets the pace for the others, and as a result, the regional contracts vary only at the margins. Similarly, negotiations for the various sectors of the economy formally take place independently, but in practice the contract results from the metalworking industry—and occasionally the public service or chemicals sector—set the pace for all the others (Necker 1993, 205).

Statutes also promote uniformity in the labor market. Collective bargaining agreements are legally binding only on the signatories to the contract. Since in most sectors membership in employers' associations in terms of employment exceeds 70 percent, collective accords cover a large majority of employees. Most nonmembers voluntarily pay their employees at least the contractual rate. Nonetheless, German labor law provides further means to dampen competition on the basis of wages. The 1949 Collective Bargaining Act *(Tarifvertragsgesetz)* permits the German federal labor minister to issue a "declaration of universal applicability" *(allgemeine Verbindlichkeitserklärung,* AVE). An AVE requires all firms from an individual sector within a single collective bargaining district to respect the existing sectoral agreements, so long as firms employing at least a majority of the employees from that sector and in that district have already concluded contracts stipulating those conditions.

Over the past twenty years, between five hundred and six hundred declarations of universal applicability have been in force at any given time. Although this number is low in comparison to the typical number of collective agreements in the Federal Republic (i.e., between 35,000 and 40,000), the mere possibility that the labor ministry could implement an AVE encourages firms that do not participate in collective bargaining to meet at least the contractual minimums.

Thus, despite a piecemeal structure, the German collective bargaining regime has proved far more powerful in promoting uniform compensation than a universal, nationwide minimum wage because of the informal links within and across sectors and its reliance on actual collective bargaining provisions to set minimums rather than a political determination of a minimum acceptable floor for wages nationwide (Bispinck 1993, 529–30).

German labor law also protects collective agreements from potential free-riders by requiring that any firm leaving an employers' association remain bound by the contracts concluded while it was a member for as long as the contracts remain in force. For wage agreements this is not so burdensome; their length is typically one year. For contracts regulating matters such as vacations, working time, wage scales, and sick pay, however, the duration can be considerably longer (Schroeder 1993, 701). Consequently, in most sectors of the western German economy until recently, only a handful of firms were willing to undercut compensation standards set in collective bargaining. Thus, when functioning properly, the postwar German industrial relations regime took labor costs out of competition at the domestic level and dampened income differentials across the economy. In essence, it produced a "leakproof" solidaristic wage (Streeck 1991, 25–31).

In its heyday during the first four decades of the Federal Republic, Germany's educational system also helped to reduce imbalances in employment and income distribution. Its much admired apprenticeship system trained those students not planning to study at a university by allowing them to spend half of their time learning theoretical knowledge in the classroom and the other half gaining practical experience in actual enterprises. This system made hiring young employees worthwhile for firms, thereby avoiding the disproportionately high youth unemployment that has plagued most other European nations and that has produced considerable inequities in the distribution of income.

From the late 1950s to the late 1970s, the collective bargaining order and educational system combined with strong domestic and international economies to provide most job seekers with employment at a wage that produced a relatively even national distribution of income. This began to change in the 1980s, however.

GERMAN EMPLOYMENT TRENDS SINCE 1980

The 1980s marked a return to mass unemployment in West Germany for the first time in several decades. Joblessness rose to levels not seen since the 1950s and remained stubbornly high throughout the decade. The unemployment rate, which averaged 2.8 percent in the 1970s and stood at 3.8 percent in 1980, climbed to 9.1 percent in 1983 as a result of the 1981–82 worldwide recession.[2] The simultaneous influx onto the job market of unprecedented numbers of youths who comprised the West German baby-boom (which came a decade later to the Federal Republic than in most other countries), exacerbated the problem. Joblessness remained at 9 percent or above for three more years, and by the end of the decade, it had fallen only to 8.7 percent.

Economic unification on July 1, 1990, sent the western German economy into a series of severe gyrations from which it has yet to recover. Unity fueled a short, sharp economic boom. Western Germany's gross domestic product spiked upward, expanding by 5.7 percent in 1990 and 4.5 percent in 1991, before it slowed to a growth rate of 1.6 percent in 1992. A decline of 1.9 percent followed in 1993. The unification boom swiftly reduced western unemployment to a ten-year low of 6.3 percent by 1991, but the 1992–93 recession abruptly reversed this trend. By 1996, the western jobless rate was at 9.1 percent (10.4 percent for all of Germany).

The decline in the share of employment dedicated to goods production picked up considerable momentum in the first part of the 1990s, raising the specter of deindustrialization in western Germany for the first time. During

---

2. All data, unless otherwise noted, come from Statistisches Bundesamt, *Statistisches Jahrbuch für die Bundesrepublik Deutschland,* various years.

the 1970s and the 1980s, these sectors' share of employment declined each year on average by 0.4 percent; in the first part of the 1990s, the annual contraction in manufacturing employment accelerated to 0.6 percent.

Job loss in the traditionally declining western German industries accelerated. For example, during the eight years between 1982 and 1990, employment in the steel industry fell by 30 percent. During the 1990s, it took only *half* as long (from 1990 to 1994) to lose a comparable proportion of jobs. Unemployment in the western German textiles sector suffered an even greater acceleration (37 percent) over the same four years (*direkt* 06/95, March 29, 1995; and *textil-bekleidung*, June 1995).

Unemployment also spread to the core of western German manufacturing, the chemical and metalworking industries. Between 1990 and 1994, employment in the western German chemical sector declined by 10.3 percent and in metals by 15.8 percent. As a result, the pools of long-term jobless (those unemployed for more than one year) and discouraged workers expanded. Between 1993 and 1994 alone, long-term unemployment grew by 36 percent to 721,200 out of a total of 2.2 million jobless (32.5 percent of total unemployment). This pattern is likely to persist. For example, statements by chief executives at two recent "summits" between the heads of Germany's major automobile producers and several state prime ministers indicate that this sector will continue to cut back its domestic workforce significantly regardless of market developments at least until the year 2000 (*Ausblick*, March 1995; Deutsche Presse-Agentur, August 11 and 15, 1995; *direkt* 09/95, May 10, 1995; and *The Week in Germany*, July 21, 1995).

Employment developments in eastern Germany are replete with even sharper gyrations, as one would expect from a former nation making a transition to capitalism after forty years of "real existing socialism," which was built upon the rubble of an autarkic, war-ravaged economy. Like all other communist states, the former German Democratic Republic (GDR) guaranteed full employment. This policy severely distorted the labor market, producing vast overstaffing in some segments of the economy and labor shortages in others. An extremely low birthrate and periodic episodes of massive flight to West Germany primarily by younger, skilled workers exacerbated already severe shortages of skilled workers.

The transition from state socialism to capitalism has not been easy for eastern Germany. Unification also brought with it radical deindustrialization. Industrial production in eastern Germany fell to one-third and industrial employment to one-fourth of pre-unification levels. Before unification, somewhere between 50 and 60 percent of the workforce was employed in goods production. By 1994, this had dropped to under 20 percent, which was roughly 60 percent of the western rate.

Several factors combined to produce the employment catastrophe in eastern Germany after communism collapsed: (1) the rapid establishment of economic and monetary union of the two Germanies on July 1, 1990 (less than four months after the communists had been voted out of office), which gave eastern Germans virtually no time to prepare their economy for market competition; (2) the overvalued average exchange rate of 1.7 eastern marks for every deutschmark, which undercut the former GDR's export competitiveness and saddled many eastern firms with heavy debts; (3) the dissolution of the Council on Mutual Economic Cooperation and Assistance (CMEA, or "Comecon"), to which all of the former GDR's major export markets were signatories; (4) the suspension of the "transfer ruble" as a regionally convertible currency among the former Comecon members, which made exporting far more difficult; and (5) the political and economic collapse in 1991 of the Soviet Union, which was by far the GDR's single largest foreign customer.

As a result of these five blows to the eastern German economy in rapid succession, its gross "regional" product (GRP) dropped by 13.4 percent in 1990 and 31 percent in 1991. Employment in eastern Germany fell by almost half between 1989 and 1994 (from 9.8 to 5.5 million). The official unemployment rate in eastern Germany rose from a negligible amount at the start of 1990 to an average of 910,000 (10.8 percent) for 1991. In the following year, joblessness advanced to 1.17 million, or 14.8 percent. Since 1992, the official unemployment rate in the five eastern states has remained stable at about 15 percent despite two successive years of high economic growth. In 1994, 1.14 million eastern Germans were officially unemployed. A further shrinkage in the eastern labor market translated this into a 15.7 percent unemployment rate in 1996. Long-term unemployment in eastern Germany rose by 9 percent in 1994 to 362,000, that is, 31.8 percent of total unemployment (*The Week in Germany,* July 21, 1995).

The unprecedented nature and immensity of the task of restoring markets to a planned economy understandably overwhelmed every institution, public and private, including those responsible for the labor market. Undoubtedly, mistakes were made. Still, massive government intervention has held the eastern German unemployment rate down considerably. If the federal and state governments had not implemented a series of active labor-market measures, the eastern unemployment rate would have exceeded 40 percent (Kühl 1994, 14–15).

The German government played the most prominent role in managing both the preservation and elimination of eastern jobs through the use of active labor-market policies and the direction of the state-owned Treuhandanstalt (THA, Trust Holding Agency). The THA was either directly or indirectly implicated in the elimination of three-quarters of all of the lost eastern jobs.[3] Evaluating the effectiveness of the Treuhandanstalt is beyond the scope of this paper. At the outset in early 1990, the Treuhand employed 4.1 million employees, or approximately 40 percent of the eastern workforce, most of whom were involved in manufacturing. By the end of 1995, when it was liquidated, it employed less than 100,000. The Treuhand's privatized progeny retained an additional 900,000.

Three active labor-market policies and trends have kept joblessness down. First, 1.4 million eastern German employees have either moved to West Germany or commute there. Since only 372,000 western employees have gone in the opposite direction, the net outflow equals over one million.

Second, the German government enacted an expanded series of active labor-market policies. These include subsidized early retirement, training and retraining programs, employment promotion and structural development corps (*Arbeitsförderung, Beschäftigung und Strukturentwicklung Gesellschaften,* ABS Gesellschaften), and employment-creation measures (*Arbeitsbeschaffungsmaßnahmen,* ABM). The ABS Gesellschaften and ABM effort created a sizable second labor market in the five new states. In 1991, these measures absorbed almost two million workers, directly created 400,000 jobs, and cost 23 percent of the GRP (the western German peak all-time expenditure on active labor-market programs was 2 percent of GRP). By the end of 1995, more than one million eastern employees were still engaged in various active labor-market programs and almost 50 percent of the eastern German working population had been involved in at least one active labor-market policy, if short-time payments are also included (Adamy, Bosch, and Knuth 1993, 331).

Third, "women in eastern Germany were systematically and against their will forced out of the work world" (Bosch, Weinkopf, and Adamy 1994, 284). Eastern German work units had employed women in almost the same quantities as men. Women worked in both production and numerous staff and support roles, such as operating day-care centers and providing for an extensive set of social activities for employees. Eastern women had a labor force participation rate of 85 percent in 1989, which was much higher than that of western women (55 percent). Once westerners began to take over the management of eastern facilities, one of the first things they did was eliminate the social support apparatus. Consequently, hundreds of thousands of women lost their jobs. Two-thirds of the eastern German unemployed have been women; eastern German women have an unemployment

---

3. Assessments of the work of the Treuhandanstalt, in particular its impact on employment, vary widely. They range from the largely positive (e.g., Lichtblau 1995), to the moderately critical (e.g., Sinn and Sinn 1992), to the highly critical (e.g., Flug 1992, Hankel 1993, Hickel and Priewe 1994, and Liedke 1993).

rate twice that of eastern German men; and nine out of ten of the long-term unemployed in the five new states are women (*direkt,* no. 08/95, April 26, 1995). Nonetheless, women are badly underrepresented in the programs designed to absorb the unemployed. When most eastern German production units laid off redundant line workers, the managers and works councillors usually chose to retain married males over females when they had to decide who would lose their jobs (*Quelle,* April 1995).

Despite the virtuous and less-than-virtuous means that government officials have used to reduce unemployment east of the Elbe, the employment outlook is not bright for the foreseeable future in either part of Germany. Virtually every long-term assessment of the German labor market predicts that mass unemployment will persist in western Germany well into the next century and that only massive public and private investment for at least a decade, in amounts greatly exceeding current levels, could reduce eastern unemployment to the current western rate (e.g., Fuchs and Hoffmann 1993). Immigration as well as increases in productivity and in the female labor-force participation rate will more than counteract the anticipated absolute decline in the size of the male labor force. Moreover, government cutbacks to meet the fiscal criteria laid out in the Maastricht treaty of European Union have reduced government subsidies to eastern Germany, which has exacerbated the weak economy and labor market.

Countries such as the Czech Republic, Slovakia, Hungary, and to a lesser extent Poland and the Baltic states offer German businesses a highly educated and well-trained labor force, which is extremely close to Germany, at a small fraction of the cost of domestic employees. German managers in manufacturing and some services have found operating in central and eastern Europe particularly attractive because they can integrate these facilities far more closely into their domestic production networks than they ever could those on the periphery of western Europe. Thus the opening of central and eastern Europe has exposed several German industries to wage competition, from which they had been largely shielded for decades. This could cut into domestic employment directly and indirectly.

The Federal Republic's famed apprenticeship system has also begun to suffer as a result of rising unemployment. Fewer and fewer employers are accepting apprentices. In 1986, West German employers concluded 700,000 contracts with apprentices, but by 1994 this had dropped by 36 percent to 450,000. A 1993 study by the *Institut für Arbeitsmarkt- und Berufsforschung* (IAB, Institute for Labor Market and Occupational Research), the research arm of the Federal Agency for Employment *(Bundesanstalt für Arbeit),* found that only 36 percent of all German firms were training apprentices, an all-time low. Portions of this decline are simply a function of smaller age cohorts and the increasing share of young Germans going on to university studies instead of apprenticeships, but these factors by no means account for the entire drop (*arbeitgeber*, June 23, 1995).

In the past, many employers saw training as both a moral obligation and an opportunity. When unemployment was lower, training apprentices gave firms an edge in both assessing and recruiting new employees that was well worth the cost of running a training program. Now that many skilled workers have also fallen victim to unemployment in several core sectors of the German economy, particularly in eastern Germany, firms can save on training costs simply by hiring them. As a result, in 1994 there were only 47.3 percent as many apprentices working in the western German metalworking industry, for example, as there were in 1986. This problem is even more acute in eastern Germany, where unemployment is much higher (*direkt* 07/ 95, April 12, 1995; *direkt*, 11/95, June 7, 1995).

In early 1995, when talk of replacing the current voluntary system of apprenticeships with a mandatory training tax on all enterprises began to circulate publicly, employers' representatives responded with a commitment to increase the number of places offered to apprentices by at least 10 percent over the upcoming two summer placement rounds. Employers made progress toward this goal in the summer of 1995, accepting 20,000 more apprentices in the West and 13,000 more in the East than in 1994. Still, the shortage of apprenticeships worsened in 1996 and 1997.

The wrenching impact of German unification and the lifting of the Iron Curtain in the early 1990s combined with the economic and demographic pressures that had already begun to erode the unitary German labor market in the 1980s to strain the previously unitary labor market for skilled, blue-collar workers (Schmitthenner 1992, 11). Large pockets of severe joblessness have spread from the older declining industries to the center of the German economy, and unemployment has become increasingly concentrated geographically and demographically. How have the stewards of the German economy—namely, employers' associations, trade unions, and the government—reacted to these pressures?

POLICY RESPONSES

Ideological, political, and structural differences have restricted the scope of cooperation between the government and the associations representing business and labor in combating labor-market turbulence primarily to efforts aimed at shoring up the status quo. Nonetheless, some of these endeavors have had some success, for example, the government's program to reduce long-term unemployment and the 1994 agreement in the metalworking and other industries to accept short-time work (typically thirty hours per week) in exchange for employment guarantees. Beyond these measures, each participant has primarily attempted to resolve the unemployment problem unilaterally, relying on its own perception of its causes. These individual efforts, in contrast, have produced minimal results at best.

The solo efforts by business and labor associations to reduce unemployment represent less a challenge to the current industrial relations order than experimentation at its fringes. This stands in stark contrast to the independent actions of individual employers and employees, many of whom have responded to market pressures in ways that have already damaged the industrial relations regime.

To reduce unemployment, labor leaders have called for Keynesian counter-cycle demand stimuli, the subsidization of research and development, an expansion of training programs, and the creation of a "second labor market"[4] to act as a bridge to regular employment (Deutscher Gewerkschaftsbund, 1994). Since the strategies above all required government participation, organized labor made little progress in implementing them, except for the creation of a second labor market. Labor instead continued to favor "relying on its own power," a strategy begun in the early 1980s, by using collective bargaining to push for wage parity in eastern Germany and working-time reduction throughout the FRG. Union officials justified this strategy by pointing out that the government had failed to act either to promote work sharing or to inject a Keynesian demand stimulus into the economy. Opinions vary widely and largely along ideological lines regarding the success of working-time reduction as a means to dampen unemployment (Hampe 1993). It is obvious, however, that working-time reductions combined with increases in hourly wages have *not* eliminated the problem. The more drastic working-time reduction of the 1990s—which, unlike that implemented in the 1980s, came without increases in hourly compensation —have proved to be only stopgap measures.

For the past ten years, and as a result of division and uncertainty within their ranks, German employers have pursued erratic and contradictory policies. For over a decade, employers' associations have lobbied in vain for cuts in the payroll, corporate-income, and capital-gains taxes, which they argue would enable firms to hire more employees and thereby reduce unem-

---

4. The central concept of a "second labor market" *(zweiter Arbeitsmarkt)* is simple. Instead of paying people unemployment benefits not to work, the government pays the jobless to fill needs that private firms will not, such as the provision of social services, improvements in infrastructure, and environmental renewal. The objectives of the second labor market are to enhance the general quality of life, save the taxpayers money, and preserve the pride, discipline, and skills of the unemployed. Proponents of the second labor market agree that it should promote rather than preclude a quick and easy return to the "first" labor market. Hence, most advocates support strictly limiting the time that participants can spend in such a program (Kühl 1983, 111–13).

ployment. Consequently, in the past few years, employers' associations have increasingly attempted to turn collective bargaining into an alternate forum for attaining cost reductions. Many employers profess a desire for additional flexibility to use part-time employees and to set hours unilaterally according to fluctuations in demand for their products even though few have taken advantage of the limited flexibility available to them already. In early 1993, the metal employers' association even violated an existing labor agreement and provoked a strike in eastern Germany in an effort to make modest progress toward achieving these ends. Nonetheless, German employers have made little headway in attaining additional flexibility, largely because the preponderance of them in the mid-1990s has been unwilling to risk disrupting workplace relations to attain it (Silvia 1993).

In 1995, employers, trade unionists, and the government presented a common front in support of the renewal of a government program designed to reduce long-term unemployment. The program fell somewhere between cooperation and unilateral action, because the government did consult with labor and management representatives regarding the program's design and depended to some degree on cooperation from employers and good will from trade unions, but the government provided all of the funding (*Frankfurter Allgemeine Zeitung,* January 27, 1995).

The social partners and the government all have good individual reasons to want to cut joblessness. Full employment has always been one of organized labor's goals. It not only helps those currently unemployed (whom unionists assert they represent as well) but also increases the size of the pool of potential union members and strengthens labor's hand in collective bargaining (*Handelsblatt,* June 4/5, 1993). German employers have expressed little interest in recreating a tight labor market, but they do wish to reduce joblessness, primarily to avoid the additional tax burden it generates (Bundesvereinigung der deutschen Arbeitgeberverbände, *Kurz-Nachrichten-Dienst,* January 24, 1995). Germany funds its unemployment and welfare programs through a joint payroll tax on employers and employees. These taxes have risen dramatically since the early 1980s, increasing Germany's labor costs. Higher employment would also boost demand. German government officials would like to reduce the financial burden of mass unemployment on the state coffers and please the electorate, particularly in the five eastern states, which rank unemployment among Germany's most pressing problems. Beyond these immediate concerns, the social and political dangers of mass unemployment, in particular the rise in criminality and intolerance, have distressed labor, management, and government alike.

In early 1995, Helmut Kohl met with representatives from German business and labor to iron out the finishing touches for the renewal of a program, which had begun without much fanfare, to promote the hiring of

130,000 long-term unemployed through temporary wage subsidies paid directly to private firms. Hence the program resembled a second labor market, but it promoted employment in the private rather than the public sector. The renewal legislation envisions allocating DM 3.1 billion through to the end of 1998 to assist 180,000 additional long-term jobless back into productive employment. At a gathering marking the renewal of the program, which included influential representatives from the ranks of organized labor, business, and government, long-time federal labor minister Norbert Blüm (CDU) stated, "Our goal should be to build bridges to the primary labor market for those who have problems reaching it. . . . We do not want a split of our labor market with the skilled and the healthy in the primary labor market and the old, sick, and handicapped in the secondary labor market. That cannot be a solution for our labor market" (Deutsche Presse Agentur, March 13, 1995).

The renewal of the program to aid the long-term unemployed has won praise from both the employers and organized labor. The employers support it because the program preserves their right to chose their own employees and because it pays a sizable subsidy directly to the firms. Labor leaders support the program because it preserves the minimums set in collective bargaining agreements and it resembles their own proposal to establish a second labor market. This program to reduce long-term joblessness, like the government's active labor-market measures for eastern Germany, is a stopgap measure designed to contain unemployment while preserving the institutional and political status quo.

During the first few months of 1996, Helmut Kohl took up an offer made by IG Metall president Klaus Zwickel in late 1995 to form a tripartite "alliance for jobs." Despite much fanfare, these talks broke down as a result of employer intransigence. As a result, in the spring of 1996 Helmut Kohl seized on the demand of German employers to reduce non-labor costs by passing legislation that reduced the statutory minimum sick pay for employees from 100 to 80 percent of average pay (including overtime, vacation money, and bonus payments). In the fall of 1996, several German employers' associations pushed beyond the mandate of the revised law and announced that they planned to cancel the collective agreements governing sick pay before the agreements had expired. A combination of protest strikes and a public denunciation from Helmut Kohl forced the employers to back down, to return within the confines of the postwar economic order and to negotiate the matter with the trade unions.

On a more explicitly independent tack, Kohl's government has also experimented with the artificial introduction of further segmentation into the labor market in a bid to reduce joblessness. On January 27, 1993, the *Bundestag* amended the Employment Promotion Act (*Arbeitsförderungsge-*

setz, AFG), the central piece of German employment legislation, by adding Article 249h. This amendment promotes the development of a limited "secondary labor market"[5] in which compensation would be held significantly below the minimum set in collective bargaining contracts.

Employees hired under the provisions of Article 249h, which is valid only for eastern Germany and expires at the end of 1997, must have been unemployed for at least a year. Article 249h provides a financial incentive to the collective bargaining parties to create a secondary labor market by making available a government subsidy to cover the portion of the wage payment for qualified new hires that exceeds the rate of unemployment insurance (namely, 68 percent of the employee's previous net wage) so long as the new hires receive *no more* than 90 percent of the weekly minimum wage set out in the collective bargaining contract for the relevant sector. Employees can either earn the full *hourly* wage agreed to in the appropriate collective accord by only working for 80 percent of the standard work week or 90 percent of the hourly collective bargaining rate for working the full work week. The government also set a maximum annual level of subsidization at DM 15,120 per employee (Wagner 1993, 464–66). Three sectors are eligible: environmental recovery, the demolition of antiquated factories, and emergency social services (Emmerich 1994, 130).

Employers and trade unionists alike have a mixed opinion of Article 249h of the Employment Promotion Act. Currently, over 60,000 employees are working under the provisions of Article 249h in eastern Germany, which is close to the maximum of 70,000 set out in the legislation (Bosch, Weinkopf, and Adamy 1994, 288). IG Chemie and IG Metall signed special collective bargaining contracts with the Treuhandanstalt in order to gain access to the wage subsidy, but IG Metall simultaneously filed suit, claiming that Article 249h was a violation of collective bargaining autonomy, which is enshrined

---

5. The concept of a secondary labor market *(sekundärer Arbeitsmarkt)* is familiar to most North American students of industrial relations and political economy. It develops spontaneously when imperfections in the labor market accrue that generate enduring segmentation among employees. Under these circumstances, larger, more affluent firms tend to pay higher wages and to offer more secure employment in order to attract and to retain the best employees. These well-off companies also rely heavily on internal promotion ladders to fill positions above the entry level. The combined effect is to produce a "primary" segment within the work force that is largely insulated from adverse economic developments.

The residual employers outside the primary sector comprise the "secondary" labor market; they have neither the financial resources to offer highly paid long-term employment nor the organizational depth to permit substantial internal advancement. Hence, employment in the secondary labor market tends to be contingent and low paid (Doeringer and Piore 1985; Gordon, Edwards, and Reich, 1982).

The difference in this case is that the German government is explicitly attempting to *create* a controlled version of a secondary labor market.

in Article 9, paragraph 3, of the German constitution (*Handelsblatt,* April 5, 1993).

In 1994, German employers and unions turned down a government offer to extend Article 249h to western Germany. The North Rhine-Westphalian branches of IG Metall and Gesamtmetall, the employers' association in the metalworking industry, supported the measure because it would provide immediate financial relief to their constituencies. The national offices of both these organizations rejected the proposal, however, because they feared that extending Article 249h of the Employment Promotion Act could be the first step toward a permanent nationwide secondary labor market that would undermine pattern bargaining, and with it the traditionally pivotal roles of employers' associations and trade unions. The Kohl government, ever sensitive to the accusation that it was violating collective bargaining autonomy—particularly when it came both from labor and management—retracted the offer.

Despite (or perhaps because of) the objections to Article 249h, labor and management in several sectors have recently constructed a far larger version of a temporary secondary labor market of their own. The impetus for this effort began with the automobile producer Volkswagen. In the fall of 1993, a severe cost crisis at Volkswagen forced management to propose a series of cuts in its relatively generous company contract with IG Metall. These included early retirement incentives, a cut in benefits, and a radical reduction in weekly working time to thirty hours *without* compensatory increases in the hourly wage as an alternative to the loss of 30,000 jobs. IG Metall officials accepted the offer, even though it slashed nominal compensation by over 10 percent and deviated from pattern bargaining, because it preserved jobs and its duration was limited, so it did not represent a permanent disruption of pattern bargaining (Hartz 1994). Yet in 1996, IG Metall and VW agreed to extend the agreement for another two years because employment problems had only marginally diminished.

The 1993 Volkswagen accord served as a model for the 1994 collective bargaining talks in the entire western German metalworking sector and in several other sectors as well. One component of these agreements was a two-year side accord that introduced a modest escape, or "hardship," clause for western firms experiencing economic difficulties. In exchange for a firing freeze, firms in financial trouble were permitted to cut their employees' work week to thirty hours with no obligation to pay compensatory increases in the hourly wage, so long as all employees were equally subject to the reduction. The agreement proved effective. By mid 1994, over one million employees were working short time under some version of the Volkswagen model. In 1997, IG Chemie agreed to let firms undercut wages by as much as 10 percent in exchange for a layoff freeze.

German unification is perhaps the single biggest example that illustrates both the potential and the actual limits of cooperation among labor, management, and government in the Federal Republic. In the spring of 1990, once it became clear that German unification would proceed quickly, the Kohl government worked closely with both the *Bundesvereinigung der deutschen Arbeitgeberverbände* (BDA, Federal Organization of German Employers' Associations) and its member associations as well as the *Deutscher Gewerkschaftsbund* (DGB, German Trade Union Federation) and its member unions to extend an unaltered version of the western German industrial relations order eastward. This included the adoption of not only all of the existing legislation and public institutions but also the western trade unions and employers' associations.

Four considerations account for this decision. First, the legacy of the failed Weimar Republic made most Germans extremely hesitant to tinker with the successful western system. As in most other areas of German society, westerners, initially with substantial eastern support, reasoned that the least risky means to unify Germany while preserving the Federal Republic's postwar success would be simply to transfer eastward the laws, organizations, and institutional arrangements of the Federal Republic without changing them. (Yet, it is important to note that this reasoning failed to take into account the fundamental differences between the old and the new Federal Republic).

Second, by 1990, the West German industrial relations order had become an extraordinarily complex and interconnected amalgamation of five decades of deals, legal precedents, understandings, and compromises. This eliminated the option of transferring some portions of the western industrial relations order eastward but not others, because the different components were too closely intertwined. Third, although most employers, unionists, and government officials are dissatisfied with elements of the industrial relations order, there was no consensus regarding how to change it. Thus it was impossible to attain the critical mass of support needed to implement even minor changes.

Fourth, the constitutional protection of collective bargaining autonomy effectively prevented the government from unilaterally altering the industrial relations regime because a disgruntled party would most certainly undertake legal and perhaps even direct action (e.g., a strike) to block it. Thus the joint effort of employers' associations, trade unionists, and the government to transfer the industrial relations order eastward without adjusting it to match the new circumstances of a united Germany is an expression of both the capacity of the social partners and the government to cooperate and the ease with which one of these parties can exercise a veto.

Gridlock has produced a great deal of dissatisfaction among the rank-and-file membership of both the employers' associations and the trade unions over the failure of the government and the social partners to meet their needs. Consequently, increasing numbers of employers and employees have been "fleeing" their associations. This trend, if left unchecked, could eventually transform employers' associations and trade unions in the eyes of the public from representatives into special interests (cf. the Chamber of Commerce or American Iron and Steel Institute in the United States).

Dissatisfaction has also prompted unprecedented numbers from both sides to take matters into their own hands. More and more employers, especially but by no means exclusively in eastern Germany, have been concluding informal (and often illegal) agreements with their workforces that set compensation below the collective bargaining rate in exchange for preserving employment. Employers see these informal accords as a far less troublesome way to cut costs than haggling with a union. The employees see the exchange as a price that must be paid to preserve jobs. The net effect, however, could be to weaken the power of the collective bargaining regime to take wages out of competition if more than the current small percentage of firms in a few sectors engage in these practices.

Thus far, however, employers' associations and trade unions have managed to curtail these arrangements and are likely to be able to continue to do so in the future. Containing the recent outburst of dissent within employers' associations may ultimately prove to be far more difficult (Silvia 1997). Nonetheless, a long and solid economic recovery, if it materializes, would go a long way toward lessening the temptation to resort to either of these options in the future.

GERMAN INDUSTRIAL RELATIONS IN THE COMING CENTURY

The tumult of the past five years has strained the dense network of economic institutions that regulate the German labor market to an unprecedented degree. Although these institutions have become less inclusive as a result, they have thus far weathered the strain of both German unification and Germany's sharpest recession, showing a remarkable resilience that has once again proved skeptics wrong. This success is largely the product of flexibility that is not readily apparent under normal circumstances. For example, the collapse of eastern Germany's economy prompted the Kohl government to suspend its ideological suspicion of active labor market policies and to widen the margin for experimentation within a context of continuing support for the existing industrial relations order. Although the government's measures have by no means resolved all the problems in the labor market, they have successfully managed a severe labor-market crisis with a minimum of social unrest. Trade unions and employers' associations have also proved willing at times to make sacrifices in order to preserve the status quo.

Nonetheless, the far greater danger to the German industrial relations order in the long run is not collapse but slowly declining relevance. As long as high unemployment and association flight persist, fewer and fewer employees will fall under the purview of the collective bargaining regime. There is no easy solution to either of these problems, and if Germany's net deficit in foreign direct investments remains as large as it has been over the past five years, they very well could get worse. Furthermore, the cost of high unemployment is proving both politically and economically difficult to sustain. Hence, although German institutions have weathered the worst of the immediate labor-market crisis, there is no guarantee that they will also withstand the more insidious trends of secret deals between employers and their workforces and association flight as well as the punishing economic pressures of tremendous investment flight and huge transfer payments.

REFERENCES

Adamy, Wilhelm, Gerhard Bosch, and Matthias Knuth. 1993. "Arbeitsmarkt." In Michael Kittner, ed., *Gewerkschaftsjahrbuch 1993. Daten—Fakten—Analysen*. Cologne: Bund.

Altvater, Elmar, Jürgen Hoffmann, and Willi Semmler. 1979. *Vom Wirtschaftswunder zur Wirtschaftskrise*. Berlin: Rotbuchverlag.

Bispinck, Reinhard. 1993. "Daten und Fakten zum bundesdeutschen Tarifsystem." *WSI-Mitteilungen* 46, no. 8: 148–95.

Bosch, Gerhard, Claudia Weinkopf, and Wilhelm Adamy. 1994. "Arbeitsmarkt." In Michael Kittner, ed., *Gewerkschaften heute. Jahrbuch für Arbeitnehmerfragen 1994*. Cologne: Bund.

Deutscher Gewerkschaftsbund, Bundesvorstand. 1994. *Fünf-Wege-Strategie zu mehr Beschäftigung. Positionen des Deutschen Gewerkschaftbundes*. Düsseldorf: DGB.

Doeringer, Peter B., and Michael J. Piore. 1985. *Internal Labor Markets and Manpower Analysis*. Armonk, N.Y.: M. E. Sharpe.

Emmerich, Knut. 1994. "Mega-Arbeitsbeschaffungsmaßnahmen in den neuen Bundesländern—Bestandsaufnahme und Perspektiven." In Hubert Heinelt, Gerhard Bosch, and Berndt Reissert, eds., *Arbeitspolitik nach der Vereinigung*. Berlin: edition sigma.

Flug, Martin. 1992. *Treuhand-Poker. Die Mechanismen des Ausverkaufs*. Berlin: Ch. Links.

Fuchs, Johann, and Edeltraud Hoffmann. 1993. "Der Arbeitsmarkt in

Deutschland bis 2010—quo vadis?" In Werner Fricke, ed., *Jahrbuch Arbeit und Technik 1993*. Bonn: Verlag J.H.W. Dietz.

Gordon, David M., Richard Edwards, and Michael Reich. 1982. *Segmented Work, Divided Workers*. Cambridge: Cambridge University Press.

Hampe, Peter, ed. 1993. *Zwischenbilanz der Arbeitszeitverkürzung*. Tutzinger Schriften zur Politik 1. Munich: von Hase & Koehler.

Hankel, Wilhelm. 1993. *Die Sieben Todsünden der Vereinigung. Wege aus der Wirtschaftsdesaster*. Berlin: Siedler.

Hartz, Peter. 1994. *Jeder Arbeitsplatz hat ein Gesicht. Die Volkswagenlösung*. Frankfurt: Campus.

Henschel, Rudolf. 1980. "Arbeitslosigkeit. Folge einseitig quantativ orientierter Wachstumspolitik." *WSI-Mitteilungen* 33, no. 4: 206–16.

Hickel, Rudolf, and Jan Priewe. 1994. *Nach dem Fehlstart. Ökonomische Perspektiven der deutschen Einigung*. Frankfurt: S. Fischer.

Kühl, Jürgen. 1983. "Aspekte der Zweiten Arbeitsmarktes." *Arbeit und Beruf*, no. 4: 109–22.

———. 1994. "Zur Veränderung der arbeitmarktpolitischen Instrumente seit 1990." In Hubert Heinelt, Gerhard Bosch, and Bernd Reissert, eds., *Arbeitsmarktpolitik nach der Vereinigung*. Berlin: edition sigma.

Lichtblau, Karl. 1995. *Von der Transfer- in die Marktwirtschaft. Strukturpolitische Leitlinien für die neuen Ländern*. Cologne: Deutscher Instituts-Verlag.

Liedke, Rudiger. 1992. *Die Treuhand, die zweite Enteignung der Ostdeutschen*. Munich: Edition Ch. Links.

Mahnkopf, Birgit. 1991. "Pessimistische Spekulationen über die Zukunft der Gewerkschaften in der neuen Bundesrepublik." In Andreas Westphal, Hansjörg Hert, Michael Heire, and Ulrich Busch, eds., *Wirtschaftspolitische Konsequenzen der deutschen Vereinigung*, 269–95. Frankfurt: Campus.

Necker, Tyll. 1993. "Sozialpartnerschaft und Standortqualität." In Michael Fuchs and Horst-Udo Niedenhoff, eds., *Sozialpartnerschaft. Meinungen, Visionen, Vorschläge*. Cologne: Deutscher-Instituts Verlag.

Reissert, Bernd. 1985. "Der zweite Arbeitsmarkt—Begriff, Umfang, Erfahrung, Konflikte, Perspektiven." In Evangelische Akademie Mülheim/Ruhr, ed., *Arbeitslos nicht wehrlos. Wege aus der Arbeitslosigkeit. Der zweite Arbeitsmarkt. Chancen, Gefahren, Grenzen*. Mülheim: Evangelische Akademie Mülheim/Ruhr.

Schmitthenner, Horst. 1992. "Die Renaissance der sozialen Fragen. Sozialpolitische Rahmenbedingungen, Konfliktfelder und Perspektiven für Gewerkschaften in vereinigten Deutschland." In Horst Schmitthenner, ed., *Zwischen Krise und Solidarität. Perspektiven gewerkschaftlicher Sozialpolitik*. Hamburg: VSA-Verlag.

Schroeder, Wolfgang. 1993. "Politik und Programmatik der Unternehmer-verbände." In Michael Kittner, ed., *Gewerkschaftsjahrbuch 1993*. Cologne: Bund.

Silvia, Stephen J., 1993. " 'Holding the Shop Together': Old and New Challenges to the German System of Industrial Relations in the mid 1990s." Berliner Arbeitshefte und Berichte zur Sozialwissenschaftlichen Forschung, no. 83, Freie Universität Berlin, Zentralinstitut für Wissenschaftliche Forschung.

——. 1997. "A House Divided: Employers and the Challenge to Pattern Bargaining in a United Germany." *Comparative Politics* 29: 187–207.

Sinn, Gerlinde, and Hans-Werner Sinn. 1992. *Jumpstart: The Economic Unification of Germany*. Cambridge, Mass.: MIT Press.

Strauss-Kahn, D. 1979. "Eléments de comparaison internationale des patrimonies des ménages." *Economie et Statistique*, no. 92 (September): 1–21.

Streeck, Wolfgang. 1991. "On the Institutional Conditions of Diversified Quality Production." In Egon Matzner and Wolfgang Streeck, eds., *Beyond Keynesianism: The Socio-Economics of Production and Employment*. London: Edward Elgar.

——. 1994. "European Social Policy after Maastricht: The 'Social Dialogue' and 'Subsidiarity.' " *Economic and Industrial Democracy* 15, no. 2: 151–77.

Vitols, Sigurt. 1994. "German Banks and the Modernization of the Small Firm Sector: Long-Term Finance in Comparative Perspective." Paper presented at the Ninth International Conference of Europeanists, Chicago, Illinois, March 31-April 2.

Wagner, Alexandra. 1993. "Der Paragraph 249h AFG. Ein neues arbeitsmarktpolitisches Instrument in Ostdeutschland." *WSI-Mitteilungen* 46, no. 7: 464–66.

Wolff, Edward N. 1995. *Top Heavy: A Study of Increasing Inequality of Wealth in America*. New York: Twentieth-Century Fund.

8 • The Limits of German Manufacturing Flexibility

Gary Herrigel

Renewed competitiveness of small and medium-sized producers, timely decentralization on the part of large producers, and a robust infrastructure for supporting decentralized flexible production contributed to a very heady atmosphere within many German industrial regions during the later half of the 1980s. The southwest province of Baden-Württemberg in particular was heralded within Germany as a *Musterländle* (a model or showpiece state) and was widely admired throughout Europe and North America for its dynamic, high-quality producers and its effective industrial policy (Cooke and Morgan 1990a, 1990b; Funck and Becher 1994; Semlinger 1993; Hassink 1992; Herrigel 1993). Moreover, at a time when it seemed that things could not get much better, the Berlin Wall fell and Germany was unified, giving a new boost to the business cycle and longer life to the already very extended boom. As the 1990s began, it truly appeared that Germany, and in particular Baden-Württemberg, had hit upon the secret for enduring competitive success in a turbulent, rapidly changing international market environment (Katzenstein 1989; Simon 1992).

This impression did not last long. By 1992 the German economy had

I thank Lowell Turner, Richard Locke, Charles Sabel, Jonathan Zeitlin, Peter Katzenstein, Nick Ziegler, David Finegold, Tom Ertman, Horst Kern, Bruce Kogut, and two anonymous reviewers for help and comments. All mistakes are the sole responsibility of the author. I also thank the Center for European Studies, Harvard University, and the Akademie für Technikfolgenabschätzung in Baden-Württemberg for support during the conduct of the research upon which this chapter is based. This chapter was published in earlier form in *European Urban and Regional Studies* 3:1 (1996) and appears here by permission of the journal's publisher, Addison Wesley Longman.

fallen into the deepest recession of the entire postwar period, and the *Musterländle* Baden-Württemberg was by no means spared (Heilemann 1993; Isaak 1992; Association 1992; Atkinson 1994). Indeed, in 1991, the GDP growth rate in Baden-Württemberg (2.8 percent) fell beneath the Federal average of 3.4 percent for the first time since 1978, placing it behind all other western German provinces except the Rheinland-Pfalz. Investment rates and job growth, especially in investment goods, fell off dramatically: the total number of jobs in the Baden-Württemberg investment goods industries fell by 11.4 percent between 1991 and 1993. Large and small firms in a variety of sectors, especially machinery, auto, and electronics, announced sometimes dauntingly large losses and layoffs. Daimler Benz, for example, announced in 1992 that it planned to lay off 29,000 workers and engage in massive internal restructuring. Berthold Leibinger, a prominent machine tool industry executive, was so alarmed by the dramatic downturn in orders for German machine tools in 1993 that he predicted that nearly half of the industry's jobs would have to be cut by mid decade (Iwer 1994; Engelmann et al. 1994; Cooke, Morgan, and Price 1993; Cooke 1994).[1] Bankruptcies (both personal and business) increased dramatically in the Federal Republic during this period. From a low of 12,437 in 1990 totaling DM 6.82 billion, the number of bankruptcies increased to 19,264 in 1993, totaling some DM 29.03 billion (*Industrie-und Handelskammer* 1994, 14).

Most interesting about this recession is that virtually no one in Baden-Württemberg believed that it was simply a cyclical downturn. On the contrary, most observers clearly understood the recession to be some kind of structural crisis, and there was nearly universal agreement on its primary symptoms. For example, both the elite, heavily business dominated *Zukunftskommission*[2] which was appointed by the government of Baden-Württemberg to study the economic problems of the region, and a study by the IMU Institute commissioned by IG Metall traced the crisis to the incapacity of regional producers to keep pace with increasing international competition. Relative to their main competitors in Japan, the rest of the Pacific Rim, and North America, the two studies agreed that Baden-Württemberg producers, large and small, had the following failings:

1. They brought new products to market more slowly than their foreign rivals.
2. They had more difficulty continuously and quickly integrating new technologies into their products.

---

1. Iwer (1994) points out that average annual rates of job growth fell even more precipitously in the narrower Stuttgart/Böblingen region. Investment goods industries had 15.5 percent fewer jobs in 1993 than they did in 1991.
2. *Zukunftskommission* can be translated as "Commission for the Future."

3. They had a tendency to "overengineer" their products.
4. They are unable to lower their production costs into competitive ranges.

Both parties further agreed that producers had become overly rigid and bureaucratic (Iwer 1994, esp. 50–59, 66–82; Zukunftskommission 1993). Finally, though both groups were writing about Baden-Württemberg, both indicated that the problems they identified applied to German manufacturing as a whole.[3]

Despite this surface consensus on the symptoms of the crisis, fundamental disagreements existed between the parties regarding its underlying causes and possible remedies. The Zukunftskommission, which represented government and management, claimed that the decisive problem for German competitiveness was the high comparative level of German production costs and in particular wage costs. Labor and academics sympathetic to labor, on the other hand, claimed that the real problem lay not in wages but in the failure of government and management to raise productivity and engineer a shift within the economy to more modern and growth-intensive industries and technologies, such as information technology, biotechnology, new materials technologies, and energy, aerospace, and environmental technologies (Naschold 1994; Iwer 1994). In short, each wanted to shift the blame and ultimately the burden of adjustment onto the other.

As politically weighty as each of these positions may be, neither is altogether satisfactory. Though it is true that German wages are higher than those of most of their major competitors, the gap is moderate and, moreover, has not changed appreciably from the 1980s when German competitiveness was being celebrated (Iwer 1994, 30–43). Likewise, German productivity levels have always been out of line with many of their foreign competitors in many sectors, largely because traditionally Germans have very successfully emphasized the production of lower-series, high-quality niche products that their international competitors did not or could not produce. The manufacture of such products has always been cost-intensive and has always resisted productivity-enhancing rationalization. The difference now is that the distinction between a niche product and a volume product has begun to collapse, and Germany's competitors have been able to maintain their higher levels of productivity while entering German high-quality markets (Naschold 1994). This, moreover, has nothing to do with a

3. Indeed, the Zukunftskommission solicited members from all over Germany, not just Baden-Württemberg. The IMU study was sponsored by IG Metall, which obviously regards events in Baden-Württemberg, its strongest and most prosperous district, as crucial for developments elsewhere in the Federal Republic.

failure by German manufacturers to enter new "growth" markets: Germany's competitors are gaining market share in traditional German markets such as machine tools and automobiles! Nor is the problem simply that the German employers have been unable to maintain levels of productivity. Rather, it is that German manufacturers cannot compete in world markets using the market strategies and production practices that have made them successful in the past.

AN ALTERNATIVE VIEW

I suggest that the current crisis afflicting German producers stems from the fact that their international competitors are better and more flexibly organized than they are. Adapting to and adopting some or all of the features of these new forms of organization will involve a profound restructuring of at least two of the fundamental characteristics of German industrial practice: the central structuring role of skill distinctions within German workplaces, and the divisions between functions within the managerial structures of German firms. Reforming these dimensions of the German industrial order will force the Germans to reconsider the adequacy of institutional solutions to labor and product-market processes that have been in place for much of the current century and, moreover, which have long been considered to be sources of Germany's competitive strength in world markets.

The current crisis in German manufacturing, in other words, cannot be resolved by shunting the burden of adjustment onto either labor or management. Instead, successful adjustment will have to involve the collective reconsideration of the institutional mechanisms that define and regulate relations among *all* parties in labor and product markets. Crises are moments of collective self-redefinition in which the order of relations, roles, and institutions in social life is recomposed: The current crisis in German manufacturing is provoking a set of debates and experiments that aim at nothing less than the reconception of the actors within and the boundaries of industrial practice in the German political economy.

A general argument about industrial transformation in Germany through a close analysis of the experience of producers in Baden-Württemberg may appear paradoxical to those familiar with the arguments for the peculiarity of Baden-Württemberg's industrial structure during the 1980s, but the paradox is easily clarified: the significance of Baden-Württemberg during the 1980s largely had to do with the striking success of its dense networks of small and medium-sized firms. Baden-Württemberg was constructed in public debate as an industrial district and contrasted with the competitive and organizational strategies of larger-scale firms elsewhere in Germany (and, indeed, within Baden-Württemberg itself)(see e.g. Herrigel 1989).[4]

Currently, however, both large-scale producers and the dense networks of small and medium-sized producers are suffering competitive decline in international markets. Thus it is at least plausible that the problems that large and small firms have in common stem from their similarities, not their differences. Baden-Württemberg, unlike many other German regions, has important concentrations of both large-scale and decentralized small and medium-sized producers; thus close analysis of the experience of producers there can be taken to be characteristic of the experience of producers throughout the German Federal Republic.

THE CASES OF AUTOMOBILES AND MACHINE TOOLS

The experiences of the machine tool and the automobile industries are typical of what has happened to flexible decentralized production in Baden-Württemberg in the 1990s. In both cases, the traditional strategy for success had been to aim for the high-quality segments of markets for particular technologies or products and attempt to narrow (or, as in the case of Mercedes Benz, manage) the price gap between their higher-quality goods and the standardized variants produced by their competitors. This strategy was made possible by a unique array of social roles, political and economic practices, and institutional mechanisms that shaped and regulated labor and product markets among producers in the region:

1. In general there were relatively high levels of skilled labor in production.
2. Significant dimensions of the specialty production processes utilized craft or batch production organizational principles and not mass production ones.
3. Among industrial workers and managers in the region, in large and small firms, there existed a strong social norm according social honor to the successful performance of a *Beruf* or skilled vocation.
4. Relations among producers were constituted vertically through extensive and collaborative subcontracting relations and horizontally through long-standing arrangements for the stabilization of competition and the coordination of specialization.

---

4. Indeed, much of the debate about Baden-Württemberg during the 1980s involved whether or not this claim was true—or at least to what degree it was true relative to other German regions. For important dissenting views see Cooke and Morgan 1990a and 1990b.

5. Finally, many costs and risks that especially smaller and medium-sized producers encountered were socialized across a supportive exoskeleton of institutions for technology transfer, vocational training, export promotion, market stabilization, and so on.

This system of industrial order in southwest Germany relied on quality and customer satisfaction to compensate for what were traditionally considered to be, given the way they were produced, the *invariably* higher costs of the products it manufactured.[5]

The Achilles' heel of this strategy and possibly of the entire supportive social economy, it now appears, was that it depended on the existence of a relatively stable space in markets for higher quality and/or customized products that were more expensive than standard variants. This space seems to have disappeared, not because consumers are no longer interested in high quality and customization but because a whole host of producers in these industries, particularly in Japan and the United States (though not only there), have adopted production methods that enable them to supply this demand at a much lower price than the Germans can. Moreover, these competitors can do this while driving the pace of innovation to levels even the historically highly innovative Germans are not accustomed to (see e.g. Schumann et al. 1994).[6]

The key advantage the new alternative production methods have over the traditional German-form of decentralized industrial order is that they organize production in ways that break down boundaries not only *between* firms, as the decentralized Germans have done, but *within* firms as well. Extremely flexible organizational forms have emerged, in different ways in different countries, which bring together production, purchasing, sales, development, and often suppliers, to cooperate in the "simultaneous engineering" of products. These changes have been accompanied by and are integrated with the broad diffusion of group or team work in direct production, modular production, U-shaped production lines, and the institution of zero-defect and continuous-improvement policies managed by teams them-

5. For an elaboration of the concept of industrial order in the Baden-Württemberg context, see Herrigel 1993 and Sabel et al. 1989.

6. It is important to emphasize that these "new production methods" cannot be identified with all the practices of all the producers in a particular country—such as Japan or the United States. As the world and European economies become more integrated and national boundaries become less significant, best practice in manufacturing is increasingly located everywhere and nowhere. Examples of highly successful new style flexible production can be found all over the advanced industrial world (even, as we shall see, in Germany). Producers in different national and regional environments implement the new methods in distinctive ways, and they encounter distinctive obstacles to adaptation and adoption. The focus here is on the German chapter of this story.

selves. All of this is organized around and enforced by the maintenance of extremely low inventories throughout the production process (Shingo 1987, 1992; Nishigushi 1992; Koike and Takenori 1987; Womack et al. 1990; Aoki 1988; Rommel et al. 1995).

Such systems attempt to orient the entire process chain in production, from development and design to final assembly, around the needs and desires of the customer. The key to the system's tremendous flexibility is that it reunites the conceptual development of product and production design with their actual manufacture within production units by removing all fixed roles in the workplace. The product teams define and allocate specific tasks of design and manufacture through the process of development and production itself. The key to the system's remarkable innovativeness rests in the close and continuous self-monitoring practices that the new product teams engage in under conditions of extremely low inventory. Because buffers are extremely small, each position in the production process has an incentive to get information about and communicate with the entire set of positions in the process to optimize flow and avoid bottlenecks. This structure engenders continuous discussion within and among product teams about the organization of production and the nature of the product. At its limit, the logic of this alternative system causes the old style "firm" to disintegrate entirely into an infinitely recombinable set of roles and relations that the participants themselves continuously define and structure (Sabel 1994).[7]

Experience in direct competition has proven the superiority of these alternative methods over the traditional German forms of decentralized flexible high-quality production. The significance of the growth in popularity of Toyota's *Lexus* and Nissan's *Infiniti,* for example, has been widely appreciated as a threat to German luxury automobile producers. Without (at least the perception of) any drop in quality, Nissan and especially Toyota, using the alternative production methods, managed to produce luxury cars much more cheaply than Daimler Benz and quickly captured a very large section of the American luxury market during the latter half of the 1980s. By the early 1990s, the Japanese had begun to invade European markets.

If there had been any doubt at Daimler Benz that the production methods deployed by the Japanese were superior to those in its own factories, these doubts were dispelled when it was revealed that their main assembly plant in Sindelfingen was the notorious "anonymous high quality but low produc-

---

7. I am not suggesting that the system described here in the text exists anywhere in the full form outlined in the text, or that it must be adopted in the same way in all places. On the contrary! But it is the case that the principles mentioned in the text are at the center of debate worldwide about the reorganization of production. For a discussion of the diffusion of these principles, with examples taken from throughout the advanced industrial world, especially Japan and the United States, see Sabel 1995.

tivity European plant" in the MIT Automobile Project's famous study of the world automobile industry, *The Machine That Changed the World* (Womack, Jones, and Roos 1990, 91; Cooke, Morgan, and Price 1993). According to the MIT report, this plant was "expending more effort to fix problems it had just created than the Japanese plant required to make a perfectly new car the first time."[8] Daimler Benz itself estimated in 1993 that its production costs were roughly 35 percent higher than those of its main competitors in Japan. In that same year, the company announced a record DM 1.8 billion net loss (Morgan 1994).

The competitive disadvantages of the decentralized German craft manufacturing system relative to the more flexible and lower cost system being adopted by the best of their major competitors is if anything even clearer in the case of the machine tool industry. Here too, the Germans performed badly relative to the Japanese and rejuvenated U.S. producers during the 1990s (Finegold et al. 1994; Schumann et al. 1994, 371–528, esp 406f). Here as in automotive sector, high German production costs and the high quality, greater flexibility, and relentless innovation of competitors have been to blame. Producers of high-quality standardized computer-guided tools, such as Traub Maschinenfabrik of Reichenback/Fils and the Index-Werke of Eßlingen, have been radically outproduced by Asian, especially Japanese producers. The Japanese have been able to match the quality of the German machines at a much better price and with better service and delivery conditions (Schumann et al. 1994, 404–5). At the high end of lower-volume specialty machines, German producers are being squeezed on the one hand by the ever improving quality and flexibility of Japanese standard machines, which can be used in more and more areas formerly accessible only to specialized machinery, and on the other, by resurgent American producers (Finegold et al. 1994; USDC 1994).

The inefficiency of German production relative to the Japanese can readily be seen in the fact that despite a 74 percent increase in production between 1983 and 1990, rates of labor productivity (value-added per employee) in the German industry were well below those in the Japanese industry, which grew at an even more spectacular rate (see Tables 8.1 and 8.2). Labor productivity in the German industry, moreover, did not keep pace with increases in output over the period, while in Japan they did. The gravity of this trend appears, however, only when German performance in international markets in the 1990s is taken into account. The incursion of Japanese and American producers into markets the Germans once dominated is indicated by the movement of world production and trade figures in the 1990s (see Tables 8.3 and 8.4). Since 1990, both Japanese and German

---

8. Daimler's reaction to this news is discussed in Morgan, Cooke, and Price 1992, 13f.

TABLE 8.1. Performance and Costs of German Machine Tool Enterprises

					% Share of Sales	
Indicator*	Unit	1980	1985	1989	1980	1989
Sales	Mill.DM	118	134	183	100.0	100.0
Material Consumption	Mill.DM	59	73	102	50.0	55.9
Value-added	Mill.DM	59	61	81	50.0	44.1
Out of which:						
Depreciation	Mill.DM	4	4	7	3.1	3.7
Staff Expenditure	Mill.DM	48	53	67	40.8	36.7
Other Costs	Mill.DM	3	3	4	2.8	2.5
Total Employees		1081	971	1053		
Data per employee:						
Sales	Thou.DM	109	138	174		
Staff expenditure	Thou.DM	45	55	64		
Value-added	Thou.DM	55	63	77		

* Average values for firms with more than 500 employees. In 1990, these producers represented 19.7 percent of all firms in the industry. 63.3 percent of all employment, a significant proportion of production and the bulk of exports in the industry.
Source: IFO Institut, Statistisches Bundesamt; table adapted from Engelman et al. 1994, 37.

production levels have fallen relative to the United States, Italy, and China, but the German descent has been much more precipitous than the Japanese. More ominous for the Germans, between 1992 and 1993, Germany's total share of world machine tool exports declined by 17 percent, while the

TABLE 8.2. Performance and Costs of Japanese Machine Tool Enterprises †

					% Share of Sales	
Indicator*	Unit	1980	1985	1989	1980	1989
Sales	Mill.DM	298	458	514	100.0	100.0
Material Consumption	Mill.DM	186	285	323	62.4	62.7
Value-added	Mill.DM	112	173	192	37.6	37.3
Out of which:						
Depreciation	Mill.DM	7	13	16	2.3	3.2
Staff Expenditure	Mill.DM	45	69	77	15.2	15.0
Other Costs	Mill.DM	23	38	34	7.7	6.5
Employees	Number	945	1171	1152		
Data per employee:						
Sales	Thou.DM	315.4	390.7	446.6		
Staff expenditure	Thou.DM	48.0	59.0	67.0		
Value-added	Thou.DM	118.6	147.3	166.4		

† Converted using 1989 exchange rate.
* Average values for firms with more than 500 employees.
Source: IFO Institut, Japan Development Bank, Ministry of International Trade and Industry (MITI); table adapted from Engelman et al 1994, 37.

TABLE 8.3. World Shares of Machine Tool Production, 1990–1993 (%)

Country	1990	1991	1992	1993
Japan	23.3	32.9	25.1	25.3
Germany	18.9	25.0	22.7	18.2
USA	6.7	9.3	9.2	11.6
Italy	8.5	9.8	8.8	8.4
China			5.0	6.2
Switzerland	6.8	5.7	4.9	4.8
Taiwan		2.7	2.8	3.8
UK	3.7	3.6	3.0	3.4
South Korea		2.1	1.8	2.2
France		2.9	2.9	2.2
Others		6.0	13.8	13.9

Source: Cooke 1994, 8.

TABLE 8.4. Export Share of World Machine Tools, 1992–1993 (%)

Country	1992	1993
Japan	21.0	26.5
Germany	27.8	22.9
Italy	8.1	9.6
Switzerland	8.6	8.2
USA	5.9	7.0
Taiwan	3.8	4.7
UK	3.5	3.4
France	3.1	2.1
Belgium		2.1
Others	18.1	13.7

Source: Cooke 1994, 8.

Japanese share increased by 25 percent (despite nearly constant appreciation of the yen) and that of American industry increased by 20 percent. The attractiveness of German products in export markets is simply falling off. By 1994, Japanese producers of CNC (computer numerically controlled) lathes accounted for 25 percent of the *German* market for such machines (Cooke 1994).

INTERNAL REORGANIZATION: THE END OF GERMAN-STYLE DECENTRALIZED CRAFT MANUFACTURING?

The decisive difference between the systems of production increasingly being deployed by successful producers throughout Japan, the United

States, and elsewhere and the system of production practiced by large and small producers within the industrial district of Baden-Württemberg is the greater openness and flexibility of the production practices in the former systems. This is extremely paradoxical because it was thought during the 1980s that, in addition to the capacity to utilize specialized subcontractors, the flexibility of small and medium-sized German firms (and even some large-volume producers in the region such as Robert Bosch) rested on the tremendous resourcefulness and autonomy of broadly skilled workers in production and the close, cooperative relations between those skilled shop-floor workers and higher levels of management within the firm. The "lean" or "open" or "simple" forms of flexible organization diffusing in Japan, the United States, and elsewhere, however, rely on far greater worker autonomy and cross-functional and cross-departmental cooperation within the firm than is currently possible within the traditional internal organization of German craft producers (Herrigel and Sabel 1994; Naschold 1994; Kern and Sabel 1993; Rommel et al. 1995).

The sticking points within German firms are roles, jurisdictions, and hierarchies that date back to an earlier period of recomposition in the industrial system. In my book *Industrial Constructions* (Herrigel 1996, chaps. 2 and 5). I show that through the construction and elaboration of an industrial structure of coordinated specialization in the first part of this century, small and medium-sized specialist producers in Germany imposed a degree of stability on themselves that allowed them to rationalize the organization of work within their factories. Homologous processes of rationalization also occurred within large firms at that time (Herrigel 1996, chaps. 3 and 6).[9] Out of this rationalization process emerged two clusters of roles and institutions that have become so pervasive in the organization of German industrial order that they are taken for granted as quasi-natural features of the organization of industrial work: (1) broadly defined yet distinct skill divisions within the production process, and (2) functional divisions within German managerial hierarchies. These institutionalized features of German industrial life played a very significant role in the post-World War II success of German producers, but they now constitute, at least in their current form, obstacles to effective adjustment to the challenge of alternative forms of flexibility.

---

9. It is perhaps obvious, but I think nonetheless important to remind the reader that rationalization should not be understood as the implementation of mass-production techniques. Rather, rationalization involves the clarification and definition of procedures, norms, and roles in *any* kind of production process. Werner Abelshauser makes the point that most of the rationalization in the interwar period occurred in batch-production processes and involved the optimization of the deployment of skilled labor. See Abelshauser 1994, 2.

The Creation of Specific Skills

The first outcome of the early-twentieth-century rationalization process was a system of specific and circumscribed skill categories in production, each with internal hierarchies based on experience and expertise that were supported by an infrastructure of vocational education. Prior to that first great period of rationalization at the beginning of the twentieth century, the internal structure of most small and medium-sized producers and many large-scale craft producers as well, was very open. Skilled workers were cut off, both socially and physically, from the old craft *(Handwerk)* system and deployed their abilities and developed their skills according to the needs of the firm and its customers. Since firms themselves tended to produce a wide variety of specialized products, skilled workers within the firms developed very general and broad skills. Just as in the old craft system, where artisans learned all the operations associated with the craft, the transplanted industrial craftsman learned as many operations as was necessary for the production of specialties associated with the enterprise that employed him (Adelmann 1979; Lee 1978).

During the period of rationalization, firms collectively limited themselves to the manufacture of a limited range of products in order to stabilize product market competition in a broad array of specialized manufacturing industries (Herrigel 1995, chap. 2). These reforms in the structure of product markets had significant consequences for the organization of production and labor markets within specialized producers. In particular, it made obsolete the very broad and general knowledge typical of nineteenth-century skilled craftsmen. Through a long and intense process of social and workplace struggle between management and labor, rationalization ultimately transformed the identity and the role of the skilled worker in specialist production. Skills were newly constituted as discrete and clearly bounded with focused hierarchies of learning that were accorded differentiated degrees of status in society and the workplace. Masters in factories, for example, went from being generalists in broad areas of craft production (such as machine making or ironworking) to specialists with particular, circumscribed areas of vocational expertise, such as lathe operation, tool making, or the repair of electrical circuitry. This process of rationalization was further refined in the early post-World War II decades when many industrial markets became more concentrated and product cycles changed more slowly. Relative stability encouraged the proliferation of specialized jurisdictions at the workplace (on these processes see Herrigel 1996, Seyfert 1920, Preller 1949, Freyberg 1989, and Kern and Schumann 1970).

Through this process, very specifically circumscribed skills and associated job ladders were gradually naturalized and integrated into the way that people thought not only about industrial work and its organization but about virtue, honor, and status for industrial actors in German society.[10] A skilled worker *(Facharbeiter)* demonstrated his or her integrity and acquired prestige through the perfection of his or her craft. Social standards for the evaluation of achievement existed because it was possible to distinguish one group of people's special skills and contributions to the production process from others, both on the shop floor and in the formal negotiations with employers. Moreover, job hierarchies within skill distinctions gave rise to social status distinctions both in the workplace and outside (Kern and Schumann 1970; Mooser 1984).

These relatively rigid role identities formed the basis for the emergence of the estate-like (what the Germans call a *ständische*) position of skilled industrial workers within Germany today. Skilled machinists, for example, are inculcated with a belief in the value of their own expertise for the firm and the significance of their skills for the prosperity of the German economy in the postwar period from the very beginning of their apprenticeships. Their identity as skilled workers provides them with a measure of dignity, and their capacity to exercise their skill and develop it contributes to their elan not only within the factory among their fellows but also in society at large as word and evidence of their expertise spreads throughout their communities. Skilled workers form the backbone of the strong German labor movement and dominate the institutions of workplace representation in German factories.

Finally, although the status of *Facharbeiter* groups skilled workers from all trades equally within the general space of social positions within German society, within each individual skill category there is a fairly rigid paternalistic hierarchy. Older master toolmakers, for example, direct less experienced ones and supervise the shopfloor training of apprentices. They organize the labor market and transfer by example and through instruction the values associated with their trade. Once the status of skilled worker has been achieved, moreover, hierarchy continues to structure the careers of the *Facharbeiter*, as those with greater dexterity or energy (or both) are allocated greater responsibility and given more challenging tasks (Weltz, Schmidt, and Sass 1974; Hildebrandt 1991).

This social world of skilled workers has been periodically modified over the course of the postwar period and quite significantly in the 1980s. In

---

10. For a theoretical description of this kind of deeply entrenched social understanding as an institution, see DiMaggio and Powell 1991, especially the introduction. Bourdieu (1977) refers to such deeply entrenched understandings of the world of practice as "doxa," while Schutz (1962) uses the term "cultural sedimentation" to describe social understandings and practices, such as those described here, which have become a kind of grammar for social behavior in a historically specific social formation.

order to facilitate workplace flexibility, the number of discrete skill designations has been decreased (Streeck 1987). Nevertheless, the underlying principle of specialized skill as a particular role with its attendant jurisdiction and inherent hierarchy continues to structure practice in German workplaces and the institutions that attend to them.

Functional Departments in Management

The second feature of the German manufacturing system that emerged out of the first great period of rationalization in the early twentieth century was the division of management into formal departments specialized by function: purchasing, marketing, development, finance, and production. These departments, which exist in all but the very smallest of enterprises, are typically staffed by a mixture of managers who have been recruited from the shop floor and those with more academic training. They too have particular conceptions of the role their particular department plays in the success of the company and career and status hierarchies based on and cultivated by performance and experience within the milieu of the department itself (Chandler 1990; Hartmann 1959). Initially, such divisions within firms had relatively modest consequences for the degree of bureaucratization within functional departments. But as firms grew larger, particularly with the diffusion of mass production during the Second World War and in the 1950s, bureaucratic hierarchies made up of tiers of specialized managerial positions within each of these functional departments grew very large and the ranks of middle management swelled tremendously (Thannheiser 1975; Pross and Boetticher 1971; Guillen 1994).

If not quite an estate like their blue-collar counterparts, management in Germany has, nevertheless, a very robust sense of its own position in society and of the kinds of achievements, credentials, and social entitlements that should be associated with its role in the economy. Unlike their American counterparts who, with the typical MBA, receive very broad and largely nontechnical business educations, most German managers are technically trained, either as engineers or as *Betriebswirten,* the latter being the far more specialized and technical German variant of the American business degree (Locke 1989 and 1984; Lawrence 1980). Once employed, German managers are typically both mentored and inculcated by their superiors with the traditions and nuances of life in the department and the firm. Technical expertise and seniority are the prerequisites for promotion and for the acquisition of social status.

During much of the postwar period, the German manager was unique for the degree of familiarity he or she showed with the production process and the technical characteristics of the products his or her firm produced. Indeed, the confluence of technical expertise and status in the career path of managers appears to have had the interesting result of facilitating vertical communication within German firms without jeopardizing the hierarchy of distinctions. Many outside observers have noted the ability of German managers to communicate and cooperate with production workers and their representatives, while no one confuses even the lowest levels of management with industrial workers. Such communication allowed for considerable flexibility in production, because production management and labor were able to quickly reach agreement about problems and work together to adapt standard procedures to particular market needs.

Paradoxically, the same factors allowing for vertical communication within firms worked against effective horizontal or cross-functional communication and cooperation. Technical expertise was always specific, and then it was made even more specific as one gained experience in the firm. For example, mechanical engineers learned about the manufacture of a particular area of machine-tool making; accountants, the ins and outs of financial and tax regulations for the particular sector and size of firm that employed them. The process of gaining expertise and status turned managerial heads away from one another and focused them on the functional world in which expertise could be gained and careers made. All of this, naturally, contributed to the maintenance of hierarchy within firms as a whole because the only ones able to coordinate the operations of the various functional departments were those at the very top of the firm (Pross and Boetticher 1971; Lawrence 1980).

For all the success these two "doxic" features (Bourdieu 1977) of specific skill jurisdictions and functional divisions within management have enjoyed over the course of the twentieth century, these clusters of roles and institutions within the German industrial system are proving to be a liability under the current conditions of extremely short product cycles and rapid technological change (Herrigel 1996; Kern and Sabel 1993; Schumann et al. 1994, 643–64; Naschold 1994). The vulnerabilities of the system become clearest in the case of the introduction of new products. Each time a new product or a new technology is introduced—as opposed to an old one that is modified for a particular customer—the roles that each skill category and management function will play in the production and development of the new product must be bargained out. Each currently existing cluster of expertise and institutional power wants to participate; each has its own ideas and solutions; each defends its turf against encroachments from the others; each takes for granted the legitimacy of its claim on a place in the new arrangement within the firm. Electrical masters and technicians, for example, will fight with mechanical ones both on the shop floor and in the design studios over different kinds of technical or manufacturing solutions to problems that have direct consequences on the amount and character of work that each will be able to do and on the contribution each will be able to make to the value of the product.

If the new product involves the increasing interpenetration of formerly distinct areas of technology and expertise—such as microelectronics and mechanical engineering—it will take some time to iron out all of the potential areas of conflict. If the market is stable, it might be possible, even preferable, to wait until these conflicts have been resolved before deciding on the final design of the new product. But, as has been the case in the 1990s, if the market is turbulent and unstable and the lifespan of the current technology is clearly going to be limited, firms are forced to bring their products to the market while these internal conflicts are still being worked out. More often than not, impatient, nervous senior managers pressed for time but no less ignorant of the technology or the market than the contending specialists, are forced to broker compromises between the players in a way that allows the solutions of each—to the extent that they are not contradictory—to be built into the product, simply to get the new product to market before the next wave of even newer products and technologies (Schlichter 1994). It should not be surprising that the products of such compromises will appear inelegant, overpriced, and "over-engineered"—they are.

DEALING WITH SELF-BLOCKAGE: SUCCESSES AND FAILURES

In German factories today the need to introduce new products more and more quickly has eroded the boundaries between traditional skill and management divisions and given rise to jurisdictional disputes that are driving up costs and driving down quality. Such jurisdictional conflicts do not exist in the alternative flexible systems that the Germans are competing against because these systems have fewer fixed jurisdictions and occupational identities in the first place. By combining development and production (simultaneous engineering) and utilizing modular sourcing and U-shaped, team-managed production lines, many Japanese and American competitors are bringing out new products relatively rapidly and cheaply that are elegantly designed, of high quality, and attentive to customer needs.

This is extremely difficult to do in the German system as it is constituted today in Baden-Württemberg. To implement more boundary-blending forms of cooperation (both vertical and horizontal) in development and production, the system of discrete skill jurisdictions, career hierarchies, and functional pillarization within firms must be deconstructed and recomposed in a more flexible way. Given the centrality of skill and technical expertise within the social organization of small, medium-sized, and large producers in Germany, however, this has not been proving easy to do.

Firms throughout the manufacturing economy have recognized the need to change, especially since the onset of crisis in the early 1990s and the emergence of the remarkable gaps between German levels of productivity and those of competitors.[11] Yet few producers, large or small, have been able to overcome the opposition of entrenched groupings of skilled workers who when threatened with the loss of status through incorporation into teams that deny the boundaries of former jurisdictional specializations or independent departments, have resisted the redefinition and dilution of their functional areas of power. It is difficult, after all, to tell workers and managers who with considerable legitimacy understand themselves as having contributed significantly to the traditional success of high-quality manufacturing in Germany that their roles have become obstacles to adjustment.

In many cases such conflicts have given rise to furtively self-undermining efforts of adjustment in formerly successful specialized German firms. The two examples of self-blockage to be discussed here were drawn from a pool of firms examined during a research sojourn in Baden-Württemberg in the summer of 1994.[12] Both cases show a dynamic of resistance to change on the part of entrenched jurisdictional interests, yet in one it is labor that is the primary sticking point, while in the other it is management.

These two examples of self-blockage will then be followed by two cases in which the resistance of entrenched interests has apparently been overcome. These cases make the important point that the absolute decline of German industrial competitiveness in the current environment is not inevitable, but that successful adjustment can be achieved if labor and management find a way to reconceptualize the fundamental features of social identity and industrial governance that have heretofore been considered central to German competitiveness.

TWO CASES OF SELF-BLOCKAGE

The first example of self-blockage is that of an electric turbine works in southwest Germany belonging to a large European electromechanical

---

11. Naschold (1994, 16) claims that despite the skepticism that emerged around the debate about lean production in Germany there is a consensus within the current discussion of work reorganization on the need for a fundamental reorientation. In particular, most people agree on the need for zero-defect manufacturing, customer-oriented process chains, decentralized responsibility in production, new constitution of the relationship between conception and execution within the firm, and the institution of processes of continuous improvement in production.

12. These cases were selected from over thirty interviews with German manufacturers, trade unionists, government officials, and association bureaucrats conducted in Baden-Württemberg in June and July of 1994 by the author and Charles F. Sabel of Columbia University Law School.

multinational (interview, June 1994—name of firm withheld by request). The globally active parent concern has systematically attempted to implement many of the characteristics of the alternative form of open flexible system mentioned above. It has cultivated the development of a new kind of management career in which individual managers move cross-functionally throughout the organization, accumulating knowledge of the company, its products, its suppliers, and its customers. Promotion within the parent firm is increasingly becoming contingent on having successfully participated in cooperative product development teams made up of members of different departments as well as key suppliers. To encourage this, the parent company has introduced what it calls a Customer Focus Program (CFP) throughout its subsidiaries. This CFP brings managers together across subsidiaries as well as across functional departments on a regular basis to foster dialogue on how to improve company products and develop new technologies. This is not simply a discussion group, however. Because it reconstitutes itself regularly, the CFP also acts as a kind of monitoring forum for projects and subsidiaries throughout the organization. In many subsidiaries, this collaborative, team-and product-oriented organizational practice has been taken right down to the shop floor in the form of group work and product-oriented, low-inventory production.

Not so in the turbine works under discussion. Hierarchy flattening has occurred within the departmental structures above the shop floor, where a number of CFP groups exist. But the production process itself remains dominated by the old workshop system of skill distinctions and hierarchies. The plants in southwest Germany continued to be organized around specialized machine and/or part production. Typically, any given work station operates with an inventory of up to five days. Operators working on particular machines dedicated to the production of a specific range of parts had little idea where their work object fit into the larger product the plant was constructing—one machinist had no idea where the parts he was making were going to go next in the line of production. Masters and foremen set up machines.

Why has this system of skill jurisdictions continued to exist beneath an increasingly open, flexible, management structure? In part the answer stems from the strategy that the local firm pursued after the former parent company of the German turbine works merged with another European electromechanical producer in the late 1980s. Prior to the merger, the German plant was capable of making complete electrical turbine generators. After the merger the plant was broken up and parts of the production process were shifted to facilities in other locations. The southwest German plant was specialized on large-part production. Thousands of layoffs resulted from these changes in the location of production. Perhaps understandably, given the massive job losses, the works council and trade unions have been reluctant to engage in additional restructuring within the production lines that remain for fear of additional layoffs. The local labor representation was persuaded that additional losses would redound to its disadvantage and therefore defended the traditional job structure. Labor representatives resist the new structures, in other words, because they believe they must defend the traditional roles and status of the workers they represent if they are to retain their own power and position within the firm and their institutional position in the labor market. But management, which is committed to the larger European parent company, but not to the southwest German location, is becoming increasingly frustrated and is currently considering relocating.

The second case of self-blockage is a medium-sized machine tool company in southern Württemberg. Here, an important obstacle to the adoption of the new system has been management, not labor (interview, June 1994 —name witheld by request). This machine tool company manufactures large-scale stamping machines for the automobile industry. The company has made tremendous strides toward completely revamping its production process through the introduction of integrated product islands and group work. The traditional workshop system has been modified so that machines are now grouped around the production of particular groups of products rather than around parts for all products. All set-up, production-planning, and delivery-scheduling tasks, formerly carried out by the masters and foremen of the individual machine shops, or by a level of middle management located directly above the floor of the plant, have been integrated into the new product islands. Members of product-development teams, moreover, now continually move between activity in the production teams and the relocated engineering rooms on the shop floor. Technicians, programmers, engineers, and skilled machine operators now work side by side in close cooperation and to some extent interchangeably within the teams. Groups within the islands have begun electing their own representatives to facilitate the coordination of their own internal duties as well as to maintain contact with the operations of the other groups and other product islands.

There are two factors within the firm, however, which significantly disturb the operation of these islands and constrain their ability to produce significant gains in efficiency and cost reduction. First, the changes in production have only been introduced in the areas of direct mechanical production—areas of work preparation, such as tool making and materials purchasing, have neither been organized into teams nor adapted to the needs of teams. As a result, teams have only limited control over their overhead costs. Since the idea of the introduction of teams is to devolve responsibility for holding down costs to the teams themselves, lack of control over overheads engenders frustration on the shop floor—and skepticism regarding the effectiveness of the new system. Changing this arrangement, however, involves attacking the privileges of some of the most highly skilled workers in the plant (toolmakers) and the prerogative of purchasing managers—something the management of the firm, at least until now, has been unwilling to do.

Second, changes in production have not been accompanied by corresponding efforts to deconstruct the hierarchical relations between top management departments and the newly emergent product-team structure. Management has retained the right to veto group decisions that it believes will not result in the cost savings it desires. It has also retained control over the budgets of the product islands: company management, not the teams, make investment decisions and ultimately evaluate the performance of the teams. A speaker for one of the product islands as well as the head of all manufacturing at the firm claimed that this limitation on local autonomy and the continued existence of hierarchy threatened to undermine the effectiveness of the product islands and teams. When members of the group believe that their success or failure is the direct result of their collective efforts, all have an incentive to make continuous improvements. Without local autonomy, however, such incentives do not exist, and the commitment of team members to the success of the team is undermined.

Both examples show that a partial movement away from the old principles of specific skill jurisdictions and functional departments diminishes the credibility of the new organizational principles in the eyes of the participants. Making a full commitment, however, means taking privilege and authority away from those with little desire to give them up. Clearly there is no equilibrium with the current arrangement. Doing nothing leads to the gradual erosion of morale and enthusiasm within the new product islands; returning to the old system of specific skill jurisdictions and functional divisions within management prices the firm out of the market; moving forward requires the spilling of blood. Someone is going to lose this battle, and the stakes in the world market at the moment are such that it may be the firm itself. Given that conflicts of this kind are legion at present throughout Baden-Württemberg and the German industrial economy generally, it is easy to see that the current situation is a grave one for German industry.

SELF-BLOCKAGE TRANSCENDED: GERMANY REINVENTED?

There is a ray of hope in the gloomy picture the preceding examples have painted. In two other cases, producers have been able to overcome entrenched interests and transform the entire organization and structure of how they produce industrial goods. Both cases also demonstrate, however, that successful adjustment poses very profound questions about identity, authority, and institutional design in labor and product markets narrowly and in German society more broadly. Indeed, moving from these isolated cases of success to a general process of successful adjustment ultimately will have to involve a collective process of self-reinvention on the order of the kind of transformative social discussion that took place during the first great period of rationalization at the beginning of the twentieth century.

The first example of a producer that has apparently been able to successfully break from the old system of skill jurisdictions and functional departments and adopt a more open and flexible alternative is the medium-sized family firm, Getrag, located in northern Württemberg. The firm is a manufacturer of high-performance gear units for standard-shift automobiles. Getrag began to initiate major changes in its organization in 1987 in order to meet stringent cost and quality terms being demanded in a new contract with BMW (itself a company that has made great strides toward the adoption of the alternative system, see Sabel, Kern, and Herrigel 1991, and Herrigel 1996, chap. 6). According to a spokesman for Getrag, the reorganization was to be guided by the idea that the new organization would be defined more by a process of change than by a specific organizational structure. The company literally and somewhat naively set out to constitute "trusting" relations among all actors within the firm, regardless of role or position, based on mutual respect. It discouraged thinking in terms of hierarchy and status and made all information about the company (its finances, its products, its suppliers, its customers) available to everyone within it.

To realize this, product teams were created that combined the previously separate departments of development, planning, purchasing, and production. The many levels of management hierarchy in the old system between top management and shop floor were reduced to three. Relations with Getrag suppliers were also reformed so that their parts and materials would be delivered according to the stringent cost and quality standards of the *Kanban* system.

It is at the level of the production process, however, in which the departure from the old system can be seen most clearly. In the restructuring, the production process was broken down and completely reorganized. All line and workshop organization was eliminated, and production and assembly islands, governed by autonomous work teams, were introduced. Members of the teams allocate work among themselves and take responsibility for most aspects of their quality control and maintenance. Island teams possess a small budget to help them perform these tasks. Teams also have the option of turning to different suppliers—inevitably also outsiders—to ensure that their quality responsibilities are met. Workers in the teams are not constrained by old skill categories: their responsibility is to keep the island performing at exacting cost and quality standards in the best way that they can.

One of the ways they do this is to interact with the other work teams and with suppliers in order to continually optimize and improve the entire production flow. In an effort to encourage this kind of cross-boundary communication, even the old apprenticeship system is being broken down. Rather than train workers in specific trades away from the production process under the stewardship of masters, the firm attempts to integrate the apprentices into the teams from the start. Rather than learn a specific craft skill, newer apprentices are trained in the much more demanding trade of general problem solving and cooperation.

The new system, which the firm has been introducing piecemeal over the last seven years, has been tremendously successful. The firm has rates of machine utilization above 80 percent in the teams, while serviceability rates on the same production machinery (time not spent in repair) are over 90 percent. Moreover, over the course of the last seven years, the firm has introduced three new generations of its product.

A second example of successful adjustment is the small machinery firm Mettler Toledo, a maker of electronic scales and weighing devices in the Schwäbische Alb in southern Württemberg. Reorganization at Mettler Toledo was brought on by a financial crisis associated with an unsuccessful shift to new microelectronic variants of their product during the mid-1980s. New management was brought in with a mandate to restructure the company radically. Management made two major moves. First, all production was shifted onto area suppliers so that the company could focus its energies fully on product development, product assembly, and sales. Relations with suppliers, which were already very close and cooperative before the reorganization, were intensified; important providers were drawn directly into the development process.

Second, all remaining activities within the firm were reorganized into teams. No functional divisions or departments survived the reorganization, and all levels of formal middle management associated with those areas were dissolved. The company was reorganized around products and process. Teams organized by themselves the development and production of new products and dealt with the continuing needs of existing customers. The emphasis was on total process optimization and improvement. Teams maintained intimate and open contact with the assembly workers about individual orders. Assemblers worked as individuals and had responsibility for the complete assembly of a product. They could call on team members for advice and service at any time. As at Getrag, this reorganization at Mettler Toledo led the firm to attempt to get away from the old specific skill jurisdiction-based system of apprenticeship and to integrate apprentices right from the beginning into production and team work.

Neither of these successes were painless. Both were initiated in periods of financial and market crisis for the firms. The elimination of hierarchy involved the dislocation of many unnecessary jobs in middle management. The introduction of teams made it possible for fewer workers to perform more operations—which made many other workers redundant. Hundreds of workers and managers lost their jobs at Getrag and Mettler Toledo over the course of the long transition to the new system. Moreover, the cases are fairly isolated within the landscape of German industrial producers, and their situation is unique because of the early onset of crisis. Nevertheless, they are important to note because they make it difficult to claim that the Germans cannot change and that they must live or die by the old system of specific skill jurisdictions and functional departments.

Movement beyond these isolated cases, however, will require that all actors in the German industrial system reevaluate their own roles and their relations to one another. The effect of team work on how firms view vocational training is one example of how processes of reform within firms also involve institutional systems that go well beyond the firm's boundaries. At both Getrag and Mettler Toledo, teams are flirting with illegality by integrating apprentices into actual team work—there has been a long taboo against using apprentices for productive labor. It is by no means clear that the vocational system will be reformed to accommodate this kind of behavior. Reform would make it easier for other producers to do the same, as well as remove an institutional support for the old system of jurisdictions. There is likely to be opposition to this not only among skilled workers and their representatives but from instructors in *Berufschulen* and *Fachhochschulen* as well, who themselves possess identities and roles in the educational system that correspond to the old system of skill jurisdictions (as well as to old distinctions between management and labor in production). Accommodation at a general institutional level in a way that would allow experiments to become generalized would invariably call these secondary identities, roles, and relations within the supporting infrastructure of institutions surrounding the industrial economy into question.

Will the creation of new kinds of workers and new institutional arrangements within firms result in the creation of new kinds of educators and a new system of disciplines in the academy capable of serving the industrial economy? It is not possible to answer this question now, but it is easy to see in this case how debate and experimentation about the reform of roles and positions within firms must lead to reevaluation and debate about the relationship between the firm and the identities, roles, and structures of supporting institutions in society. Failure to engage in this process of collective self-redefinition could ultimately be devastating for German international competitiveness; doing so will involve a massive reconceptualization of the German industrial order.

This example of the relationship between internal reform of production and the reform of vocational training is only one among a myriad of interconnected changes currently taking place in Germany. With more space, it would be possible to show how teams are creating a system of workplace representation that could potentially rival, if not supplant, the one that currently exists in German workplaces. How will trade unions deal with self-governing work teams in which the old distinction between management and labor no longer applies? What will happen to traditional conceptions of the firm and private property if existing firms recompose themselves into self-governing production teams with their own budgets? None of the old actors in the German industrial system are unaffected by the current changes, and all will be participating in the public dialogue that will invariably accompany it. It seems fairly clear that whatever happens, the roles and identities of actors and the institutional structures that help to support and govern them will be (re)constituted simultaneously in and through the process of dialogue itself.

TOWARD A NEW SYSTEM OF FLEXIBLE PRODUCTION?

This is a crucial period for German manufacturing. If firms, large and small, succeed in adopting and adapting within themselves the same kind of low-inventory, low-cost, high-quality manufacturing of their most sophisticated competitors, it could very well result in the complete transformation in the kind of decentralized industrial production that has existed in regions like the southwest of Germany for much of the twentieth century. Already extensive external decentralization (the existence of collaborative ties beyond the boundaries of the firm) will be matched by the dissolution of the internal architecture of the firm in a way that integrates development and purchasing with the shop floor in the form of self-recombinatory teams.

If, on the other hand, the entrenched interests in the old departments of management and among the various skilled groupings on the shop floor succeed in blocking movements in this direction, it is difficult to imagine, given the dramatic productivity and cost differentials currently separating German producers from their major competitors, how the decentralized industrial order can continue to reproduce itself in the form it adopted in the 1980s. German flexible manufacturing finds itself at a crossroads not unlike the situation it faced at the beginning of the twentieth century during the great period of rationalization and the subsequent diffusion of mass production. An unprecedented and extremely strong challenge from abroad is creating the conditions as well as the incentives for producers to break out of and recompose existing arrangements. Time will tell how plastic the current system actually is and how much of it, if any at all, will survive.

REFERENCES

Abelshauser, Werner. 1994. "Two Kinds of Fordism: On the Differing Roles of the Automobile Industry in the Development of the Two German States." Unpublished manuscript, Bielefeld.

Adelmann, Gerd. 1979. "Die berufliche Aus-und Weiterbildung in der deutschen Wirtschaft, 1871–1918." In H. Pohl, ed., *Die berufliche Aus- und Weiterbildung in der deutschen Wirtschaft seit dem 19. Jahrhundert*. Wiesbaden: Franz Steiner.

Aoki, Masahiko. 1988. *Information, Incentives, and Bargaining in the Japanese Economy*. New York: Cambridge University Press.

Association of German Economic Research Institutes. 1992. "The Economic Situation in Germany." *Intereconomics* 27, no. 6: 301–4.

Atkinson, Rick. 1994. "Germany Forced to Reexamine Key Elements of Economy." *Washington Post*, August 9, p. A12.

Bourdieu, Pierre. 1977. *Outline of A Theory of Practice*. New York: Cambridge University Press.

Chandler, Alfred. 1990. *Scale and Scope*. Cambridge: Harvard University Press.

Cooke, Philip. 1994. "The Baden-Württemberg Machine Tool Industry: Regional Responses to Global Threats." Center for Advanced Studies, University of Wales, Cardiff, May.

Cooke, Philip, and Kevin Morgan. 1990a. "Industry, Training and Technology Transfer: The Baden-Württemberg System in Perspective." British Council, Cardiff City Council, Welsh Development Agency, Welsh Office.

———. 1990b. "Learning through Networking: Regional Innovation and the Lessons of Baden-Württemberg." Regional Research Report, University of Cardiff.

Cooke, Philip, Kevin Morgan, and Adam Price. 1993. "The Future of the Mittelstand: Collaboration versus Competition." Regional Industrial Research, Department of City and Regional Planning, University of Wales College of Cardiff, Report 13; April.

DiMaggio Paul, and Walter Powell, eds. 1991. *The New Institutionalism in Organizational Analysis*. Chicago: University of Chicago Press.

Engelmann, Frank C., Christian Heyd, Daniel Köstler, and Peter Paustian. 1994. "The German Machine Tool Industry." Appendix 2 of Finegold et al. 1994.

Finegold, David, Keith Brendly, Robert Lempert, Donald Henry, and Peter Cannon. 1994. *Machines On the Brink: The Decline of the U.S. Machine Tool Industry and Prospects for Its Recovery.* RAND DRR-496-OSTP, prepared for the Office of Science and Technology Policy.

Freyberg, Thomas von. 1989. *Industrielle Rationalisierung in der Weimarer Republik.* Frankfurt: Campus.

Funck, R., and G. Becher. 1994. "Regional Development and Technology Policies: Some Lessons from the German Experience." *European Planning Studies* 2:81–96.

Guillen, Mauro. 1994. *Work, Authority, and Organization in a Comparative Perspective.* Chicago: University of Chicago Press.

Hassink, Robert. 1992. "Regional Innovation Policy: Case Studies from the Ruhr Area, Baden-Württemberg and the North East of England." Ph.D. diss., Faculteit Ruimtelijke Wetenschappen Rijksuniversiteit Utrecht.

Hartmann, Heinz. 1959. *Authority and Organization in German Management.* Princeton: Princeton University Press.

Heilemann, Ulrich. 1993. "Mo' Money? Medium-Term Perspectives of the West German Economy." *Economie Appliquée* 46, no. 1: 63–82.

Herrigel, Gary. 1989. "Industrial Order and the Politics of Industrial Change." In Katzenstein 1989, 185–220.

———. 1993. "Large Firms, Small Firms and the Governance of Flexible Specialization." In Bruce Kogut, ed., *Country Competitiveness. Technology and the Organizing of Work.* New York: Oxford University Press.

———. 1996. *Industrial Constructions: The Sources of German Industrial Power.* New York: Cambridge University Press.

Herrigel, Gary, and Charles Sabel. 1994 "Craft Production in Crisis: Industrial Restructuring in Germany during the 1990s." Paper presented at the conference "Globalization and Regionalization: Implications and Options for the Asian NIEs," East-West Center, Honolulu, Hawaii, August 15–17.

Hildebrandt, Eckhardt, ed. 1991. *Betriebliche Sozialverfassung unter Veränderungsdruck. Konzepte, Variante, Entwicklungstendenzen.* Berlin: edition sigma.

Industrie-und Handelskammer Heilbronn: Wirtschaftsdienst. June 1994.

Isaak, Robert. 1992. "Germany: Economic Powerhouse or Stalemate?" *Challenge* 35, no. 5: 41ff.

Iwer, Frank. 1994. *Industriestandort Stuttgart 1994. Entwicklung und Perspektiven der Metallindustrie.* Regionale Branchenanalyse im Auftrag der IG Metall Verwaltungsstelle Stuttgart. Munich: IMU-Institut für Medienforschung und Urbanistik, April.

Katzenstein, Peter, ed. 1989. *Industry and Politics in West Germany: Toward a Third Republic.* Ithaca: Cornell University Press.

Kern, Horst, and Charles Sabel. 1993. "Verblaßte Tugend. Die Krise des deutschen Produktionsmodells." *Umbrüche gesellschaftlicher Arbeit,* Special issue of *Soziale Welt.*

Kern, Horst, and Michael Schumann. 1970. *Industriearbeit und Arbeiterbewusstsein.* Frankfurt: Europaische Verlagsanstalt.

Koike, Kazuo, and Takenori Inoki, eds. 1987. *Skill Formation in Japan and Southeast Asia.* Tokyo: Tokyo University Press.

Lawrence, Peter. 1980. *Managers and Management in West Germany.* New York: St. Martin's Press.

Lee, J. J. 1978. "Labour in German Industrialisation." In Peter Mathis and M. M. Postan, eds., *The Cambridge Economic History of Europe. Vol. 7, The Industrial Economies: Capital, Labor and Enterprise. Pt. 1, Britain, France, Germany, and Scandinavia,* 442–91. Cambridge: Cambridge University Press.

Locke, Robert. 1984. *The End of the Practical Man: Entrepreneurship and Higher Education in Germany, France, and Great Britain, 1880–1940.* Greenwich, Conn.: JAI Press.

———. 1989. *Management and Higher Education since 1940: The Influence of America and Japan on West Germany, Great Britain, and France.* New York: Cambridge University Press.

Mooser, Josef. 1984. *Arbeiterleben in Deutschland, 1900–1970.* Frankfurt: Suhrkamp.

Morgan, Kevin. 1994. "Reversing Attrition? The Auto Cluster in Baden-Württemberg." Paper prepared for the workshop Explaining Regional Competitiveness and the Capability to Innovate: The Case of Baden-Württemberg, Stuttgart, 29/30 June.

Morgan, Kevin, Philip Cooke, and Adam Price. 1992. "The Challenge of Lean Production in German Industry." Regional Industrial Research, Department of City and Regional Planning, University of Wales, Cardiff, Report no. 12.

Naschold, Frieder. 1994. "Jenseits des baden-württembergischen 'Exceptionalism': Strukturproblem der deutschen Industrie." Unpublished manuscript, Berlin.

Nishigushi, Toshihiro. 1992. *Strategic Industrial Sourcing.* New York: Oxford University Press.

Preller, Ludwig. 1949. *Sozialpolitik in der Weimarer Republik.* Stuttgart: Franz Mittelbach Verlag.

Pross, Helge, and Karl W. Boetticher. 1971. *Manager des Kapitalismus.* Frankfurt: Suhrkamp.

Rommel, Günther, Jürgen Kluge, Rolf-Dieter Kempis, Raimond Diederich, and Felix Brücke. 1995. *Simplicity Wins: How Germany's Mid-Sized Industrial Companies Succeed.* Boston: Harvard Business School Press.

Sabel, Charles F. 1994. "Learning by Monitoring: The Institutions of Economic Development." In Niel Smelser and Richard Swedberg, eds., *Handbook of Economic Sociology*. Princeton: Russel Sage and Princeton University Press.

———. 1995. "Bootstrapping Reform: Rebuilding Firms, The Welfare State and Unions." *Politics and Society* 23, no. 1 (March): 5–48.

Sabel, Charles, Gary Herrigel, Richard Deeg, and Richard Kazis. 1989."Regional Prosperities Compared: Baden-Württemberg and Massachusetts in the 1980s." *Economy and Society* 18, no. 4 November 374–404.

Sabel, Charles, Horst Kern, and Gary Herrigel. 1991. "Kooperative Produktion. Neue Formen der Zusammenarbeit zwischen Endfertigern und Zulieferern in der Automobilindustrie und die Neuordnung der Firma." In Hans Gerhard Mendius and Ulrike Wendeling-Schroeder, eds., *Zulieferer im Netz. Neustrukturierung der Logistik am Beispiel der Automobilzulieferung*, 203–27. Köln: Bund Verlag.

Schlichter, Carsten. 1994. "Karriere im Schlanken Unternehmen. Veränderte Rahmenbedingungen für die Mitarbeiterentwicklung." *Personalführung* 5:386–95.

Schumann, Michael, Volker Baethge-Kinsky, Martin Kuhlmann, Constanze Kurz, and Uwe Neumann. 1994. *Trendreport Rationalisierung. Automobile Industrie, Werkzeugmaschinenbau, Chemische Industrie*. Berlin: edition sigma.

Schutz, Alfred. 1962. *Collected Works. Vol. 1, The Problem of Social Reality*, ed. Maurice Natanson. The Hague: Martinus Nijhoff.

Semlinger, Klaus. 1993."Economic Development and Industrial Policy in Baden-Württemberg: Small Firms in a Benevolent Environment." *European Planning Studies* 1: 435–64.

Seyfert, E. W. 1920. *Der Arbeiternachwuchs in der deutschen Maschinenindustrie*. Berlin: Julius Springer.

Shingo, Shingeo. 1987. *Non-Stock Production: The Shingo System for Continuous Improvement*. Cambridge, Mass.: Productivity Press.

———. 1992. *The Shingo Production Management System: Improving Process Functions*. Cambridge, Mass.: Productivity Press.

Simon, Herman. 1992. "Lessons from Germany's Mid-Sized Giants." *Harvard Business Review,* March-April.

Streeck, Wolfgang, Josef Hilbert, Karl-Heinz von Kevelaer, Friederike Maier, and Hajo Weber. 1987. *The Role of the Social Partners in Vocational Training and Further Training in the Federal Republic of Germany*. Berlin: CEDEFOP.

Thannheiser, Heinz. 1975. "Strategy and Structure in Germany." In H. Thannheiser and Gareth Dyas, eds., *The Emergence of the European Enterprise*. London: MacMillan.

U.S. Department of Commerce, International Trade Administration. 1994. *Industry Outlook 1994*. Chap. 16, *Metalworking Equipment*. Washington, D.C.: U.S. Government Printing Office, Department of Commerce.

Weltz, Friedrich, Gert Schmidt, and Jürgen Sass. 1974. *Facharbeiter im Industriebetrieb. Eine Untersuchung in Metalverarbeitenden Betrieben.* Frankfurt: Athenaeum Verlag.

Womack, James P., Daniel T. Jones, and Daniel Roos. 1990. *The Machine That Changed the World. The Story of Lean Production.* New York: Rawson Associates.

Zukunftskommission Wirtschaft 2000. 1993. *Aufbruch aus der Krise.* Bericht der Zukunftskommission Wirtschaft 2000 von Baden-Württemberg. Stuttgart: Staatsministerium Baden-Württemberg.

9 • Renegotiating the German Model: Labor-Management Relations in the New Germany

Kirsten S. Wever

The key strength of German employment relations is inclusiveness (Turner 1998; Wever 1995a; Soskice 1991; Thelen 1991; Keim and Unger 1986). The chief weaknesses are the institutional, organizational, and strategic rigidities that limit the substance of what can be negotiated among the different actors (Herrigel, Chapter 8 in this volume; Silvia, Chapter 7 in this volume; Link 1993; Busch 1992; BDA 1991; Lane 1989; Maurice, Sellier, and Silvestre 1986). For example, German labor and management face peculiar problems in developing the kinds of flexible new forms of employment relations and work and production organization necessary to competitiveness in the international marketplace. Moreover, key institutions underlying the collective, centralized framework for employment relations are under pressure. Indeed, some observers who question the viability of the German model of industrial relations contend that these institutions are eroding.

Do changes in the German model represent a shift toward the "cowboy capitalist" end of the continuum—the Anglo-American model, characterized by a free (as opposed to social) market, relatively decentralized employment relations and management-driven (unilateral, as opposed to negotiated) industrial relations (see, for example, Wever and Turner 1995, Gazdar 1995, and Locke, Kochan, and Piore 1995)? My argument is that although relationships and dynamics in the German political economy (and particularly in the arena of employment relations) represent important departures from past practices, what we are seeing is not wholesale decline but renegotiation of the model. The essentially negotiated model of adjustment remains in place because of the articulation between employment relations and actor strategies. The key institutions of German employment relations remain inclusive and flexible, for the most part because the chief actors have an *interest* in maintaining them. Because they are flexible, the main actors also have the ability to develop adjustment strategies that *can* maintain them.[1]

BACKGROUND: THE ARGUMENT IN BRIEF

The government and the labor and employer communities can all be credited with upholding critical aspects of the negotiated postwar German model of capitalist democracy. The government has provided a strong and stable institutional infrastructure—*Rahmenbedingungen* (framework conditions)—within which both business and labor have found ample incentives to engage in a collaborative relationship from the micro to the macro level (see Allen 1989). The business community takes full advantage of the stability offered by a relatively quiescent labor movement and the supportive framework offered by the social market economy, including prominently a highly skilled workforce. Sure and steady management practices harness extensive worker and manager skills based on functional specialization and favoring concrete technical competence over general managerial qualifications (Berg 1993). In a sort of tacit pact with the employer community, the unions, led by IG Metall, actively try to influence technological change (Turner 1991). The German unions are prepared to modify their wage demands when the overall economic good seems to require it, and they allow the works councils (which are formally independent, enterprise-based, and legally mandated) to negotiate the terms of change in concrete ways that fit the needs of a specific company. This dynamic remains essentially in place in the new (unified) Germany (Turner 1998).

However, the breath-taking events that began with the symbolic fall of the Berlin wall in 1989 and resulted in German unification less than a year later introduced a great deal of uncertainty, a host of unfamiliar challenges, a vast economic burden, and an entirely new political landscape. The terms

1. This chapter is based in part on field research (interviews and case studies) undertaken in Germany between 1990 and 1994. The research involved over 100 interviews with union officials, works councillors, operations and human resources (HR) managers at all organizational levels, employer association representatives, and workers in both eastern and western Germany. Interviews were conducted in a variety of companies operating in a range of sectors, including the banking, metalworking, chemicals, and software industries. The research included eight in-depth case studies of local labor-management relations in the context of industrial restructuring, changing work practices and production/service delivery reorganization. I detail the methodology and elaborate this argument at length in Wever 1995a. I also draw on the recent research of many colleagues—some of whom also contributed to this book (see, for instance, the chapters by Herrigel, Turner, Silvia, and Knuth).

of economic and political competition have changed; traditional forms of production organization have been called into question; the cost of German labor remains high; the German service industries and high-technology sectors are weak in international markets; and the pressure for Germany to conform to the less "social" market standards of other European Union countries (and the rest of the world) is mounting (Streeck and Vitols 1994; Link 1993; Streeck 1991; Vogel 1988). The German employer community is increasingly uneasy about the continued viability of Germany as a site for investments—a problem known in Germany as *Standort Deutschland.*

FUNCTIONAL RIGIDITIES WITHIN THE FIRM

Much research points to the existence of profound functional rigidities in German organizations (Herrigel, Chapter 8 in this book; Hofstede, 1980; Lane 1989; Walgenbach 1993). While these rigidities are significant I argue that increasing flexibility is possible so as to accommodate changing external pressures. Empirical evidence in support of this position can be drawn from changes in the nature of union-works council relations and local labor-management relations over the postwar period; German managers' adoption of foreign organizational policies (particularly human resource policies); and current debates within Germany about the nature of management training and its impact on organizational innovation and structure.

The Evolution of Local Industrial Relations in the Postwar Era

Thelen (1991) has exposed the profound changes in the nature of union–works council relations over the postwar period. The Works Constitution Act of 1952 established Germany's "second channel" of worker representation: nationally mandated works councils, which can be elected by blue- and white-collar employees at all workplaces with five or more employees, formally independent of the unions, and responsible for the implementation of collective bargaining agreements between industry unions and employer associations at the regional level.

At the time of the passage of this act, both unions and employers were suspicious of the councils. Unions viewed them as potential competitors, and employers saw them as potential agents of the unions. Over time, however, both unions and employers came to see the councils in a much more favorable light. In the 1970s unions began to appreciate the importance of workplace-level negotiations with employers over the nature of work and production organization, prompting them to develop alliances with the councils. Working together, councils and unions analyzed workplace structures and their influence on job definitions, skills, and internal labor markets. With these linkages and dynamics in mind, they developed strategies to counter management efforts at workplace rationalization. Many of these innovations were spearheaded by the metalworking union (IG Metall, see also Turner 1991), but they were also adopted and expanded by other unions, including prominently the service union (Gewerkschaft Handel, Banken und Versicherung, or HBV; see, for instance, Duwe and Becker-Töpfer 1988). The nature of labor-management relations at the workplace level necessarily changed as a result of these new union–works council alliances and strategies. In many cases, changes in workplace training, the allocation of human resources, job definitions, and worker-supervisor relations (and so on) were either initiated or strongly influenced by workers and their representatives, in both councils and unions.

Three brief examples illustrate the point. At VW, the union and the councils developed far-reaching training innovations linked to changes in the organization of production and the workplace (Kakalick 1989). Management negotiation and cooperation with the works councils took on entirely new dimensions as the main local actors adjusted to the new strategies of the representatives of labor (see also Turner 1991). Recent agreements involving shorter working hours, more flexibility in how management can utilize labor, and employment security are based on the structures erected by these earlier innovations (Bispinck 1993).

At Betrix Cosmetics, a small firm in the chemicals sector, the works council pressured management to introduce a job rotation scheme, in order to enhance the quality of jobs and change the nature of worker-supervisor relations. In this case the chemical workers' union (IG Chemie) not only failed to help the works council but may have tried to prevent it from implementing its proactive strategy of work reorganization. In other words, the council's redefinition of its roles and responsibilities in the firm (and management's response) occurred even in the absence of institutional support from higher levels (the union or the employer association; see Wever 1994).

At the Commerzbank, HBV (the union) and the works councils at various branches developed strategies linking work organizational changes to particular new technologies in an attempt to influence management's information systems strategy. Here, the union worked with individual employees, including but not limited to works councillors, to define how technological and organizational change repositioned them in the firm (e.g., with respect to the internal labor market, worker-supervisor relations, and job definitions) and to develop a reorganization plan that would accommodate the new technologies as well as employees' workplace interests (Duwe and Becker-Töpfer 1988).

In short, the roles of German workers, their representatives, and managers, and the relationships among them underwent fundamental redefinition over the postwar period.[2] The unions, led by IG Metall, saw that as production processes and associated aspects of local labor-management relations came under pressure to change, they would need to intervene more and more in local "managerial" decision making if they were maintain their influence. Doing this meant ceding some power to the councils (Thelen 1991). At the same time, however, the unions developed consultative capacities regarding technological and organizational change, which the works councils came to rely on, in order to represent workplace interests effectively. Thus the unions developed new sources of influence even as they ceded certain "traditional" powers to the councils.

Many works councils, formerly seeing themselves simply as the administrators of the Works Constitution Act, began to take on the roles of strategic representatives of the workforce in all sorts of matters traditionally left to management. Many managers have also come to see the councils as necessary allies and partners in a dynamic and increasingly competitive environment.[3] That is, traditional self-conceptions and understandings of the relationships among the main actors at the local level have changed fundamentally and continue to change, with the times. Organizational processes have necessarily changed with them.

U.S. Influences on German Managers

Further evidence of the malleability of actors' roles and self-conceptions at the workplace level can be found in the sharp contrasts between managerial styles and human-resource practices at four German- and three U.S.-owned chemicals companies all operating on German soil. This comparison is based on interviews with production managers, chemists, and human resource (HR) managers at German-owned Henkel, BASF, Hoechst, and Bayer and at U.S.-owned 3M, Rey, and A&B.[4]

The pattern of management in the German firms is slow, stable, and

2. There is no question that many—perhaps most—works councils and managers continue to have more traditional self-conceptions (see, for instance, Kotthoff 1981 and 1994). The point here is not that these role and relationship shifts occurred everywhere but that they occurred thoroughly and irreversibly in many places.

3. For instance, the director of technology at Henkel, a large family-owned chemicals company, argued in a personal interview that given the need for rapid organizational change in response to dynamic external pressures, reactive and bureaucratic works councils present a real liability, while strategically proactive works councils—even if they disagree with management strategies—can be much more helpful in ensuring firm competitiveness (personal interview, Düsseldorf, March 1990).

4. Hoechst, BASF, and Bayer are in fact the remnants of the giant IG Farben chemicals concern, which collaborated closely with Hitler and was therefore broken up after World War II by the occupying powers. Rey and A & B are not the real names of these companies, which managers requested be withheld.

collectively oriented (see also Adler 1991, Lane 1989, and Maurice, Sellier, and Silvestre 1986). The works councils' primary contacts are with the HR or personnel departments, not production managers. The relationship between HR and the works councils is seen as the appropriate focal point of labor-management relations. Managers place a high premium on legal rights and responsibilities and on the need to maintain smooth relations with the council. Production managers claim that conflicts with works councils are rare because these are preempted in dealings between the council and personnel managers. Basic human resource practices emphasize collective, rather than individual, features of the employment relationship. Compensation tends not to be performance-based except for higher-level managers. Employment security is the norm. Individual performance is deemed less important than stable collective employee relations. Selection processes are fairly crude by U.S. standards, and there is a widespread belief that what really matters is how well people are trained within and integrated into the company once they are hired. Managerial promotions are slow, and cross-functional movement is rare (see also Walgenbach 1993). The chief executives of all four of the German companies—but none at the U.S. firms—are chemists. Hierarchy is excessive in comparison with flatter U.S. organizations. Labor-management relations, human-resource policies, and even corporate cultures at the large German chemical concerns are substantially similar.

The U.S.-owned, German-based firms are run very differently. Compensation is linked to individual performance. Employment security is not guaranteed. Performance appraisals are frequent and strongly emphasize individual achievement. Employee development through individual goal setting is common. Recruitment and selection of employees is extremely careful, targeting highly motivated individual achievers, rather than people with specific types of formal training.

The relative unimportance of formal skills is reflected also in the management career patterns at these companies. Managers report rapid movement through the organization, by German standards, and in particular many lateral career moves. Mobility across functional areas is justified on the basis that general management skills are more valuable than narrow functional expertise. The prevalence of cross-functional movement can be traced in part to the fact that there tend to be relatively few levels in the managerial hierarchy. Managers are assigned heavy responsibilities at low levels of the organization, relative to colleagues at German-owned companies. They link this phenomenon to their employers' emphasis on individual, rather than collective, achievement. The U.S. top managers of these firms have little interest in or time for the works councils. Corporate cultures at these firms emphasize open communications, an informal work atmosphere, an open-door policy on the part of high-level managers, and relatively high levels of responsibility and autonomy for middle and lower-level managers. Team work is widespread, and organizational changes are seen as being rapidly implemented. The HR function is substantially integrated into the rest of the organization. Managers are encouraged to communicate directly with employees, rather than through the works council.

Clearly there are numerous sharp contrasts between the managers' attitudes and practices, as well as the organizational policies and structures found at the U.S.- and German-owned companies. American multinationals operating in Germany do so not simply for local market access but also in order to take advantage of Germany's skilled labor pool and stable industrial relations. Certainly they attempt as far as possible to bypass the constraints of the German model (e.g., employer association membership and hence voluntary collective bargaining coverage). But there are limits to the extent to which these institutional constraints can be avoided. If these limits were unacceptable, employers would set up shop elsewhere, in eastern Europe, for example. Those who do this, however, also forgo some of the benefits of skills and stability available on German soil.

It is also noteworthy that almost all the managers of both groups of firms have essentially the same backgrounds, cultures, histories, and education. Almost all are German nationals and attended the same schools, apprenticeship training programs, and universities. It is not only their practices but also their attitudes—for instance, about organizational change, the proper role of the works council, and the nature and importance of corporate culture—that differ substantially across the two groups. These variations in managers' beliefs and practices speak for the potential for similarly profound changes also in the attitudes of managers and workers in other German settings.

Current Debates about Management Training

The German employer community is aware of the problems of functional specialization and organizational rigidity. That this is the case is made clear by a large and growing literature on the need for changes in managerial education and training—much of it emanating from the employers' own think tanks, and from research institutions close to the business community —and by interviews with German managers themselves. Debates within the employer community and the political arena on the reform of managerial educational institutions and organizational structures and practices have gained importance with the continuing integration of the single European market.

Numerous employer publications have documented how German management education falls short. The system is seen as failing to deliver adequate levels of creativity and communication skills (Konegen-Grenier and List 1993). It is dominated by public institutions that are believed to lack the incentives to meet the changing needs of students and employers. Employers on the whole favor a partial privatization of the colleges and universities and a shortening of the period of study (Schlaffke and Konegen-Grenier 1991). Managers are seen as receiving insufficient general (as opposed to functionally specialized) skills, especially in light of the increasing internationalization of many business activities, which in turn has been sped up by the integration of the single European market. Other calls for changes in how German managers manage have to do with the need for a "life-long" model of learning (reflecting the limitations of a one-time apprenticeship or formal educational training), individually geared compensation plans, more direct employee participation (e.g., through quality circles), and improvements in the management of innovation (see also Zedler and Koch 1992, Falk and Weiß 1993, BDI/BDA/IW 1990, and Gesamtmetall 1989).

Moreover, individual German managers are also aware of how the problems associated with functional specialization, a sharp hierarchical division of labor, and low levels of autonomy can interfere with their effectiveness. Managers at all organizational levels in medium-sized and large organizations across sectors agree on certain widespread problems. They cite excessive bureaucracy, which can stifle individual initiative and creativity; the fact that changes (and even common procedures) take too long to carry out; that keeping labor on (as opposed to laying off workers) in economic downturns is costly; that organizational change is slow; and that there is inadequate communication and cross-fertilization across departments (see Wever 1995b).

In short, the employer community as a whole and individual managers within that community are alive to the key challenges facing German organizations. They recognize the limitations of traditional, rigid organizational and communications structures; and they are addressing those limitations. But they are not, in the process, abandoning their traditional sources of strength—deep skills and technical excellence. Rather, they are building on historical strengths by adapting aspects of more flexible models.

THE WEAKENING OF COLLECTIVE EMPLOYER ACTION

The centralization of employer interests and their collective actions represent a cornerstone of the German model of political economy and industrial relations. Yet membership in employer associations has declined since 1990, especially in the new states (Silvia, Chapter 7 in this book; Mahnkopf 1993). Some companies, anticipating that they will not be able to meet the terms of regionally negotiated collective bargaining agreements, are deciding that the benefits of nonmembership outweigh its costs (for instance, the cost of not receiving financial support in the event of a strike, or of not receiving technical assistance available from the employer associations).

If this were a widespread and permanent phenomenon—if German companies were moving *en masse* to the adoption of more individualistic and unilateral strategies of U.S. firms—there would be considerable reason to doubt the viability of the German model, whose central pillar is the collectivization of employer and worker interests. However, there is no reason to believe that shifts in employer preferences concerning association membership reflect a movement toward a unilateral (management-dominated, non-negotiated) model of employment relations, or that they are necessarily permanent. On the contrary, it seems likely that these developments in fact reflect discontent with the substance of precisely what is negotiated at the central level, and what should be left to the parties to determine at the local level. There is no reason why employers' membership in associations should not increase again as the competitive circumstances of German firms and industries change. In fact, many—perhaps most—employers continue to have powerful structural reasons for preferring collective employer action to a more free-market model; recent collective bargaining agreements indicate new measures of flexibility and significant innovation on both sides; and developments in the new states—where employer association membership is lowest, suggest a need to search for *new forms* of collaboration and negotiation, rather than abandon the negotiated approach to employment relations altogether.

Incentives for Collective Employer Action

Centralization takes many of the costs of labor out of competition. Individual companies are not forced to compete against each other—as many organizations in the United States are—on the basis of labor costs. Moreover, the many public sector and para-public forums (see Katzenstein 1987) in which labor and management come together to negotiate different aspects of employment relations create regular contact around consensual goals between representatives of labor and management, from the micro to the macro levels of the economy. As well as promoting negotiation over the terms of institutional and organizational change, these circumstances facilitate the diffusion of innovations across workplaces, enterprises, and even industries. As such, they provide collective economic benefits to employers. Thus the Confederation of Employer Associations (BDA) and many of the main employer associations are on record as emphatically supporting the continuation of the centralized system of wage bargaining (BDA 1991). What is called for is change within the system, not rejection of the system itself.

Some of the main benefits of the centralized system are captured by the following statement of the (then) president of the BDA:

> If there were no Works Constitution Act, then the . . . differences across enterprises would be much greater. . . . I would take the German system [over the American]. . . . American capitalism's understanding of the free market doesn't reflect my preferences. . . . I think with technological developments we need, more than in past years, employees who are not only highly qualified but also motivated. . . . Manchester liberalism can't be realized in this kind of world. Basically even in just economic terms a progressive employer strategy will pay off better anyhow. In this regard, a preventative strategy is the best strategy. Though if we were only competing with Korea or Taiwan it would be a different matter.[5]

The caveat at the end of this statement refers to the fact that German employers do not in fact compete "only" or directly against Korean and Taiwanese companies—with their substantially lower labor costs. This view contrasts sharply with U.S. employers' frequent justification of lower labor costs precisely because of the imperative of meeting low-cost competitors in the international marketplace. Many German employers see themselves as competing not against other firms but against foreign countries or industries —one of the core byproducts of collective employer organization, with its ability to take labor costs out of direct competition among firms.[6] Put differently, for most German employers the collective institutions of employment relations provide benefits that in turn create incentives for their maintenance. This is possible only through adjustments, albeit *within* the framework provided by those institutions. The battle currently raging within the employer community certainly indicates that some employers do not believe that these benefits offset the costs of association. The task confronting the employer associations resembles the challenge facing the unions: to cede some power to more local levels while building new sources of influence at the central level.

New Flexibility in Collective Bargaining

The 1993 conflict between employers and the union in the metalworking industries of the new states serves as an example of how German labor and business are coming to terms with the need to tailor collective bargaining

---

5. Personal interview, Dr. Fritz-Heinz Himmelreich, Cologne, February 1990.
6. Casper (1997) shows how employer and industry associations can help institutionalize effective relations among German firms and their suppliers in ways that are not available to American companies. His argument speaks to some of the competitiveness benefits of collective employer organization.

agreements to the increasingly varied needs of different employers. The conflict revolved around employers' legal but unprecedented early opening of the existing collective bargaining agreement. Their argument was that the schedule for bringing the wages of eastern workers into line with those of western workers had to be lengthened in order to take into account the financial struggles of eastern firms. The union, alarmed at the unprecedented early opening of a contract, and concerned with maintaining the principle of solidaristic wages, called a strike. Eastern workers came out in full force, surprising even union officials with their militancy (see Turner 1998).

The resolution of the strike proved an important turning point in German industrial relations. The contract contained a "hardship clause" *(Öffnungsklausel)*, allowing employers to petition for exemption from certain aspects of the collective agreement. This clause amounted to the union's explicit acknowledgment that some firms might not be able to meet the minimum standards set by the regional agreement. However, the clause continues to give the parties to collective bargaining (the unions and employer association) the power to accept or reject the petition for exemption. By creating the possibility for a more thorough exchange of information about the particular circumstances of a particular firm, the clause calls for intensified labor-management negotiation over individual firms' competitiveness problems and various means of addressing these. The agreement retains the institutional integrity of regional and industry-wide collective bargaining, while at the same time rendering microeconomic contingencies subject to negotiation.

Other collective bargaining contracts tend in the same direction, with unions agreeing to contract revisions in light of the fact that economic circumstances were less favorable in 1993 than had been projected (see Bispinck 1993). Recent collective bargaining agreements in the metalworking, printing, clothing and textile, construction, and transport industries (among others) contain opening clauses that allow for a deferral of wage increases or a temporary lowering of agreed wage minimums (WSI 1993 and 1995). A 1993 enterprise-specific collective bargaining agreement between IG Metall and VW entailed a temporary reduction of the work week to four days in order to allow the company to reorganize, to make up for losses, and to take better advantage of its skilled workforce. Another contract innovation that has gained popularity in the 1990s allows workers to chose their preferred combination of shorter hours and lower pay, with the amount of pay per hour decreasing marginally in inverse proportion to the number of hours worked.

While the German wage bargaining system is still centralized by international standards, the unions' general willingness to consider the special circumstances of employers in the new states suggests a new measure of flexibility. The system has also become more fluid in other regards. The number of sectoral/regional agreements and firm-specific agreements ("house" contracts) increased significantly in the early 1990s (Bispinck 1993). Pay differentiation across regions and sectors is at least as high in the western part of Germany as in the east (BDA 1992). The western metalworking agreements of 1994 and 1995—accounting for 12 percent of the western workforce but fully 50 percent of German exports—accepted wage restraint, a variety of measures such as work sharing and flexible forms of employment, and cuts in workers' paid hours for a period of up to two years, in return for employment security. Contracts in the public sector follow similar patterns.

These adjustments to the wage bargaining system reflect both an increase in the sharing of information and joint consultation about the scope of collective agreements, on the one hand, and a safeguarding of the institutional integrity and security of the centralized approach, on the other.

Negotiation and Innovation in the New States

The ability of labor and management to devise new mechanisms for coping with the unfamiliar challenges of the day is illustrated by the emergence of various new kinds of tripartite local and regional adjustment and development initiatives. While there are many such experiments, two in particular illustrate the potential for labor and management to balance the benefits of collective action against the requirements of local flexibility (see also Röbenack and Hartung 1992, Stöhr 1992, Grabher 1993, and Mickler 1992).

The IG Metall-inspired ATLAS experiment in Saxony is a regional development and industrial policy initiative that grew out of IG Metall's dissatisfaction with the lack of investment in and restructuring of eastern companies that had not yet been privatized (IW 1992; Kern 1993). The union called for the creation of a holding company in which firms that could be saved would be separated from the remainder of the holdings of the Treuhand (the semipublic body charged with privatizing the eastern German economy) and given the necessary resources to turn them around. This plan was developed in the context of a detailed industrial policy. The union began a series of discussions with the state government, gaining political support to proceed. The state then concluded an agreement with the Treuhand, in which the former agreed to fund, and the latter promised to help make possible an industrial policy modeled after the union's ideas. A council made up of representatives from labor, management, finance, and government was charged with exploring, together with the managers and works councils at individual Treuhand companies, and restructuring avenues that might be pursued, as well as developing new organizational, product, and market strategies. These efforts were financed jointly by the state and the Treuhand.

The concrete proposals of the union included the restructuring of the companies in core industries; local-content agreements favoring suppliers within the state; maquilladora-style cooperative agreements with local producers; involvement of the states' Employment and Training Companies (see below) in the restructuring efforts; and the establishment of a network linking state-level institutions and programs of economic development, and focusing these on the preservation of core industrial capacities. The implementation of this state-level industrial policy provided a model for similar efforts elsewhere (Kern 1993).

Another new institution—the Employment and Training Company (ETC)—was developed (again, on a tripartite basis) to cope with job losses as well as pressing environmental and infrastructural problems in the eastern part of the country (see Knuth 1993 and Chapter 3 in this book). The ETCs target specific regional needs and try to meet them through the establishment of pseudo-companies, providing valuable training to workers who would otherwise be out of a job. A July 1991 agreement between business, labor, government, and the Treuhand stipulated that the ETCs were to aid structural development, economic reorientation, and the founding of new enterprises. The unions worked together with eastern works councils to develop the ETCs for the purpose of acting as employers while engaging in socially and economically useful activities, most of which would probably not be undertaken by private-sector actors. The ETCs act more or less as substitute employers, using various public and even some private funds—from the Treuhand, the local and state governments, the Federal Employment Agency, and sometimes including employee contributions in the amount of severance pay they would have received if they had simply been laid off. The areas in which the ETCs have become active include laboratory and databank services aimed at clarifying and solving environmental problems, construction and repair activities to accommodate projected tourism, and databank services for investors and regional economic development efforts. They illustrate the capacity of the unions and local social and political groups for political as well as economic innovation.

Notably, these innovations are occurring in the very landscape in which some employers are withdrawing from employer associations, or trying to take increasing advantage of the *Öffnungsklauseln* in industry collective bargaining contracts. Not surprisingly, then, we are seeing a variety of approaches aimed at meeting unfamiliar and significant economic and social problems. Decentralized and more unilateral efforts exist alongside ATLAS and the ETCs, in which the social partners, in collaboration with local allies, are changing strategies and structures, shifting the substance of what is negotiated centrally and what is agreed upon at the local level, and developing new organizational and institutional forms and networks in the process.

RE-NEGOTIATING THE GERMAN "MODEL"

We are living in the era of the (U.S.-led) internationalization of "lean production" (see Womack, Jones, and Roos 1990). Many believe that there are certain "best" organizational practices—best in terms of delivering firm competitiveness. The quality of "best-ness" attaching to a certain organizational practice is widely seen to cut across differences of history, culture, or political economic context (see Kotter and Heskett 1991; Peters and Waterman 1982). With the U.S. free-market model once again in first position, it is hardly surprising that problems with other prominent ways of organizing democratic capitalism, such as the German model, would be critiqued in "American" terms. Questions about the viability of the German model ease almost naturally into the idea that Germany is undergoing a shift toward "cowboy capitalism." Indeed, many of the features of that model appear opposed to the U.S. model, especially to the extent that the two are seen on a continuum from free to social market capitalism. Much of the U.S. management literature is widely available in German bookstores and seen on German top managers' bookshelves. U.S. innovations ("best practices," e.g., the organization of large companies into smaller profit centers) and refinements of innovations originating in other countries (such as Just-In-Time, imported from Japan) are being adopted and adapted. German companies setting up shop in the United States (for instance, the new Mercedes Benz plant in Alabama and the BMW plant in South Carolina) are leaving behind many policies associated with the negotiated model of employment relations, preferring more U.S.-style policies, organizational forms, relationships with suppliers, and so on (*Ward's Automotive Reports*, 1993–95).

Against this background, it makes sense that observers of Germany might see rigidities hampering firm-level change and declines in cornerstone institutions like employer associations as vindications of the free market model and of flexible U.S. "best" practices. German managers feel they have much to learn from U.S. managers, as illustrated by the perceptions and practices of the German nationals running German-based U.S.-owned firms in the chemicals industry.

But does learning from U.S. organizational forms and strategies require rejecting the German model? On the contrary, the evidence could be interpreted as suggesting just the opposite. This process of learning—sped up by the economic strains imposed by unification—has both challenged certain particulars and reaffirmed the basic strengths of the German model. What is happening in Germany is not the rejection, one company at a time, of centralized "constraints" and negotiated labor-management adjustment processes, but rather a widespread effort to renegotiate that model using aspects of the U.S. model as deemed appropriate. Under the current circumstances, experiments with various approaches make sense. But the dominant process of renegotiation—seen in recent collective bargaining rounds, in the varied and changing practices of German managers, and in the new forms of negotiated adjustment emerging in the new states—actually assumes certain key features of the German model. It assumes collaboration between labor and management, albeit in different forms and forums, and over different substantive issues. It assumes the tripartite pooling of resources and ideas to solve pressing problems, albeit different kinds of problems than have had to be solved in the past. The conditions for successful, though evolving, forms of negotiated change and adjustment at the firm level are not at risk.

REFERENCES

Adler, Nancy. 1991. *International Dimensions of Organizational Behavior.* 2d ed. Boston: PWS Kent Publishing.

Allen, Christopher S. 1989. "Regional Governments and Economic Policies in West Germany: The 'Meso' Politics of Industrial Adjustment." *Publius* 19, no. 4: 147–64.

BDA. 1991. "Tarifpolitik in den neuen Bundesländern—eine kritische Zwischenbilanz." *Der Arbeitgeber* (special issue), December, 86–97.

——. 1992. *Jahresbericht.* Cologne.

BDI/BDA/IW. 1990. *Hochschule 2000: Wirtschaft und Wissenschaft im Dialog.* Bundesverband der Deutschen Industrie, Bundesvereinigung der Deutschen Arbeitgeberverbände, Institut der deutschen Wirtschaft. Cologne: Deutscher Instituts-Verlag.

Berg, Peter. 1993. "The Restructuring of Work and the Role of Training: A Comparative Analysis of the United States and German Automobile Industries." Ph.D. diss., University of Notre Dame.

Bispinck, Reinhard. 1993. "Der Tarifkonflikt um den Stufenplan in der ostdeutschen Metallindustrie." *WSI Mitteilungen* 46, no. 8: 469–81.

Busch, Berthold. 1992. *Die EG nach 1992: Die Gemeinschaft vor neuen Herausforderungen.* Institut der Deutschen Wirtschaft, Beiträge zur Wirtschafts- und Sozialpolitik, no. 203. Cologne: Deutscher Instituts-Verlag.

Casper, Steven. 1997. "How German Industrial Associations Help Diffuse Innovative Economic Organization: The Case of JIT Contracting." Paper prepared for the German-American Project Follow-up Conference, Wissenschaftszentrum, Berlin, December.

Duwe, Ursula, and Elisabeth Becker-Töpfer. 1988. "Gruppenarbeit in der Bank? Überlegungen der Interessenvertretung in der Commerzbank." In Sigfried Roth and Heribert Kohl, eds., *Perspektive Gruppenarbeit.* Cologne: Bund Verlag.

Falk, Rüdiger and Reinhold Weiß. 1993. *Zunkunft der Akademiker.* Institut der deutschen Wirtschaft, Beiträge zur Gesellschafts- und Bildungspolitik, no. 186. Cologne: Deutscher Instituts-Verlag.

Gazdar, Kaevan. 1995. "The Sleeping Giant." Unpublished manuscript, Munich.

Gesamtmetall. 1989. *Mensch und Arbeit: Gemeinsame Interessen von Mitarbeitern und Unternehmen in einer sich wandelten Arbeitswelt.* Cologne: Gesamtverband der metallindustriellen Arbeitgeberverbände.

Grabher, Gernot. 1993. "Rediscovering the Social in the Economics of Interfirm Relations." In Gernot Grabher, ed., *The Embedded Firm: On the Socioeconomics of Industrial Networks.* London: Routledge.

Hofstede, Gustav. 1980. *Culture's Consequences.* Beverly Hills: Sage.

IW. 1992. "ATLAS: Ein Projekt des Sächsischen Staatsministeriums für Wirtschaft und Arbeit." Internal memorandum, Institut der deutschen Wirtschaft, Cologne, August.

Kakalick, Gerhard. 1989. "Qualifizierungsprogramm für Produktionsarbeiter im Zusammenhang mit der Einführung neuer Technologien im Volkswagenwerk Kassel." Paper given at conference "Neue Technologien, Lernen und Berufliche Weiterbildung," Universität Bremen, no. 18, Beiträge zur Fachtagung Berufliche Weiterbildung, 14–16 February.

Katzenstein, Peter. 1987. *Policy and Politics in West Germany: The Growth of a Semi-Sovereign State?* Philadelphia: Temple University Press.

Keim, Rüdiger, and Hans Unger. 1986. *Kooperation Statt Konfrontation: Vertrauensvolle Zusammenarbeit zwischen Arbeitgeber und Betriebsrat.* Cologne: Infomedia.

Kern, Horst. 1993. "Gewerkschaftliche Industriepolitik: Beiträge der Gewerkschaften in Ost und West zur Erneuerung des deutschen Produktionsmodells." Working paper, SOFI, Göttingen, October.

Knuth, Matthias. 1993. "Employment and Training Companies: Bridging Unemployment in the East German Crash." Paper prepared for the Conference of the Society for the Advancement of Socio-Economics, New York, March 26–28.

Konegen-Grenier, Christiane, and Juliane List. 1993. *Die Anforderung der Wirtschaft an das BWL Studium.* Institut der Deutschen Wirtschaft, Beiträge zur Gesellschafts- und Bildungspolitik, no. 188. Cologne: Deutscher Instituts-Verlag.

Kotter, James, and William Heskett. 1991. *Corporate Culture.* Boston: Harvard Business School Press.

Kotthoff, Hermann. 1981. *Betriebsräte und betriebliche Herrschaft: Eine Typologie von Partizipationsmustern im Industriebetrieb.* Frankfurt: Campus Verlag.

———. 1994. *Betriebsräte und Bürgerstatus: Wandel und Kontinuität betrieblicher Mitbestimung.* Munich: Rainer Hampp Verlag.

Lane, Christel. 1989. *Management and Labour in Europe.* Aldershot: Edward Elgar.

Link, Franz Josef. 1993. *Lohnpolitik in Ostdeutschland aus ökonomischer und sozialer Perspektive.* Institut der Deutschen Wirtschaft, Beiträge zur Wirtschafts- und Sozialpolitik, no. 207. Cologne: Deutscher Instituts-Verlag.

Locke, Richard, Thomas Kochan, and Michael Piore. 1995. *Employment Relations in a Changing World Economy.* Cambridge: MIT Press.

Mahnkopf, Birgit. 1993. "Ex Orient Risk: The Impact of Unification on the German System of Industrial Relations." Working paper, Wissenschaftszentrum Berlin.

Maurice, Marc, François Sellier, and Jean-Jacques Silvestre. 1986. *The Social Foundations of Industrial Power: A Comparison of France and Germany.* Cambridge: MIT Press.

Mickler, Otfried. 1992. "Modernization of East German Industry and the Development of New Structures of Industrial Relations in Enterprises— The Case of the Auto Industry." Working paper, University of Hannover, Institut für Soziologie, October.

Peters, Tom, and Robert Waterman. 1982. *In Search of Excellence: Lessons from America's Best-Run Companies.* New York: Warner Books.

Röbenack, Silke, and Gabriele Hartung. 1992. "Strukturwandel industrieller Beziehungen in ostdeutschen Industriebetrieben: Herausbildung neuer Beziehungen zwischen Arbeitgebern und Betriebsräten sowie Wandel in der Austragung von Interessenkonflikten." Kurzstudie AG 3/3. Leipzig: Kommission für die Erforschung des sozialen und politischen Wandels in den neuen Bundesländern e.V.

Schlaffge, Winfried, and Christiane Konegen-Grenier, eds. 1991. *Streitsache: Wettbewerbsstrategien für die Hochschulen.* Cologne: Deutscher Instituts-Verlag.

Soskice, David. 1991. "The Institutional Infrastructure for International

Competitiveness: A Comparative Analysis of the U.K. and Germany." In A. B. Atkinson and R. Brunetta, eds., *The Economics of the New Europe.* London: Macmillan.

Stöhr, Andreas. 1992. "Interessenwahrnehmung und Interessenvertretung in Ingenieurbetrieben." Kurzstudie. Leipzig: Kommission für die Erforschung des sozialen und politischen Wandels in den neuen Bundesländern e.v.

Streeck, Wolfgang. 1991. "More Uncertainties: German Unions Facing 1992." *Industrial Relations* 30, no. 3: 317–49.

Streeck, Wolfgang, and Sigurt Vitols. 1994. "European Works Councils: Between Statutory and Voluntary Adoption." In Joel Rogers and Wolfgang Streeck, eds., *Works Councils: Consultation, Representation, Cooperation.* Chicago: University of Chicago Press and NBER.

Thelen, Kathleen A. 1991. *A Union of Parts: Labor Politics in Postwar Germany.* Ithaca: Cornell University Press.

Turner, Lowell. 1991. *Democracy at Work: Changing World Markets and the Future of Labor Unions.* Ithaca: Cornell University Press.

——. 1998. *Fighting for Partnership: Labor and Politics in Unified Germany.* Ithaca: Cornell University Press.

Vogel, Otto, ed. 1988. *Deregulierung und Privatisierung.* Cologne: Deutscher Instituts-Verlag.

Walgenbach, Peter. 1993. "Führungsverhalten mittlerer Manager in Deutschland und Grossbritannien." *ZEW Newsletter.* Mannheim. no. 2: 16–19.

Ward's Automotive Reports, various issues.

Wever, Kirsten. 1994. "Learning from Works Councils: Five Unspectacular Cases from Germany." *Industrial Relations* 33, no. 4 (Fall): 467–81.

——. 1995a. *Negotiating Competitiveness: Employment Relations and Organizational Innovation in Germany and the United States.* Boston: Harvard Business School Press.

——. 1995b. "Human Resource Management and Organizational Strategies in German and U.S.-Owned Companies." *International Journal of Human Resource Management* 6, no. 3: 606–20.

Wever, Kirsten, and Lowell Turner, eds. 1995. *The Comparative Political Economy of Industrial Relations.* Madison: IRRA.

Womack, James P., Daniel T. Jones, and Daniel Roos. 1990. *The Machine That Changed The World: The Story of Lean Production.* New York: Macmillan.

WSI (Wirtschafts-und Sozialwissenschaftsinstitut des DGB). 1993. *Tarifpolitisches Taschenbuch 1993 — Zahlen, Daten, Fakten.* Cologne: Bund Verlag.

——. 1995. *Tarifpolitisches Taschenbuch 1995 — Zahlen, Daten, Fakten.* Cologne: Bund Verlag.

Zedler, Reinhard, and Rita Koch. 1992. *Berufsschule — Partner der Aus-bildungsbetriebe.* Institut der deutschen Wirtschaft. Beiträge zur Gesellschafts- und Bildungspolitik, no. 178. Cologne: Deutscher Instituts-Verlag.

10 • The Second Coming of the Bonn Republic

Douglas Webber

"**The Bonn** republic is dead" (Glotz 1994, 269). The united Germany is "just a bigger Federal Republic" (Weiß 1993, 41). These two statements, the former by a (West German) Social Democrat, the latter by a former leader of the East German protest movement, illustrate how widely opinions diverge on the issue of how much the "old" Federal Republic has changed as a consequence of German reunification. Although the prognoses and analyses of political scientists have, on the whole, been more nuanced than those of political practitioners, their views have also differed, sometimes substantially. Gerhard Lehmbruch, for example, on the eve of unification, forecast "a far-reaching transformation of the political and social structures of the political system" (Lehmbruch 1990, 464); and Hans-Joachim Veen found, after analysing the first all-German elections, that the "social and political system has begun to move in a fundamental way" (Veen 1993, 85). Kurt Sontheimer, however, argued that unification had not brought about fundamental changes in either the institutions or structures of the political system of the "old" republic (Sontheimer 1993, 337); and Manfred Schmidt insisted in the same vein that the "governance structure" of the Federal Republic has "not fundamentally altered" (Schmidt 1992, 12). Still, most of those who observed an overall high level of continuity between the "old" Germany and the "new," including Schmidt, anticipated a major change in at least one central dimension of the old Federal Republic: a considerably higher degree of political centralization as a consequence of the relative poverty of the new federal states. Many shared Fritz Scharpf's concern that reunification would bring the Federal Republic a "big step closer" to becoming, in effect, a unitary state (Scharpf 1991, 154).

I take a radical position in this debate. I contend that reunification has led to fundamental changes in *none* of the principal traits of the "old" Federal Republic, if anything, it has reinforced them. There has been no major shift in the territorial distribution of power; there has been a renaissance of "neocorporatist" democracy; the practice of "cooperative opposition" still characterizes the party system; and the "new" Germany remains committed to multilateralism and tightly integrated in the Western community of states.

THE BONN REPUBLIC

Peter Katzenstein aptly labeled the "old" Federal Republic a "semisovereign state" (Katzenstein 1987). This concept highlights the extent to which the freedom of action of the federal government was constrained by the federal states; parastate agencies, such as the Bundesbank; and organized private interests. At the same time, the Federal Republic was a "penetrated system," in which the federal government's foreign policy autonomy was tightly constrained by the country's integration into a network of West European and transatlantic alliances. The "social partnership" at home was complemented by a "security partnership" abroad (Katzenstein 1991, 77).

In its first forty years the Bonn Republic developed four main traits that, collectively, distinguished it from other large Western liberal democracies. The first of these was the system of "cooperative federalism" in which the states and the federation were constrained to work together closely both in formulating and implementing much public policy. As policymaking powers were increasingly centralized, the state governments' collective scope to codetermine policy through the states' chamber of the Federal Parliament, the Bundesrat, was gradually expanded, giving the states a degree of influence of federal policy which, in international comparison, was "absolutely extraordinary" (Scharpf 1990, 579).

The second such trait was the extensive integration of the major organized economic interests into the formulation and implementation of public policy. Owing to institutional obstacles (the independence of the Bundesbank, the decentralization of budgetary policy, and so on), the Bonn republic did not develop a comprehensive system of neocorporatist macroeconomic management as some smaller Western European states did; however, there was a great deal of "meso-" or "sectoral corporatism." This sectoral corporatism *was the* defining characteristic of the *Modell Deutschland* of the 1970s, when according to Katzenstein, the Federal Republic was a "neo-corporatist democracy" (Katzenstein 1989, 329). Under the Kohl governments in the 1980s, neocorporatist practices declined, without, however, dying out completely.

Third, the "old" Federal Republic was a state with a comparatively low degree of political polarization and a predominantly "cooperative" style of opposition—a trait that was reinforced by the "cooperative federal" system, under which no major party was ever completely out of office and devoid of political influence (Paterson and Webber 1986). The Grand Coalition government of 1966–69 marked the high point of cooperative party politics in the Federal Republic; however, even in the subsequent two decades, notwithstanding the "Sonthofen" strategy of the CSU leader, Franz-Josef Strauß, the emergence of the Green movement, and all the sound and fury of election campaign rhetoric, the main opposition party in Bonn continued to prefer cooperative over fundamental opposition in its day-to-day practice, bargaining where possible with the government to achieve incremental changes in legislation or policy rather than maximizing the level of political confrontation.

The fourth distinguishing trait of the Federal Republic was the multilateral orientation of its foreign policy, whose objective could be characterized as "voluntary self-containment through integration," politically and economically in the EC (now European Union—EU) and militarily in the NATO. Burdened by memories of the Second World War and the Holocaust and constrained by the division of Germany along the front line of the cold war, the Federal Republic renounced traditional great-power politics in favor of participating in international institutions created in part to tie it to the West and prevent it from once again becoming a security threat to its neighbors. It developed into a "civilian power" or "trading state—a "giant" in world economic and financial affairs but a "pygmy" in the classic realms of international diplomacy, as exemplified in the Basic Law's ban on wars of aggression and the fact that West German troops never engaged in military action. The United States guaranteed the Federal Republic's military security and was its principal ally in NATO; France, on the other hand, became its principal partner in the EC, which developed into a decisive factor for the state's economic security. Accordingly, not to have to choose between the United States and France represented a basic premise of German foreign policy, irrespective of the party-political complexion of the governing coalition (Katzenstein 1991, 74).

If one were to search for a single expression to characterize the politics of the Bonn Republic, it would surely have to be *cooperation*—cooperation between the federation and the states, between the government and major organized economic interests, between the government and the opposition, and between the Federal Republic and the West—primarily through the EC and NATO. This pattern of (albeit antagonistic) cooperation in daily politics rested on legal-institutional and ideological foundations. The legal-institutional foundations of cooperation were provided by the Basic Law (with its provisions, for example, for the involvement of the states in the federal legislative process) and the multitude of other laws (for example, relating to collective bargaining and codetermination) that regulated political and economic life in the Federal Republic as well as by the organizations (in particular, the relatively highly centralized trade unions and employers' associations), which were created, in the case of the unions, as a reaction against the Third Reich or in that of the employers' and business associations, on top of its institutional legacy. The *will* to cooperation—without which the German political process, with its many built-in checks and balances, could rapidly have been prone to stalemate, deadlock, and crisis —sprang from the predominance in postwar West Germany of political movements based on ideologies (Christian and Social Democracy) favorably disposed toward inter-class cooperation or negotiation and accommodation between competing political and economic forces. One could say that the legal-institutional framework supplied the "hardware" and the dominant political ideologies the "software" that produced such extensive cooperation in pre-1990 (West) German politics.

Cooperation with the West in German foreign policy was necessitated, on the other hand, by the Federal Republic's vulnerability as the frontline Western state in the cold war as well as imposed by its Western allies. The security threat posed by the communist bloc was also an important factor of cohesion in domestic (West) German politics.

The consensus among political scientists at the time of unification was that the creation of five new, relatively impoverished states would undermine the territorial distribution of power in the old republic by enabling the federal government to trade financial concessions to the poorer states in exchange for their support for an extension of the federation's competences and for government legislation in the Bundesrat (Lehmbruch 1990, 479–81; Schmidt 1992, 3–4; Sally and Webber 1994, 19). But plausible arguments could have been made to expect significant changes in the other distinguishing traits of the Bonn republic too. Would not the lifting of the "Iron Curtain" between Western and Eastern Europe produce a surge of immigration into Germany and an upsurge in support for radical right-wing parties, of which one, the Republicans, had already risen to prominence by clearing the 5 percent barrier in the Berlin state elections in 1989? Following a sharp rise in support for the Republicans in state elections in 1991 and 1992, "further electoral successes" for the party in the "super-election year" 1994 were regarded as "almost inevitable" (Minkenberg 1994, 188). Would not political instability and radicalization, favoring the long-term consolidation of a reformed communist party to the left of the SPD in the party system, result from the exclusion of the former East German elites and mass unemployment and a widespread collective identity crisis in the east?

(Lehmbruch 1990, 479, 484–86). "The chances of democracy to take root among East German citizens faces severe obstacles," warned one observer, who feared that a "rebellious nativist (if not bluntly nationalist) socialism might rise from the ashes of the old regime and challenge the all-German republic" (Minkenberg 1993, 65–66). In other words, would not the centrifugal forces in the party system be greatly strengthened—and the practice of cooperative opposition correspondingly eroded? Would not the famed "social partnership" and neocorporatist practices be stretched beyond the breaking point by distributional conflicts arising from the costly process of unification, especially since the relationship among government, business, and labor had already grown increasingly strained in the 1980s and unification was likely to weaken organized labor by creating a large "reserve army" of unemployed in eastern Germany? (see Sally and Webber 1994, 43). Furthermore, would not the transformation of Germany's geopolitical environment following its unification and the end of the cold war and its reversion to its traditional *Mittellage* on the European continent lead to the revival of the old German tendency to "see-saw" between East and West *(Schaukelpolitik)* or even—the perennial fear of especially the French political class—a replay of the reputedly compulsive German *Drang nach Osten,* either of which policy would be incompatible with the prior orientation toward self-containment through (Western) integration?

How widely such fears were held in the capital cities of the Federal Republic's neighbors and allies is amply illustrated in various accounts of the negotiations concerning the external aspects of German unification (Thatcher 1993, 790–99; Teltschik 1991). They were nourished not least by the style in which Chancellor Kohl formulated and announced his "Ten-Point-Plan" for German unity in November 1989 (Teltschik 1991, 48–53). In the domestic political process of unification, Kohl suspended the standard operating procedures of the Bonn Republic more brutally—the party system, most of all the government, "cut its communication channels to other corporate actors . . . and assumed the position of an unconstrained sovereign decision-maker" (Lehmbruch 1992, 45–46). In short, the omens for the survival of the old Bonn republic in the new Germany did not seem at all good. If politics in the new Germany were to be much more centralized, polarized, conflict-laden, and majoritarian than in the old, then the coming Berlin republic would indeed differ substantially and qualitatively from that of Bonn.

NEOCORPORATISM

In retrospect, the (apparent) exclusion of organized interests from the policy process by the Kohl government during the turbulent year culminating in German unification seems less a pointer to the future than an exception to the rule of neocorporatist concertation. This is not to say that Germany was or has become a neocorporatist state comparable to Austria or the Scandinavian states—such a development is, in any case, precluded in Germany by the monetary policy autonomy of the Bundesbank, the fragmentation of fiscal policy responsibilities by the federal system of government, and the norm of free collective bargaining. Within the boundaries imposed by these constraints, however, the federal government has gone to great lengths to restore the "communication channels to other corporate actors" that Chancellor Kohl cut in 1989–90. Arguably, as many trade union and business leaders were coming and going from the Federal Chancellor's Office at the high point of its efforts in 1992 and 1993 as at the height of West German neocorporatist democracy in the late 1960s and 1970s.

The first significant initiative that the government took in this direction occurred within a few months of the December 1990 federal elections against the background of a rapidly intensifying economic crisis in eastern Germany. Plant closures and sweeping job cuts in the new federal states produced a growing wave of opposition to the policies of the government and its privatization agency, the Treuhandanstalt (THA). The increasing threat of political instability in the East elicited some concessions from the government, including an agreement in March 1991 to consult the eastern state governments more closely on THA decisions, and a few months later, an agreement among the THA, state governments, unions, and employers' associations to create so-called employment companies *(Beschäftigungsgesellschaften)* to mitigate the effects of impending mass redundancies. The negotiations among these actors were the "first occasion" since unification that they had all "sat together around the same table and agreed on a solution" (Breuel 1993, 259). Within a year of unification, the traditional pattern of neocorporatist crisis management in the old Federal Republic had begun to reassert itself (Webber 1994, 165).

The renaissance of neocorporatism was epitomized by the negotiations between the government and major organized economic interests over a "Solidarity Pact" in winter 1992–93. By this time, the persistent, if not deepening, economic crisis in eastern Germany, combined with an imminent recession in the West, was threatening Kohl's very survival as chancellor. In proposing the Solidarity Pact, Kohl was responding primarily to the pressures of the eastern German members of his party (Sally and Webber 1994, 22–23). He hoped to persuade the unions to exercise wage moderation in the West and to revise their policy of raising eastern wages to western levels and the business associations—which were also involved in the negotiations

—to make sacrifices, on behalf of their members, which would enable the package to be sold politically as "equitable."

Over a period lasting almost six months, the Solidarity Pact was the subject of good forty rounds of negotiations in the Chancellor's Office alone. To increase their efficiency, talks between the federal government and the other participants (including the state governments and the federal opposition) were always bilateral and, to maximize their confidentiality, the number of participants in the talks was kept to a minimum—in the case of the unions, to the leaders of the three biggest unions and the chairman of the union federation, the DGB. The government failed to persuade or coerce either the unions or the business associations to make substantial concessions. Threatened implicitly with sanctions by the government, the principal associations of the banking and manufacturing industries struck bargains concerning investments in the eastern states and the purchase of intermediate products from eastern German firms. However, given their incapacity to oblige their member firms to implement the deals, these amounted to little more than nonbinding "declarations of intent," whose principal practical significance was to legitimate the overall pact (Sally and Webber 1994, 34). The unions, for their part, suspended talks with the government until it withdrew a threat to enact legislation to enable employers to pay below-award wages. The government tried to induce union wage policy moderation by pledging to pursue a more active industrial policy in eastern Germany. Ultimately, as the government, which wanted to conclude the pact talks as rapidly as possible, saw time running out, it pledged to allocate more resources to "turn around" regionally significant, still state-owned firms in eastern Germany—without, however, securing a counterconcession from the unions.

The ensuing wage deals in Western Germany were to be relatively low and the wage-convergence agreements in eastern Germany were revised, but these outcomes had more to do with rising unemployment and employers' resistance than with the persuasive or coercive powers of the federal government. Yet if the results of the macrolevel negotiations themselves were thin, however, the federal government's undertaking to try to preserve still-existing "industrial cores" in eastern Germany accelerated a trend toward neocorporatist crisis management at the level of the states. These were encouraged to follow the government of Saxony's example and create multi-partite committees containing government, business association, and union representatives to identify "core" firms worthy of state financial support. Saxony's Atlas model has in fact been emulated in all other eastern German states (Webber 1994, 168–69).

Four years after unification, there was thus not less but more neocorporatist interaction among government, business, and labor than in the Federal

Republic during the 1980s. Initial developments after the 1994 federal elections indicated that tripartite techniques of economic management were going to be expanded rather than abandoned. Within a few weeks of having been reelected, Kohl opened employment policy talks with business and trade union leaders. Trade union leaders reacted to the government's overtures by suggesting that in exchange for government measures to cut unemployment, they would make concessions on Saturday working and wages in connection with working-time cuts aimed at safeguarding jobs. At the first of the tripartite summits—three more were scheduled for the first half of 1995—participants agreed to set up sectoral-level dialogues among business, labor, and the Federal economics minister to discuss ways of maintaining or restoring the competitiveness of German industry (*Süddeutsche Zeitung* 1995b). Far from the Solidarity Pact having been a "one-off" event, it seemed likely that during the next four years, as the chairman of the CDU labor wing, Rainer Eppelmann, anticipated, there would be a "permanent Solidarity Pact" (*Der Spiegel* 1994, 90).

In retrospect, despite its modest contents, the Solidarity Pact appears to have been a turning point in the Kohl government's post-unification economic management strategy—the point at which it recognized that it could no longer sustain the political costs (the probability of defeat in the 1994 federal elections) it would incur by relying exclusively on rising unemployment to discipline union wage demands and that it had to try to manage the unification crisis in collaboration with the big organized economic interests. It was going to be difficult for the government to deviate far from this course as long as the opposition Social Democrats occupied a dominant position in the Bundesrat—a position the results of elections in the eastern German states in 1994 had strengthened. For the trade unions, whose influence was bolstered by the Social Democrats' strong position in the Bundesrat, bargaining with the government represented a more congenial strategy than industrial militancy, which given the high costs and competitive problems of German industry, would risk increasing unemployment and—beyond the short term at least—eroding their bargaining power in the labor market (for the IG Metall chairman's positive attitude on collaboration with the federal government, see Zwickel 1994). Only the employers and their associations, exposed respectively to intense foreign competition and growing internal dissent, arguably had an incentive to break out of the neocorporatist institutional arrangements and pursue a strategy of confrontation with the trade unions (on the internal conflicts within the employers' organizations, see Silvia 1994). Yet the outcomes of the post-unification labor conflicts may have led most employers to conclude that they had little choice but to deal with the unions rather than try to defeat them. At any rate, the price that they had to pay for participating in tripartite talks was cheap; after all, they could not be obliged to implement the deals struck by their leaders in Bonn.

The fate of neocorporatist politics will depend on the evolution of the macropolitical balance of power. Thus the SPD's losses (and the consequent weakening of its position in the Bundesrat) and the FDP's recovery in several state elections in spring 1996 encouraged the Kohl government to adopt a package of austerity measures that precipitated the trade unions' suspension of their participation in tripartite summit meetings with the federal government and business. It was by no means certain that these events signaled a long-term deterioration in the unions' relationship with the government; such conflicts had also taken place—without killing German tripartism— in the 1980s. Much depends on the outcome of the 1998 federal elections. A return of the Social Democrats to the federal government will undoubtedly result in an *intensification* of neocorporatist economic management. (In 1994, the SPD had in fact proposed the negotiation of a national employment pact reminiscent of the old Concerted Action [Scharping 1994a]). If, on other hand, the Christian-Liberal coalition is reelected with a bigger majority than in 1994, the incentive for it to try to integrate the trade unions into the economic and social policymaking process will be diminished.

COOPERATIVE FEDERALISM

In no other sphere of German politics were such major changes predicted as a consequence of unification as in federal-state relations. The consensus was that the federation would exploit the financial dependence of the new eastern states to "hollow out" the cooperative federalist system, effectively creating a unitary state within what would be no more than a federal shell.

There is no doubt that the new eastern states are, and for a very long time will remain, dependent on financial transfers from the West, if not necessarily on discretionary transfers from the federal government. Also, the central role played by the federal privatization agency, the Treuhandanstalt, in shaping the economic structure of the former GDR, together with their relative poverty, has left the eastern states less scope to pursue autonomous industrial policies than their western counterparts. The federal government has also been able to exploit the financial dependence of the eastern states on *some* occasions to secure a majority for its legislation in the Bundesrat, despite the SPD majority in that chamber since the elections in the Rhineland-Palatinate in 1991. This was most notably the case in the conflict over the 1992 federal budget, which was adopted after the federal government succeeded in detaching Brandenburg from the coalition of SPD-led states opposed to an increase in indirect taxation (Sturm and Jeffery 1992, 169).

As a rule, however, the federal government has not succeeded in "dividing and ruling." Rather, all ideological, regional and financial cleavages between them notwithstanding, the states have displayed an unexpectedly strong capacity to maintain a common front against the federation. They have, for example, succeeded in securing several changes in the Basic Law improving their policymaking or codetermination powers. The rights of the states to participate in deciding German European policy have been extended in a new Article 23, which empowers the states to determine the stance taken by the Federal Republic in the Council of Ministers on policy issues that according to the Basic Law, belong to their exclusive legislative powers and gives them a right of veto over future EU treaty revisions as well as the federal government's participation in European Monetary Union.[1] The concurrent legislative powers of the federation have also been circumscribed to the states' advantage. Although these constitutional revisions fell short of the states' original aspirations and their practical impact must in any case be awaited, they go in precisely the opposite direction to what was expected following unification. Indeed, they are the first changes in the Basic Law enhancing the states' powers since 1949 (Melder 1994).

The federal government had to make these concessions to the states over Article 23 because ratification of the Maastricht Treaty's provisions concerning the right of the citizens of other EU member states to vote in German local elections and a European Central Bank necessitated changes in the Basic Law that could be adopted only with a two-thirds majority in the Bundesrat (as well as in the Bundestag). The states threatened to block these changes and, with them, the Maastricht Treaty, if the federal government did not strengthen their powers of European policy codetermination and concede them a right of veto over future EU treaties (*Der Spiegel* 1992, 37–38). Despite fears expressed in the Chancellor's Office that the states' demands, if accepted, would transform the Federal Republic from a federation into a confederation *(Staatenbund),* Kohl conceded them for fear of provoking a failure of the treaty—which would have been a catastrophe for the government's European policy.

Proponents of the thesis of an increasing erosion of German federalism as a consequence of unification also anticipated that the federation would be able to outmaneuver the states in forthcoming conflicts over federal-state

---

1. At the same time as they ratified the Maastricht Treaty, the Bundestag and the Bundesrat adopted resolutions stating that they reserved the right to vote again on Germany's entry into a European monetary union in the late 1990s. The federal government undertook to notify other member states that it would respect the votes of the two houses.

financial relations, which were regulated only temporarily (and very favorably for the western states) in the 1990 unification treaty. The issue of the reform of the financial equalization scheme, which divides tax revenues between the federation and the states, was declared to be "an acid test for the federal system" (Klatt 1992, 10). The "omens" for the states in this conflict were diagnosed to be "not good" (Sturm and Jeffery 1992, 171). For the states—western as well as eastern—the stakes involved in this issue were immense: without prior reform, the scheme would have been extended to the eastern states automatically in 1995, costing the western states DM 28 billion (roughly 10 percent of their existing budgets). However, far from dividing and ruling the states, and despite the fact that, by doing nothing, it could have unloaded a large part of the costs of unification onto the western states, the federal government suffered a resounding defeat. The largest western states, North Rhine-Westphalia and Bavaria, which also led the campaign to strengthen the states' influence on German European policy, assembled a coalition of all sixteen states around a reform plan that transferred the great bulk of the costs of raising the eastern states' revenues to the federal budget (Sally and Webber 1994, 23–27). Faced with a united front, the federal government caved in and accepted a reform by which it, in effect, financed a good 90 percent of its costs. According to one participant in the critical round of Solidarity Pact negotiations, "Kohl wanted a deal, quite literally, at any price" (as quoted in Sally and Webber 1994, 26–27). The Federal finance minister, Theo Waigel, defended the government's retreat with the argument that

> faced with the question whether we should pursue a distributional conflict over a period of months . . ., with all the uncertainty [this would have brought] for the eastern states, with the uncertainty for investors, with the uncertainty in the world as to whether we solve the problem, we decided to pay a price which, for the federation, is very high. . . . But it would not have been defensible to put this off for months, let alone years. (*Das Parlament*, June 25-July 2, 1993)

The economic conjuncture was too depressed, Kohl's political stocks were too low, and he had invested too much political capital in the Solidarity Pact to allow it to fail, regardless of the magnitude of the cost for the federal budget. What use would it have been to Kohl, after all, to wait until 1995 and have the western states pay a much higher proportion of the unification bill if, by then, as a consequence of persistent economic uncertainty and an ongoing economic recession, he had lost the federal elections in autumn 1994?

The defeats incurred by the federal government in the conflicts with the states over their European policy codetermination powers and the reform of the financial equalization scheme are not only significant in themselves as indicators of continuing collective *Länder* power. Arguably, they may also have profound long-term implications. Now that the states (eastern as well as western) have achieved such a favorable reform of the financial equalization scheme, the federal government will find it extremely difficult to revise it in its favor. Moreover, the fact that the additional revenues that the eastern states will receive through the reform are not discretionary will reduce the capacity of the federation to play the states off against each other. The federation is unlikely to get a chance to revise the 1993 reform in its favor unless the eastern German economy and, as a consequence, the eastern states' revenues develops less favorably than forecast. The concession made by the federal government in relation to the new Article 23 of the Basic Law puts the fate of future revisions of the EU treaties into the hands of the states. Thus, on both issues, the federal government bought the support of the states at the cost of a long-term deterioration of its bargaining position in federal-state relations. The (long-term) price for it was so high because, again on both occasions, compared with the states, it had a stronger (short-term) interest in averting the collapse of negotiations.

For Germany's partners in the European Union, the impact of the concessions made by the federal government to the states is ambivalent, for while on the one hand, as the prime minister of Saxony argues (Biedenkopf 1994), they contribute to preserving the "diffusion of power" in the united Germany, thus facilitating its assimilation into the European Union, the new Article 23 of the Basic Law introduces, on the other hand, a new potential obstacle to Germany's participation in the European integration process. It has made it possible that Germany's participation in this process will founder one day on the rocks not of nationalist but of regionalist resistance.

COOPERATIVE OPPOSITION

The survival and continuing robustness of German cooperative federalism, in which the major federal opposition party is always in power in some states and may also wield a majority of votes in the Bundesrat, is also conducive to the maintenance of the basically cooperative orientation of opposition in Germany (Paterson and Webber 1986, 149, 158). What is indeed most striking about the impact of unification on German government-opposition relations and the party system is that it has not weakened but rather *strengthened* this orientation.

The initial effect of unification on the party system was to accelerate processes already under way in the old Federal Republic. First, unification contributed to the decline of partisanship and thus increased electoral volatility by adding to the old West German electorate millions of new voters who had no strong identification with any of the preexisting (West German) parties. Second, it increased—although not dramatically—the level of fragmentation of the party system, as the former Communist Party, the PDS, established itself alongside the SPD and the Greens on the left side of the political system in eastern Germany, and the Republicans and the DVU (*Deutsche Volksunion*—German People's Union), riding a wave of nationalist and xenophobic sentiment fueled by a massive influx of immigrants and political refugees, emerged on the right.

It is by no means certain, however, that either of these movements has a long-term future. The PDS, although it has consolidated its position in eastern Germany, has not succeeded in establishing a foothold in the West. Unless and until it does so and as long as it is ostracized by the other political parties, it will remain a marginal national political force. For their part, the Republicans and the DVU declined rapidly after the decision was taken to revise the article of the Basic Law concerning political refugees. Like these parties, the more respectable anti-European bourgeois party created by a former chairman of the Bavarian FDP failed to make any impact in the June 1994 elections to the European Parliament, despite their campaign against the Maastricht Treaty and for the retention of the mark. Meanwhile, the results of the sixteen different elections in 1994 showed that of the "established" parties, the FDP faced the gravest problems. In spring 1995, it was represented in only one state government and no longer sat in any of the eastern German state parliaments. At the federal level, it survived on borrowed political capital: two-thirds of the voters who helped it over the 5 percent hurdle at the 1994 federal elections were Christian Democrats. In contrast, electoral support for the Christian and Social Democrats—the big "people's parties" *(Volksparteien),* whose purported crisis and decline had long been exercising the minds of political analysts—proved relatively stable in the "super-election year."

The German elections of 1990 and 1994 were not "critical elections"; unification has produced neither a dramatic shift away from the major political parties nor a significant change in their relative strength. Their ideological orientation, moreover, has remained stable and moderate—the enormous variety of coalition patterns in the states between 1990 and 1994 (Christian-Liberal, Social-Liberal, "traffic light," red-green, and Grand coalitions) testifies to the capacity of all the nonextremist parties to form coalitions with one another.[2]

2. "Traffic light" coalitions in Brandenburg and Bremen comprised the SPD (red), FDP (yellow), and the Greens. The Brandenburg coalition ended after the SPD won an absolute majority at the 1994 elections, while the Bremen coalition collapsed over a conflict between the FDP and the Greens in early 1995.

Unification has not led to a sharper polarization between the two big political parties. On the contrary, they have, if anything, moved closer together. Following the failure of the SPD's candidate for chancellor in 1990, Oskar Lafontaine, the SPD was led back toward the political center, first by Björn Engholm, and then by his successor, Rudolf Scharping. A leadership crisis in the party in 1995 led to Scharping's replacement by Lafontaine, but not to a repositioning of the SPD on the political spectrum. Confronted with the same budgetary constraints as the federation, the SPD-led state governments in particular formed a bulwark against the party's adoption or pursuit of a strategy of radical opposition to the federal government on economic policy issues. At the same time, as illustrated by Chancellor Kohl's theft of the SPD's programmatic clothes through the Solidarity Pact, the CDU has undergone a certain "social-democratization" (Sally and Webber 1994, 40).[3]

As a result of their convergence on the programmatic center, the two major parties have become almost indistinguishable, at least on socioeconomic issues. This development has facilitated the formation of Grand Coalition governments in Berlin, Baden-Württemberg (until 1996), Mecklenburg-West Pomerania, and Thuringia and reduces to a minimum the programmatic (as opposed to tactical) obstacles to a federal Grand Coalition. Since unification, the two parties have negotiated deals on a wide range of political issues: telecommunications privatization, health insurance reform, the creation of statutory insurance for old-age care, anticrime legislation, revision of the article of the Basic Law concerning political refugees, the Solidarity Pact, and energy (coal) policy. The federal government was dependent on the Social Democrats' cooperation in some cases because constitutional changes were required and in others because the SPD-led states held a majority in the Bundesrat. In most, but not in all, cases, the SPD's cooperation was (ultimately) forthcoming—party leaders explicitly rejected the polarizing kind of "Sonthofener" opposition strategy propagated by then CSU chairman, Franz-Josef Strauß, in the 1970s (Sally and Webber 1994, 40). Even on the potentially explosive issue of the deployment of German troops outside the NATO area, government and opposition leaders were concerned to try to find a *modus vivendi*. On the other hand, negotiations between the governing coalition and the SPD over a tax reform in 1997 appeared likely to fail—less, however, because of irreconcilable policy conflicts than because of the looming shadow of the 1998 elections.

Paradoxically, for at least two reasons, the pressures on the big parties to

---

3. Claus Leggewie has described the SPD's "drama" as consisting in the fact that there are two Social Democratic parties in Germany—"of which (the more successful) one is called the CDU" (Leggewie 1994, 30).

cooperate have in fact grown more intense as a consequence of unification. First, the elite and mass political cultures in eastern Germany seem to exhibit an aversion to conflict and a preference for the kind of "round table," as opposed to majoritarian, decision-making that had been practiced during the period of transition from the communist regime to parliamentary democracy in 1989–90.[4] Thus, Chancellor Kohl's Solidarity Pact was conceived and forced upon the chancellor by eastern German CDU MPs. Second, the electoral strength of the PDS in the East (and the extreme Right at the last elections in two western states) means that, in the states where neither of the major parties managed to secure an absolute majority, the formation of "small" governing coalitions has become impossible, leaving Grand Coalitions as the only alternative to minority governments or coalitions incorporating the extreme Right or extreme Left. So long as the PDS remains as strong (and the FDP as weak) as it is presently in the East, the CDU will find it difficult to retain office in several states other than in a coalition with the Social Democrats. Given the weakness of the Greens in the East, the SPD, on the other hand, will be confronted with the choice of either forming a Grand Coalition or a government tolerated by the PDS.

The formation of the Grand Coalition governments in Thuringia and Mecklenburg-West Pomerania after the elections in October 1994 heralded an expansion of cooperation and negotiations between the two main parties over government policy by further strengthening the position of the SPD in the Bundesrat, whose consent is required for the passage of most bills, including almost all taxation measures. With the CDU controlling only one state (Saxony) outright, and the CSU one other (Bavaria), and the FDP in office in only one state (the Rhineland-Palatinate) in spring 1995, the Christian-Liberal coalition clearly had little option but to seek a rapprochement with the SPD-governed states. The SPD, on the other hand, took pains to stress it would not use its position in the Bundesrat to pursue a strategy of obstruction (Scharping 1994b). It was constrained, in any case, from trying to pursue such a strategy because the states governed by the SPD alone or in coalition with the Greens controlled fewer than half the votes in the Bundesrat and such a strategy would not be supported by the states governed by the SPD in coalition with centrist parties or with the CDU.[5] Thus united Germany was governed in large measure by an unofficial Grand Coalition. If the Christian-Liberal coalition should be succeeded by a Grand

4. In an opinion poll conducted in 1993, 38 percent of eastern German respondents (compared with 47 percent of their western German counterparts) *disagreed* with the statement that "the political opposition should support the government." See Dalton 1994, 478.

5. Coalition agreements in the states typically stipulate that, in the case of the coalition partners disagreeing on the stance to be taken on legislation in the Bundesrat, the state government must abstain from voting.

Coalition government, this would be little more than a formalization of the existing state of affairs.

A WEST-ORIENTED, MULTILATERAL, AND "CIVILIAN" FOREIGN POLICY

The end of the cold war has brought about fundamental changes in the geopolitical architecture of the European continent and Germany's external environment. Not only is Germany no longer divided, but the Warsaw Pact and the Soviet Union itself have also disintegrated, and the Soviet Army has withdrawn completely from Central Europe. As a consequence of these events and of disarmament in both former cold war camps, the direct military threat to Germany was weaker by the mid-1990s than at any other time since the end of the Second World War. In response to the end of the cold war, the United States had already substantially reduced its military presence in Western Europe: the number of U.S. troops stationed in the region had been cut by more than two-thirds of the 1990 levels. A multipolar distribution of interstate power appeared to be emerging in Europe, and one of these poles was going to be constituted by the united Germany, which would possess much greater scope to pursue an autonomous foreign policy than either the Federal Republic or the German Democratic Republic had possessed in their respective blocs. How would the united Germany, the "unbound Gulliver," exploit this newfound autonomy?

It did not take very long for united Germany to exhibit the first signs of a "new assertiveness" in foreign policy. In 1991, the German government waged a vigorous campaign in favor of the diplomatic recognition of Slovenia and Croatia, cajoling other member states into agreeing to recognize the two former Yugoslavian republics, then implementing recognition three weeks before other EC members and just two weeks after the negotiation of the Maastricht Treaty in which the member states pledged to develop a common foreign and security policy.

The German campaign to secure EC recognition of Slovenia and Croatia indeed represented a break from the traditional diplomacy of the old Federal Republic—which eschewed bold leadership in European affairs. As in the case of Chancellor Kohl's ten-point plan in 1989, domestic political considerations prevailed over the value of foreign policy calculability or reliability. In both cases, the policy choice appears to have been dictated by the logic of party competition (Crawford 1993; Van Heuven 1993; Teltschik 1991, 42–58).

In the brief foreign policy history of united Germany, the case of diplomatic recognition of Slovenia and Croatia nonetheless constitutes the outlying rather than the typical case. The Kohl government's foreign policy since 1990 demonstrates the same principal traits that it did during the cold war. First, the Federal Republic's Western orientation has been reaffirmed. The German government cosponsored, with France, the Maastricht Treaty, which will lead to the abolition of national currencies, including the deutschmark, in favor of a single European currency, a move intended in part to bind united Germany more tightly to Western Europe. If Kohl had had his way, the Maastricht Treaty would have contained even bolder steps toward a political union. His government's undiminished ardor for closer integration within the European Union was demonstrated by the contents of the "Lamers/Schäuble" paper, which was published by the CDU in summer 1994. This document, which was intended to fuel the debate over the forthcoming IGC (Intergovernmental Conference—"Maastricht II"), proposed a stronger European Parliament, a downgrading of the role of the Council of Ministers, a stronger common foreign and security policy, the formation of a "hard-core" of member states prepared and able to integrate more closely and rapidly than the others, and a closer Franco-German relationship (CDU/CSU 1994).[6] Clearly, the IGC scheduled to begin in 1996 was going to witness a rerun of the Maastricht negotiations, with Germany pushing other member states to accept closer political integration rather than vice versa.

The end of the cold war created the opportunity for united Germany to try to normalize its relations with the former communist states on its eastern borders, a goal exemplified by the series of friendship treaties negotiated with these states—as well as with Russia—after unification. Bonn's policy toward postcommunist Central and Eastern Europe was a symptom not so much of a rekindled *Drang nach Osten* ("urge to go East") as of a *Zwang nach Osten* ("compulsion to go East") born primarily out of the concern that economic and political instability in this region could spread to Germany (Treverton 1992, 199–202). If the German government's objective is (once again) to transform Central and Eastern Europe into a German "sphere of influence," it is difficult to explain why Germany, among the major EU member states, is the most ardent advocate of their entry to the EU, for, once they are in the EU, with the capacity to form coalitions with other member states, if necessary against Germany, they will be less vulnerable to German pressure than they are presently. In reality, German government strategy is aimed at overcoming the tension between "West-

---

6. The CDU paper was not a statement of government policy, as the government made clear in the ensuing diplomatic row about the paper's "multi-speed Europe" proposal; however, there is little doubt that it broadly reflected the party's thinking on the future constitution of the European Union.

oriented" and "East-oriented" foreign policies by integrating the states on its eastern borders into the Western community. The "multi-speed Europe" program elaborated in the Lamers/Schäuble paper constitutes an attempt to square the prospective eastern enlargement of the EU with the goals of preserving the union's cohesion and decision-making capacity, to "deepen" the EU before it is widened—and possibly weakened.

Despite the fundamental change that the end of the cold war has brought about in Germany's security environment, there is no sign either that Germany's commitment to NATO is weakening. Rather a continued U.S. military presence in Europe is still viewed in Bonn as essential for the maintenance of German and European security (see Anderson and Goodman 1993, 29–31, 34–37, 41–45). The German government certainly wants to forge a stronger European (Union) defense identity. This strand of its security policy rests, however, on the judgment that the United States will not want to participate in the resolution of all potential post-cold war European security issues and conflicts and that the U.S. security guarantee can no longer be regarded with the same degree of certainty as it had been before 1990. Given this scenario, the development of a stronger European defense identity could serve as a "insurance policy" against the renationalization of defense policy and arrangements. If the one multilateral defense organization is to wither away, united Germany wants to ensure that another multilateral organization—however puny it might be compared to NATO—is available to fill or grow into the void.

The Second World War and the cold war bequeathed, however, a legacy to Germany that constrains its capacity to play a full part in post-cold war multilateral defense institutions: a consensus, supported by a common interpretation of restrictions imposed by provisions of the Basic Law, that German armed forces should not be deployed outside the NATO area. Following the end of the cold war, and especially after Germany's much-criticized nonparticipation in the Gulf War, this consensus rapidly disintegrated. The Federal Constitutional Court opened the door to the possible deployment of the Bundeswehr outside the NATO area, and by 1995 the government and the majority of the SPD leadership were united in approving the principle of German participation in UN peacekeeping missions (*Der Spiegel* 1995, 21; *Süddeutsche Zeitung* 1995a). The emerging elite consensus was at odds, however, with the old Federal Republic's identity as a "civilian" power and—more strongly—with the pacifist values widely held among the German Left. It was certainly not shared by all leading Social Democrats, or the party rank and file, by the other left parties (apart from some prominent Greens), or by most Germans, two-thirds of whom opposed the deployment of German military aircraft to assist in the evacuation of UN peacekeeping troops in Bosnia (Joffe 1994). The history of the old Federal Republic—replete with the emergence of social movements around security and military issues—suggested that of all the issues pertaining to the identity of the new Germany, this one contained the greatest potential to mobilize public opinion. Nonetheless, by 1997, German armed forces' participation in multilateral peacekeeping missions was no longer politically controversial, although their assignment to a combat role in foreign military conflicts probably would be. German political elites and public opinion seemed to be adjusting quickly to the new post-cold war political realities.

The continuing importance assigned by Bonn to keeping Germany integrated in both a strong EU and a strong NATO means that in its bilateral relations, it accords highest priority to maintaining close ties with its main EU partner, France, and its main NATO partner, the United States, and hence that "not to have to choose" between Paris and Washington has survived as a basic maxim of German foreign policy. Nowhere was this preoccupation more evident and striking than in the tortuous negotiations between the EU and the United States on agricultural trade liberalization in the context of the GATT Uruguay Round—the successful conclusion of which owed a great deal to the mediating role played by the German government during the decisive stage of the talks in autumn 1993.

Why have unification and the end of the cold war not (yet at least) eroded the broad consensus among German political elites—embracing Christian, Free, and Social Democrats—in favor of the Federal Republic's tight integration, via multilateral institutions, in the West? For German elites, a strong NATO and a continued U.S. military presence in Europe remains an indispensable counterweight to Russia, which they expect to remain a military great power and politically extremely unstable (*Financial Times* 1994).[7] The U.S. military presence is also a benevolent influence on security relations *among* West European states by guaranteeing them protection *from* one another. Any renationalization of defense policy as a consequence of a decline of NATO and/or a U.S. military withdrawal from Europe would likely provoke fears and suspicion among other European states concerning Germany's future foreign policy compass and, as a result, the risk of Germany's diplomatic isolation.

Together with Germany's overwhelming economic stake in the European Union,[8] the same logic—the fear of encirclement *(Einkreisung)*—explains

7. The head of the German defense staff, General Klaus Naumann, forecast a long period of "disintegration and reconstruction" in the former Soviet Union and "further reversals . . . and more violence than we are now seeing in the almost forgotten wars of Caucasus" (as quoted in *Financial Times* 1994).

8. Well over a half of German exports are to other member states of the EU. Thus German trade with the small Benelux states (combined population, around 25 million) dwarfs that

the strength of German political elites' attachment to the EU and European integration. From the national-conservative wing of the CDU/CSU across the FDP to the Social Democrats, it would be hard to find any German political leader who does not subscribe to former chancellor Helmut Schmidt's analysis that "if our country does not want to isolate itself, if Europe is not to return to a policy of forming coalitions as a counterweight to Germany, then we Germans need to be integrated into an effectively functioning EC" (Schmidt 1993). Given the incapacity of Italy (and the smaller member states), and the unwillingness of Britain, to assist Germany in enabling the EC to function effectively, only France can occupy this role. Moreover, the Federal Republic's relationship with France "protects us from the danger of isolation. . . . As long as France stands on our side, there can be no 'balance-of-power' policy against Germany as Europe's economically strongest state" (Dregger 1994). To German policymakers, the new, post-cold war Europe, in which Germany has been restored to the *Mittellage* which they see as having sown the seeds of the two world wars, opens up new opportunities for German foreign policy and diplomacy, but it also poses more risks—especially the risk of its being encircled, at the center of Europe, by a anti-German coalition. This is why the CDU views Franco-German cooperation as having become not less but rather "more important" following the end of the cold war and why the Social Democrats typically criticize the government for not cultivating the Franco-German relationship diligently enough rather than too much (CDU/CSU 1994; Scharping 1994b, 4).

CONCLUSIONS

In early 1995, large numbers of foreign-exchange holders reacted to the Mexican economic crisis by switching to the deutschmark, bringing about a sharp appreciation of the German currency. In so doing, they were, in effect, saying that they were confident that Germany was a safe haven, a country that despite unification and the end of the cold war, was and would remain economically and politically stable. In the foreign exchange markets, the new Germany inspired just as much confidence as the old. And arguably this confidence was merited. Certainly, when one compares the degree of change in the pre-and post-1990 political landscapes of Western democracies, less—ironically, given that the end of the cold war in effect brought

---

with the United States and Japan (combined population, about 372 million). Arguably, the single market ("1992") and a common currency among those states that could form a stable monetary union represent the best mechanisms for securing long-term German access to the markets that are and will remain decisive for its economic security.

new borders and sixteen million new citizens to the Federal Republic—seems to have changed in Germany than in many other countries (*Süddeutsche Zeitung* 1995c).[9] Far from having been demolished or transformed, the preexisting traits of the Bonn republic have survived or even been reinforced and strengthened. There has been a renaissance of neocorporatist concertation; the states have held their own vis-à-vis the federation in the system of cooperative federalism; and the relationship of the federal government and opposition has become, if anything, more rather than less cooperative. The federal government has remained weak, often forced to negotiate with organized interests, state governments, and the opposition from a position of weakness. Either the Bonn Republic had not died, or if it had, sometime between 1990 and 1992, it had risen again.

The distinctive characteristic of pre-1990 Federal German politics—its predominantly negotiated and cooperative character—was attributed above all to the nature of the legal-institutional framework and the prevalence of political ideologies that were congruent with this framework and thus facilitated the relatively smooth functioning of the political and industrial relations systems. The same factors are also critical to understanding why, five years after reunification, the Bonn Republic was still so robust. First, reunification was not accompanied by any radical or, indeed, significant changes in the the legal-institutional framework of the Federal Republic. Such changes or even a serious debate about them were precluded by, on the one hand, the pace at which the reunification process unfolded (or was driven) and, on the other, by the lack of any substantial support for radical changes in the Basic Law (not least since its legitimacy was strengthened by the victory of the Federal Republic over the GDR in the struggle of the systems on German soil). Second, within this framework, the same organizations kept on operating according to routines that had been established in the Federal Republic before 1990. This reflected the stability and continuity of the political class, most of the new recruits to which since 1990 have been either younger western Germans already well socialized in the norms of the Bonn Republic or token eastern Germans, who given their lack of political experience and the requirements for their personal political advancement, had first to learn the tools of the Bonn political trade. The stability of the political class—personified by Helmut Kohl and replicated in the industrial relations world—indicates that reunification has brought about fundamental shifts of power neither between nor within the political

9. One thinks in this context of Italy (split in the Communist Party, the collapse of the Christian Democrats, rise of Berlusconi's *Forza Italia* and the reformed neo-Fascists), Japan (decline of the Socialist Party and fragmentation of the Liberal Democratic Party), Austria (decline of both major parties and the rise of populist Liberal Party), France (growth of support for national-populist movements), Belgium (rise of the extreme Right in Flanders), and so on.

movements that dominated political life in the pre-unification Federal Republic.

Reunification has wrought no major changes in the Federal Republic—so far at least; however, the second united Germany is still only five years old, and it is still hazardous to try to predict the kind of adult it will become. As Peter Glotz tells us, it took forty years, after all, for the first united Germany to grow into the power that precipitated the First World War (Glotz 1994, 12–13). Peering into the future, four possible lines of fracture or principal challenges to the model of the old Federal Republic may be discerned.

The first conceivable challenge may arise from a decline in the integrative capacity of the existing political and socioeconomic institutions (parties, unions, employers' organizations, and so on). That is to say that although the elites may retain their capacity for mutual cooperation, their capacity to regulate political and social conflicts may be undermined by a decline in membership or at least membership loyalty. This danger is most acute for the employers' organizations, from which growing numbers of firms were resigning in the mid-1990s. If this is the symptom of a structural crisis and if this crisis culminates in the effective collapse of the centralized collective bargaining system, a major pillar of the "German Model" will be destroyed. Was the crisis, though, a structural, rather than a conjunctural, one? Most of the grassroots dissatisfaction within the associations seems to be attributable to some of the collective bargains struck in the early and mid-1990s and could dissipate, depending on the outcomes of future bargaining rounds. Yet there are still weighty reasons why, for all their frustration with centralized bargaining, most firms will opt to stick with the existing system. Firm-level wage bargaining would make for much more conflictual shop-floor labor relations and individual firms could be more easily played off against each other by the trade unions, which (short of a major reform of industrial relations law) would remain the firms' bargaining-counterparts. The development of the eastern German economy is central to this issue. To the extent that the eastern German states become more prosperous, employers' associations might be able to reconquer the terrain that they had lost among firms in the region after the 1991 wage-equalization agreement.[10] Nonetheless, there are, in addition to the primarily conjunctural (and hence transitory) challenges, long-term structural trends (for example, the decline in union membership and in voter loyalty to the traditional political parties) slowly, but tenaciously, chipping away at the foundations of the Bonn Republic.

The second conceivable line of fracture may consist in the emergence of

10. See Chapter 5, in this volume.

a new national identity in the united Germany. Arguably, a "European" Germany was able to develop west of the Elbe after 1945 thanks only to the division of Germany, and now that a German nation-state has been recreated, it will be only be a matter of time before the European identity that developed during the cold war will be shed in favor of a national identity that will erode the preconditions of Germany's participation in multilateral European and North Atlantic institutions. Certainly the German electorate was not immune to the mood of hostility or skepticism toward the European integration project which manifested itself in numerous EU member states in the early 1990s—although it would be precipitate to interpret this development as a symptom of a emerging new German identity. According to official EU surveys, whereas in 1990 Germans who thought that EU membership was beneficial to Germany outnumbered those who thought it was not beneficial by three to one, by 1996 the latter group outnumbered the former. The EMU project encountered grave reservations among the German public, which opposed it at a ratio of roughly two-to-one. The government's EMU policy—its insistence on the European Central Bank being located in Frankfurt and on adherence to the tough so-called convergence criteria, the provision made for the Bundestag and the Bundesrat to vote on the project's implementation again in the late 1990s, and the proposal for a "Stability Pact" to commit member states of the EMU to maintain almost balanced budgets—was clearly designed to assuage fears that a common European currency would not be as hard as the mark and avert the rise of a "DM nationalist" popular tide. This danger exists nonetheless, not least because if the Maastricht Treaty timetable is followed, the final decision concerning the introduction of a European currency will be taken in spring 1998, just a few months before the next German federal elections.

A growing tide of popular skepticism or hostility to European integration could eventually shatter the pro-European consensus among the Federal Republic's political elite and—the third conceivable line of fracture—facilitate the rise of a generation of political leaders who unlike Helmut Kohl, do not see German unification and European integration as being "two sides of the same coin." The growing divergence between a "Euro-skeptical" mass public and a pro-European political class has created a large potential market for political entrepreneurs with an anti-EU program. To be sure, some such entrepreneurs—the extreme Right parties and the party founded by Manfred Brunner—failed with their anti-Maastricht platforms at the 1994 European elections, and it may well be that new or extremist parties will not be able to break the mold of German politics. It is not inconceivable, however, that one or other of the already established parties will be tempted to try to mobilize this segment of the political market or that such a strategy could produce a substantial electoral payoff, although a first, hesitant attempt by the SPD to campaign as the "savior of the deutschmark" in several state elections in spring 1996 proved unsuccessful, as did attempts by national conservatives in the FDP to transform the German liberals into an anti-European party similar to their Austrian counterpart led by Jörg Haider.[11]

The pro-European consensus among German political elites is all the more likely to unravel and a new, more nationalistic generation of political leader is all the more likely to emerge, if Germany encounters growing difficulties in finding allies with whom to advance the European integration process. The fourth conceivable threat to the Bonn Republic thus lies abroad and consists in Germany's partners in the EU (especially France) opting out of the European project. How credible domestically would a German government policy aimed at promoting tighter European economic and political integration be if there were to be no, or too few, other member states with whose aid such a policy could be implemented? If the integration process does indeed stall or begin to unwind, leaving the united Germany more or less alone at the center of a Europe of more or less autonomous nation-states, the repercussions for the Federal Republic's foreign policy orientation could be vast. One must not adhere to the realist school of international relations to imagine, moreover, that the domestic political landscape of a Germany cut adrift from its moorings in an integrated Europe and fearful of being encircled might be less stable and predictable than it has been in the immediate aftermath of unification. This is to say that, in the longer term, the fate of the Bonn Republic may be decided not only in Germany but also, in large measure, in Europe's other capital cities: in London, in Rome, in Madrid, in Brussels, in Warsaw, and, above all, in Paris.

REFERENCES

Anderson, Jeffrey J., and John B. Goodman. 1993. "Mars or Minerva? A United Germany in a Post-Cold War Europe." In Robert O. Keohane, Joseph S. Nye, and Stanley Hoffmann, eds., *After the Cold War: International Institutions and State Strategies in Europe, 1989–1991*, 23–62. Cambridge: Harvard University Press.

Biedenkopf, Kurt. 1994. "Pflege guter Nachbarschaft" (speech in the Bundesrat). *Das Parlament,* June 10.

Breuel, Birgit, ed. 1993. *Treuhand intern.* Frankfurt and Berlin: Ullstein.

---

11. Wolfram Kaiser (1993) analyzes the alternative strategies available to the FDP, including the issue of whether it might be "Haiderized" along the lines of the Austrian Freedom Party, which he concludes is unlikely.

CDU/CSU-Fraktion des Deutschen Bundestages. 1994. *Überlegungen zur europäischen Politik* (press statement). Bonn: CDU/CSU-Fraktion des Deutschen Bundestages.

Crawford, Beverly. 1993. *German Foreign Policy after the Cold War: The Decision to Recognize Croatia.* Working paper 2.21, Center for German and European Studies, University of California at Berkeley.

Dalton, Russell. 1994. "Communists and Democrats: Democratic Attitudes in the Two Germanies." *British Journal of Political Science* 24, no. 4: 469–93.

Dregger, Alfred. 1994. "Europapolitik ist vor allem Friedenspolitik" (speech to the Bundestag). *Das Parlament,* December 2, p. 11.

Financial Times. 1994. "Bonn in call for continued support." October 22/23.

Glotz, Peter. 1994. *Die falsche Normalisierung: Essays.* Frankfurt: Suhrkamp.

Jeffery, Charlie. 1995. "The Non-Reform of the German Federal System after Unification." *West European Politics* 18, no. 2: 252–72.

Joffe, Josef. 1994. "Abschied von der 'Kohl-Doktrin.'" *Süddeutsche Zeitung,* December 16.

Kaiser, Wolfram. 1993. "Between Haiderisation and Modernisation: The German Free Democrats since Party Unification." *German Politics* 2, no. 2: 224–42.

Katzenstein, Peter. 1987. *Policy and Politics in West Germany: The Growth of a Semi-Sovereign State?* Philadelphia: Temple University Press.

———. 1989. "Stability and Change in the Emerging Third Republic." In Katzenstein, ed., *Industry and Politics in West Germany: Toward the Third Republic,* 307–53. Ithaca: Cornell University Press.

———. 1991. "Die Fesselung der deutschen Macht im internationalen System: Der Einigungsprozeß 1989–90." In Berhard Blanke and Hellmut Wollmann, eds., *Die alte Bundesrepublik: Kontinuität und Wandel,* 68–80. Opladen: Westdeutscher Verlag.

Klatt, Hartmut. 1992. "German Unification and the Federal System." *German Politics* 1, no. 3: 1–21.

Leggewie, Claus. 1994. "Die Stunde verpaßt." *Der Spiegel,* September 26, pp. 30–31.

Lehmbruch, Gerhard. 1990. "Die improvisierte Vereinigung: Die Dritte deutsche Republik." *Leviathan,* no. 4: 462–86.

———. 1992. "The Institutional Framework of German Regulation." In Kenneth Dyson, ed., *The Politics of German Regulation.* Aldershot: Dartmouth.

Melder, Heinz-Joachim. 1994. "Die Entwicklung in Richtung Zentralismus gestoppt." *Das Parlament,* January 14.

Minkenberg, Michael. 1993. "The Wall after the Wall: On the Continuing Division of Germany and the Remaking of Political Culture." *Comparative Politics* 26, no. 1: 53–68.

——. 1994. "German Unification and the Continuity of Discontinuities: Cultural Change and the Far Right in East and West." *German Politics* 3, no. 2: 169–92.

Paterson, William E., and Douglas Webber. 1986. "The Federal Republic of Germany: The Re-emergent Opposition?" In Eva Kolinsky, ed., *Opposition in Western Europe,* 137–68. London: Croom Helm.

Sally, Razeen, and Douglas Webber. 1994. "The German Solidarity Pact: A Case Study in the Politics of the Unified Germany." *German Politics* 3, no. 1: 18–46.

Scharpf, Fritz W. 1990. "Föderalismus an der Wegscheide: Eine Replik." *Staatswissenschaften und Staatspraxis,* no. 4: 579–87.

——. 1991. "Entwicklungslinien des deutschen Föderalismus." In Bernhard Blanke and Hellmut Wollmann, eds., *Die alte Bundesrepublik: Kontinuität und Wandel,* 146–59. Opladen: Westdeutscher Verlag.

Scharping, Rudolf. 1994a. "Rudolf Scharping: 'Je n'accepterai pas d'être élu chancelier avec l'apport de la moindre voix communiste.'" *Le Monde,* October 2–3.

——. 1994b. "Was hat diese Regierung denn konkretes vorzuweisen?" (speech in the Bundestag). *Das Parlament,* December 2, pp. 3–4.

Schmidt, Helmut. 1993. "Ein Rückschlag für uns—und Europa." *Die Zeit,* August 6, p. 1.

Schmidt, Manfred. 1992. "Political Consequences of German Unification." *West European Politics* 15, no. 4: 1–15.

Silvia, Stephen. 1994. "A House Divided: Employers and the Challenge to Pattern Bargaining in a United Germany." Unpublished manuscript, American University, Washington, D.C.

Sontheimer, Kurt. 1993. *Grundzüge des politischen Systems der neuen Bundesrepublik.* Munich: Piper.

Der Spiegel. 1992. "Eine Erfolgsstory." November 23, pp. 37–38.

——. 1994. "Nach allen Seiten offen." December 12, pp. 90–93.

——. 1995. "Die SPD kann kommen." January 2, pp. 18–21.

Sturm, Roland, and Charlie Jeffery. 1992. "German Unity, European Integration and the Future of the Federal System: Revival or Permanent Loss of Substance?" *German Politics* 1, no. 3: 164–76.

Süddeutsche Zeitung. 1995a. "SPD-Fraktion billigt Scharpings Außenpolitik." January 19.

——. 1995b. "Bundesregierung finanziert weiter neue Arbeitsplätze." January 27.

——. 1995c. "Eine feste Fluchtburg ist die Mark." February 23.

———. 1995d. "Über Asyl und Abschiebung einheitlich entscheiden." March 23.

Teltschik, Horst. 1991. *329 Tage: Innenansichten der Einigung*. Berlin: Siedler.

Thatcher, Margaret. 1993. *The Downing Street Years*. London: HarperCollins.

Treverton, Gregory F. 1992. *America, Germany and the Future of Europe*. Princeton: Princeton University Press.

Van Heuven, Marten H.A. 1993. "Testing the New Germany: The Case of Yugoslavia." *German Politics and Society,* no. 29: 52–63.

Veen, Hans-Joachim. 1993. "The First All-German Elections." In Stephen Padgett, ed., *Parties and Party Systems in the New Germany,* 47–86. Aldershot: Dartmouth.

Webber, Douglas. 1994. "The Decline and Resurgence of the 'German Model': The Treuhandanstalt and Privatization Politics in East Germany." *Journal of European Public Policy* 1, no. 2: 151–75.

Weiß, Konrad. 1993. "Verlorene Hoffnung der Einheit." *Der Spiegel,* November 15, p. 41.

Zwickel, Klaus. 1994. "Wir gehen neue Wege." Interview by *Der Spiegel,* December 12, pp. 93–97.

Conclusion: Uncertain Outcomes of Conflict and Negotiation

Lowell Turner

Where does all this leave us? There are some things we can say with reasonable certainty, with consensus at least among the authors of this volume. Social partnership as a framework for the regulation of a market economy has in the past been considerably successful, in the Federal Republic of Germany and elsewhere, in terms of both economic results and workplace democracy.[1] Although in the wake of German unification and other global market challenges, social partnership in Germany finds itself in crisis, all is not lost. With varying degrees of optimism, the authors of this book agree that reform and adaptation are possible, starting from existing institutions, given appropriate actor strategies aimed at both institutional reform and innovative policy. Much depends not only on innovative strategy but also on the outcomes of conflict and negotiation among key actors in business, labor, and government. This is, therefore, a moment of great uncertainty, of possibly decisive historical contingency, when alternative scenarios are possible. The openness and pivotal nature of future outcomes for a unified Germany are points on which both historical institutionalists (who emphasize the shaping power of institutions and their constraints) and political constructionists (who emphasize political processes of conflict and negotiation) can agree.[2]

1. For other cases of enduring and successful social partnership, consider, for example, Austria (Tomandl and Fuerboeck 1986) and Denmark (Dues, Jensen, and Jesper 1994).
2. See Locke and Thelen 1995 and forthcoming for a useful theoretical presentation of the contrasting perspectives of historical institutionalists and political constructionists in the social sciences—as well as the possibilities for mutual learning and synthesis.

To elaborate on each of these points, the findings presented in this book can be summarized as follows. First of all, the German model, that is, a social partnership approach to the negotiation of terms and conditions for the organization of an advanced market economy has worked in the past.[3] We believe, on the basis of extensive collective research on different aspects of the political economy of the Federal Republic, both before and after unification, that the preservation of a reformed social partnership in Germany is highly desirable as an alternative to less regulated forms of capitalism in the contemporary world economy. Thus we disagree rather sharply with both conservative and liberal analysts who see the social market economy as an expensive and outdated relic of a welfare-state past.[4]

The evidence presented in this book also shows not only that social partnership is desirable but that it remains relatively intact. We have identified problems that must be solved for this to continue to be the case, but whatever the future holds, the basic institutions and practices of social partnership have been transferred into eastern Germany and continue to characterize political-economic relations in unified Germany. This remains true even in the face of major challenges presented by European integration, intensified global competition, a rapidly appreciating deutschmark, market imperatives for production reorganization (driven by Japanese-style lean production), and escalating collective bargaining conflict. Both employer associations and unions continue to play pattern-setting roles in wage negotiations, to set the framework for firm-level codetermination, and to engage in national, regional, and local negotiations over important aspects of economic and labor-market policy.

The authors also agree, however, that these combined pressures have been exceptionally strong in the 1990s and pose major challenges for the survival of the German model. Although the doomsayers of the 1970s and 1980s turned out to be wrong, failure appears well within the range of plausible outcomes in the coming years. None of the following, for example, are inconceivable under present and future circumstances: (1) that large numbers of small and medium-sized firms could leave the employer associations, rendering collective bargaining and other social partner-negotiated outcomes less and less comprehensive; (2) that employer associations could continue and even intensify their attacks on union influence, both undermining the unions and destabilizing the social partnership; (3) that by

---

3. For a comprehensive pre-unification analysis that reaches a similar conclusion concerning the viability of negotiated adjustment, see Katzenstein 1989. For a concise post-unification analysis in the same vein, see Goodhart 1994.

4. See, for example, a steady stream of rather one-sided editorials in the *Wall Street Journal* of recent years.

failing to resolve internal East-West and other tensions and by failing to develop appropriate strategies to organize the growing ranks of white-collar professional, technical, and service workers, unions will eventually begin to lose major collective bargaining conflicts (as they have so far avoided doing) and will embark on an irreversible and prolonged decline in membership density; and (4) that because of conservatism or paralyzing conflict, employers, unions, and government, together or singly, will fail to find adequate solutions to particular pressing problems such as technology innovation, production reorganization, long-term unemployment, vocational training reform, and macroeconomic policy demands. Any of these problems, if unsolved, could reach crisis proportions and result in a serious weakening of the German social partnership.

Even the most pessimistic among us, however, believe that it is within the capacities of the social partners to solve such problems. Successful adaptation, we contend, lies within the range of choice set by institutions and the possibilities for institutional reform. This conviction runs contrary to more pessimistic analyses that identify or predict the decline of German unions and/or the social partnership under almost any foreseeable scenario (Mahnkopf 1991 and 1993; Streeck 1991 and 1997). Our findings concerning the past performance and flexibility of German institutions of bargaining, coupled with the perception that contemporary actors do have meaningful choices to make, lead us away from such hopelessness. Precisely because the institutions are flexible, because they allow regularized and complementary bargaining ranging from national, regional, and local-level policymaking processes, to comprehensive collective bargaining, to firm and plant-level negotiated codetermination, their capacity to solve new problems is strong. This does not mean they will solve these problems, but our analyses lead us to believe that solutions to the problems we have identified lie within the capacities of existing institutions, either as they are or as they could be reformed by contemporary actors.

Three examples, in addition to the evidence already presented throughout this book, illustrate how actor strategies and reform efforts are addressing contemporary challenges. First, as both Herrigel and Wever have argued, input and negotiation need to move in a more regularized way from the "functional level" down to the point of production. Astute and experienced analysts of German industrial relations, Walther Müller-Jentsch and Hans-Joachim Sperling (1995) suggest that this is precisely what is happening in German firms today; so much so in fact that the dual system (collective bargaining and codetermination) is evolving into a flexible "triple system," one that includes greatly expanded employee participation in daily, ongoing workplace decision making. Whether such negotiation can solve the major problems of reorganization that Herrigel and Wever identify remains to be seen, but the shifting locus of negotiation indicates a fundamental institutional reform that makes such adaptation possible.

Another example is afforded by the increasing openness of IG Metall to bargaining innovations (such as flexibility in working hours and corresponding compensation) as well as the escalation of internal reform efforts within this most important of German unions. On June 15–16, 1995, for example, IG Metall invited academic speakers Wolfgang Streeck, Horst Kern, and Klaus Offe to a two-day workshop led by the union's top two leaders (Klaus Zwickel and Walther Riester), to speak openly about serious problems facing the German labor movement. With a focus on the development of a process of internal organizational development *(Organisations-Entwicklung)*, IG Metallers engaged in active debate and discussed openly the problems identified by their guest speakers. At least two principal innovations in union thinking point toward possible adaptation of the sort that our research indicates is necessary: (1) a growing commitment to rank-and-file participation, both at the workplace and in the life of the union; and (2) a growing openness to a more flexible menu of alternative, firm-level bargaining outcomes (within a comprehensive collective bargaining framework).

A final example can be seen in current internal reform processes within the metalworking employers' federation, Gesamtmetall. This is particularly salient in the wake of the 1995 bargaining round. Both inside and outside the organization, Gesamtmetall leadership was widely perceived to have made a series of bargaining blunders that contributed to a (perhaps unnecessary) strike in Bavaria, massive worker/union solidarity, and a clear union victory in the final settlement. Internal criticism and leadership changes resulting from the 1995 fiasco may well lead to (1) a better awareness of the dubious wisdom of a strategy that aims to defeat IG Metall and (2) innovative and flexible strategies that aim toward realistic compromise to better serve the interests of employer association membership. This conclusion was reinforced by an important IG Metall victory in the sick-pay dispute of fall 1996 and the subsequent contract settlements of 1996–97.

If necessary reform and adaptation are within the range of institutional possibility, then the critical variable becomes actor strategy, along with the outcomes of conflict and negotiation among major actors. Strategies, of course, are limited both by broader economic circumstances (such as the appreciation of the deutschmark, which may price some German products out of world markets no matter how extensive firm-level reform may be) and by institutional constraints. Not all things are possible. Within the limits of circumstance and structure, however, actor strategies become decisive.

Here we reach the frontiers of contemporary social science research. We know much more about institutions, their development and consequences, than we do about the political processes that lead actors to choose certain strategies at the expense of others and that result in the resolution of conflict and negotiation.[5] We know that actor strategies are in part shaped by the institutional framework (Hall 1986); but we also know that actor choices are shaped by interests, identities, and leadership decisions not entirely determined by the institutions.[6] Obviously, actors make their own choices in part in response to initiatives taken by other actors. What we do not know, however, is how these and other factors combine to determine the choices that an employers' association or labor union will make in a given situation. Nor can we necessarily predict the outcomes of conflict and negotiation from actor interests, identities, the institutional framework, or even the conflicting choices that actors might make. Too much depends on the uncertain and often surprisingly unpredictable political processes of conflict and negotiation.

Thus we end up humbled not only by the sometimes contradictory yet equally persuasive analyses presented in this book and elsewhere but also by the most fundamental limits to our ability to predict the future—and especially to predict the choices that even well-organized human agents will make and the complicated means by which they will resolve their differences among themselves and with other equally organized human agents.

Although we cannot predict the future (this luxury is reserved for those who extrapolate from the past, and they are quite often wrong), proponents of social partnership in a prosperous and democratically stable unified Germany can take heart from this analysis. While the challenges are severe, the institutions have so far demonstrated a basic resilience. Continuing reform, as we have seen, is essential to the post-unification vitality of the German model. Prospects for successful adaptation and reform now reside squarely in the hands of key, well-organized actors in German business, labor, and government. The adaptation of social partnership to the most challenging circumstances of the late twentieth century and beyond is quite possibly within their grasp, but so is the failure of adaptation and the decline of social partnership.

REFERENCES

Due, Jessper, Jørgen Steen Madsen, Carsten Strøby Jensen, Lars Kjerulf Petersen. 1994. *The Survival of the Danish Model. A Historical Sociologi-*

---

5. For some of the best contemporary research on the importance of institutions, see March and Olsen 1989; Hall 1986; Streeck 1992; and Steinmo, Thelen, and Longstreth 1992.
6. See Sabel 1992, Locke 1995, and Herrigel 1996 for persuasive and well-researched perspectives that emphasize identities and local networks.

cal Analysis of the Danish System of Collective Bargaining. Copenhagen: Jurist-og Økonomforbundets Forlag, DJØF Publishing.

Goodhart, David. 1994. *The Reshaping of the German Social Market.* London: Institute for Public Policy Research.

Hall, Peter A. 1986. *Governing the Economy: The Politics of State Intervention in Britain and France.* New York: Oxford University Press.

Herrigel, Gary. 1996. *Industrial Constructions. The Sources of German Industrial Power.* New York: Cambridge University Press.

Hoffmann, Reiner, Otto Jacobi, Berndt Keller, and Manfred Weiss, eds. 1995. *German Industrial Relations under the Impact of Structural Change, Unification and European Integration.* Düsseldorf: Hans-Böckler-Stiftung.

Katzenstein, Peter J., ed. 1989. *Industry and Politics in West Germany: Toward the Third Republic.* Ithaca: Cornell University Press.

Locke, Richard M. 1995. *Remaking the Italian Economy.* Ithaca: Cornell University Press.

Locke, Richard M., and Kathleen Thelen. 1995. "Apples and Oranges Revisited: Contextualized Comparisons and the Study of Comparative Labor Politics." *Politics and Society* 23, no. 3: 337–67.

——. Forthcoming. *The Shifting Boundaries of Labor Politics.* Cambridge: MIT Press.

Mahnkopf, Birgit. 1991. "Vorwärts in die Vergangenheit? Pessimistische Spekulationen über die Zukunft der Gewerkschaften in der neuen Bundesrepublik." In Westphal et al. 1991, 269–94.

——. 1993. "The Impact of Unification on the German System of Industrial Relations." Discussion Paper FS I 93–102, Wissenschaftszentrum Berlin für Sozialforschung.

March, James, and Johan Olsen. 1989. *Rediscovering Institutions.* New York: Free Press.

Müller-Jentsch, Walther, and Hans Joachim Sperling. 1995. "Towards a Flexible Triple System? Continuity and Structural Changes in German Industrial Relations." In Hoffmann et al. 1995, 9–29.

Steinmo, Sven, Kathleen Thelen, and Frank Longstreth. 1992. *Structuring Politics: Historical Institutionalism in Comparative Analysis.* Cambridge: Cambridge University Press.

Streeck, Wolfgang. 1991. "More Uncertainties: German Unions Facing 1992." *Industrial Relations* 30, no. 3: 317–49.

——. 1992. *Social Institutions and Economic Performance: Studies of Industrial Relations in Advanced Capitalist Societies.* London: Sage.

——. 1997. "German Capitalism: Does It Exist? Can It Survive?" *New Political Economy,* forthcoming.

Tomandl, Theodor, and Karl Fuerboeck. 1986. *Social Partnership: The Aus-*

trian System of Industrial Relations and Social Insurance. Ithaca: ILR Press.

Westphal, Andreas, Hansjörg Herr, Michael Heine, and Busch, Ulrich, eds. 1991. *Wirtschaftspolitische Konsequenzen der deutschen Vereinigung*. Frankfurt: Campus Verlag.

Index

East-West tensions, 88, 98, 100, 146
East-West wage differentials, 25, 103–4
  and metal industry strike (1993), 115,
    120, 121
  and unemployment, 104, 167
Educational system, 213–14. *See also*
  Vocational training
Electronics industry, 2
Employer associations
  dissatisfaction with, 172–73
  and East-West wage differentials, 103–
    4
  former East Germany, 103–4, 124,
    128, 130, 214
  in modernization, 4, 43, 143
  and political system continuity, 233,
    234–35
  reform, 258
  unemployment responses, 167–68,
    171
  and vocational training, 43
  and West German model renegotiation,
    214–16
  See also Collective bargaining; Metal
    industry strike (1993)
Employer offensives (1993–1996), 2, 28
Employment and training companies
  (ETCs), 71, 77–78
  case-study findings, 127–28
  development of, 74–76
  operation of, 76–77
  and political system continuity, 232
  and Treuhandanstalt, 75, 76, 77, 82,
    83, 219
  and West German model renegotiation,
    219
Employment Promotion Act (AFG), 72,
  85, 104
  Article 249h, 169–71
Engholm, Björn, 240
Eppelmann, Rainer, 234
ETCs. *See* Employment and training
  companies
European integration
  and codetermination, 25–28
  and cooperative federalism, 236, 238
  and German foreign policy, 229, 242,
    243–44, 245–46, 249, 250
  and labor unions, 87
  and relocation threats, 7, 23, 27, 28
    subsidiarity principle, 26, 27
  and vocational training, 44

and West German social partnership
  model, 3
European Union. *See* European
  integration
European Works Councils (EWCs), 26–
  27
EWC. *See* Directive on European Works
  Councils
EWCs. *See* European Works Councils
Existenzsicherungspartnerschaft, 100

FDGB. *See* Freier Deutscher
  Gewerkschaftsbund
FDP. *See* Free Democratic Party
Federal Association of German
  Employers. *See* Bundesvereinigung
  der deutschen Arbeitgeberverbände
Federal Association of German Industry.
  See Bundesverband der Deutschen
  Industrie
Federal Employment Agency, 37, 51, 73,
  75, 76
  and direct job creation, 80, 81
  and downsizing, 85
Federal Institute for Vocational Training
  (BiBB), 36, 43, 51, 53
Federal Vocational Training Law (1969),
  36
Fichter, Michael, 118
Fifth Directive, 26
Financial system, 144–45
Fixed-rate subsidies, 80–81
Foreign policy, 228, 229, 230, 242–46,
  249, 250
Former East German labor market policy,
  41, 71–74, 163, 164
  Article 249h, 169–71
  and civil society, 74–75
  direct job creation, 73–74, 80–81, 84
  employment and training companies,
    71, 74–78, 79, 82, 83
  future prospects, 84–85
  and labor unions, 75, 78, 79, 82, 83–
    84
  proactive nature of, 72–73
  types of, 71–72
  See also Treuhandanstalt
Former East Germany
  ATLAS experiment, 218–19, 233
  civil society, 48
  codetermination, 24–25, 99–101, 122
  collective bargaining, 125, 128–29